MICHEL ROUX'S
Finest Desserts

MICHEL ROUX'S
Finest Desserts

TRANSLATED AND EDITED BY KATE WHITEMAN

PHOTOGRAPHS BY MARTIN BRIGDALE

RIZZOLI
NEW YORK

AUTHOR'S ACKNOWLEDGMENTS

I am very grateful to the following people who have contributed so much to this book: Chris Sellors, sous-chef at The Waterside Inn and Laurent Corcaud, my pâtissier, who skillfully tested all the recipes; M.O.R.A. for generously supplying some of the specialist equipment, and Valrhona for providing the chocolate used in my recipes; Martin Brigdale, who photographed them so artistically, and Helen Trent, who styled them; Mary Evans for her art direction; Alison Barrett for the attractive illustrations; Kate Whiteman for editing and translating the book: the rapport we have established over the past twelve years and five books has ensured that this has been done just as I would wish; John Huber, Principal Lecturer at Thames Valley University, who meticulously read and checked the recipes; Claude Grant for typing the manuscript and coping with my ego from time to time; and of course, Robyn, who continues to support me throughout the creative process.

First published in the United States of America in 1995 by
RIZZOLI INTERNATIONAL PUBLICATIONS, INC.
300 Park Avenue South, New York, NY 10010

First published in the United Kingdom in 1994 by
Conran Octopus Limited

Library of Congress Cataloging-in-Publication Data
Roux, Michel. 1941–
    Finest desserts / Michel Roux ; photographs by Martin Brigdale.
        p.   cm.
    Includes index.
    ISBN 0-8478-1857-8
    1. Pastry.   2. Desserts.   3. Cookery, French.   I. Title.
TX773.R7973   1995
641.8′6--dc20   94-35427
                                                                        CIP

Art director: Mary Evans
Design: Peter Butler
Project editor: Anne Furniss
Translation and editing: Kate Whiteman
American editor: Norma MacMillan
Illustrations: Alison Barrett
Styling: Helen Trent
Production: Jill Macey

Typeset by Servis Filmsetting Ltd
Colour reproduction by H.B.M. Print Pte Ltd, Singapore
Printed and bound by Kim Hup Lee, Singapore

CONTENTS

Page 2: Banana and Caramel Mousse Gâteau; Title page: White Chocolate Dome; Page 5: French Meringues; Page 6: Lucien Peletier; Page 7: Love Nest with a choux pastry heart; Page 8: Michel Roux

DEDICATION
TO LUCIEN PELTIER
1941–1991
My friend of yesterday, today, and forever

1980–Chef de l'Année Culinary Trophy
1981–Médaille d'Argent de la Ville de Paris
1985–Médaille d'Or de la Pâtisserie du Japon
1988–Chevalier de l'Ordre des Palmes Académiques
1989–Chevalier de l'Ordre du Mérite Agricole

LUCIEN PELTIER was the director of an exemplary business, La Pâtisserie Peltier of Paris, Tokyo, and Seoul. He was administrator of St Michel, the association for all French pâtissiers, from the youngest apprentice to owners of the grandest pastry shops. From 1982, until his death in 1991, Lucien was president of Relais et Desserts. A decisive, disciplined man, he understood how to rally our profession to give of its best. He was a perfectionist whose gaze spoke volumes, a gourmet who understood and appreciated all good food, not only pâtisserie. This master generously molded hundreds of young pâtissiers and thus ensured that the profession of pâtisserie continued to be built on firm foundations.

Farewell, Lucien. You will always remain among us. To you my friend I pay deep homage and respect.

My Secret Obsession

I catch myself smiling at her, a discreet furtive smile that I have secretly harbored for longer than I can remember. I felt its first feeble flickerings in adolescence; over the years it has heated into an incandescent furnace.

Ours is a faithful relationship, pure and bottomless, which cannot easily be expressed in words. It has deepened over many years through the senses: touch, sight, smell, and even hearing. I rarely speak to her, but communicate only by vague movements of my lips, almost like the first outline of a kiss.

I reinvent and recreate her every day, using simple ingredients. Inspired by my thoughts, my fingers model and caress her, gently dress her, apply a hint of makeup with the touch of a piping cone, and ornament her hair with a sugar rose. Her beauty takes my breath away; she thrills me and fills me with admiration.

MICHEL ROUX

INTRODUCTION

MY CHOSEN CAREER I am a pâtissier at heart and always shall be. The creation of a dessert is my passion. During my career, I have passed through various stages. When I first started, I aimed to emulate my teachers and peers and to match their skill. Then I was drawn to the artistic aspect of pâtisserie and successfully took part in many professional competitions.

Nearly all my desserts, both hot and cold, are served individually assembled on the plate. They are put together in the kitchen only when ordered and, as a result, they are always wonderfully fresh, delicate, and refined. Many years ago, I abandoned the free-for-all of the dessert cart, which all too often looks like a battlefield.

As in all cooking, I dislike mixing flavors, especially those that are diametrically opposed, on the same plate. The look and taste of the basic ingredient must be paramount. The only accompaniments that do not dominate a dessert are coulis, ladyfingers, fruit,

8

mousses, or ice creams. As you will see, my desserts range from simple to elaborate.

MY APPRENTICESHIP My apprentice master was Monsieur Camille Loyal. Originally from Alsace, he was a man of about fifty, huge, churlish yet modest, with a small graying moustache. He instilled in me a passion for cakes, chocolates, and ice cream – but only if they were well made. As he said: "It takes no longer to make something well than badly." This simple logic stuck in the mind of more than one apprentice. Another favorite saying of his was: "We don't eat sugar flowers, pastillage, or elaborate decorations, but we do eat desserts"; hence his insistence on using the very best quality ingredients and the simplest techniques for his desserts.

A MATTER OF TASTE All tastes are to be found in nature and it is up to us to discover and develop them. Personal taste should be respected, but we can share, examine, and study it in order to modify it. Those who do not develop their own tastebuds or accept the taste of others deprive themselves of the opportunity to discover the constantly changing beauty of taste.

In France, it is customary when visiting friends or relations to present your host with a cake or dessert, especially on festive occasions. France is full of pastry shops and professional pâtissiers who bring happiness to thousands of customers every day, for pâtisserie adds a little luxury to our lives. Sharing is a gesture of friendship, so why not make a dessert to offer as a gift?

HOW PATISSERIE HAS EVOLVED Like French cooking, pâtisserie has evolved in a significant way. Nowadays, many more desserts are based on fruits, be they fresh, frozen, or canned, which are refreshing and introduce a note of healthy eating. Nearly all are lighter and contain far less butter, eggs, and cream than formerly. They are also less sugary. Dark cooking or baker's chocolate and couverture range from bitter to extra-bitter, which allows us to savor the taste of the chocolate without being overwhelmed by its sweetness.

It is my pleasure to invite you to enter my magical world, the world of my favorite desserts. I do urge you to read and digest the Practical Advice section before embarking on the recipes; then with simple, clear instructions I shall help and guide you through the preparations to the final delicious result.

PRACTICAL ADVICE

These pages contain a reminder of certain basic rules and guidelines that you should follow when making the recipes. They are second nature to me, and I am sure you will find them helpful when you come to prepare the desserts in this book. I trust that they will answer some of the questions that may already have come to mind.

Silpat: Fine conical strainer: Metal spatula for spreading: Round cooling rack: Cornet cone: Cardboard cake base: Fluted nozzle: Cake rack: Cannelé molds: Madeleine tin: Spiral dipping tool for chocolate and sugarwork: 2-pronged dipping fork for chocolate and sugarwork:

THE GOLDEN RULES The three vital rules to remember before embarking on the preparation of a dessert are:

1. Have all the equipment needed for the recipe ready at hand.

2. Measure all the ingredients before you begin and keep them in separate containers.

3. Preheat the oven to the necessary temperature.

By following these golden rules, you will produce successful and delicious desserts every time.

Rodoïde plastic: Bombe mold: Hemispherical mold: Icing comb: Copper sugar pan: Pointed sculpting tool: Hemispherical mold: Aluminum pie weights: Pyramid mold: Fluted cookie cutters: Fluted modeling tool: Right-angled metal spatula.

✳ MAKING THINGS SIMPLE Many of the more elaborate recipes in the book contain a number of elements that can be prepared several hours, or even a day or two in advance. An asterisk✳ beside the Ingredients list indicates that the greater part of the dessert can be prepared beforehand.

WEIGHTS AND MEASURES All my recipes have been tested using metric measurements. For perfect results, it is worth investing in a set of electronic metric scales. If you use cup measurements for dry ingredients, remember that they are not as precise as metric weights and of necessity are the nearest equivalent, to facilitate measuring.

SPECIAL EQUIPMENT The suggested sizes of special equipment are the ideals. However, if you do not possess, for example, a flan or mold of the precise dimensions given in a recipe, use the nearest equivalent.

Rodoïde plastic: This flexible clear plastic is invaluable for giving chocolate work a high gloss. For suppliers, see page 190. Acetate makes an acceptable substitute.

Silicone paper: This is also known as parchment paper. Since it is nonstick, it is useful for baking.

Silpat: Silpat is a recently developed baking medium that is exceptionally versatile and useful for baking sponge bases, pulling sugar, etc. It can be reused many times. Use instead of conventional nonstick surfaces.

OVEN TEMPERATURES These can vary from oven to oven, so for perfect results, use an oven thermometer.

All the recipes in this book have been tested using a convection oven. If you have a conventional oven, in every case you should increase the suggested temperature by 50°F or 20°C (eg: 350°F/180°C should be increased to 400°F/200°C).

SERVING TEMPERATURES It is important to serve desserts and gâteaux at the temperature that best suits their composition and flavor. Chocolate-based desserts (filled with ganache, mousse, etc.) should be served at 42.8°–46.4°F/6°–8°C. Those based on fruit mousses, such as charlottes, at 42.8°–53.6°F/8°–12°C. Warm desserts (tarts and some feuilletés) at 95°–113°F/35°–45°C, and hot desserts (principally soufflés) at 158°–176°F/70°–80°C.

CHOOSING THE BASIC INGREDIENTS   To achieve a gastronomically and visually perfect dessert, it is essential to use only extremely fresh, top-quality ingredients. Eggs must be extra fresh and come from a reliable source; if you cannot guarantee this, use pasteurized eggs.

Fresh cream can go off quickly, so buy only the best quality. Cream should always be pasteurized to prevent the spread of any bacteria.

STORAGE   Recommended storage times are for foods kept in airtight containers or tightly wrapped or covered with plastic wrap.
COLD STORAGE   Technological advances have opened up new horizons which make for more efficiency in the field of pâtisserie.
Domestic refrigerators: 41°F/5°C.
Holding freezers: 0°F/–18°C.
Deep freezers: –13°F/–25°C.
Blast freezers: –31°F/–35°C (ideally all foods should be frozen at this temperature for 30 minutes before being transferred to the holding freezer).

HYGIENE   You are strongly advised not to wear a watch or jewelry when baking. They can cause allergies and are unhygienic, as ingredients such as flour and confectioners' sugar may get trapped inside.

SOME ADVICE ON INGREDIENTS AND CULINARY TECHNIQUES
Almonds and hazelnuts: Before using these to prepare a dessert, dry them in an airing cupboard or low oven, otherwise the moisture they contain could adversely affect the cooking.
Sliced almonds: Sprinkle with confectioners' sugar and toast lightly in a hot oven or with a salamander. They are delicious scattered over a mousse or cream just before serving.
Butter, sugar, and flour: Unless otherwise specified, always use unsalted butter, granulated sugar, and sifted, all-purpose flour for these recipes.

EGGS: *Beating egg whites:* To ensure that egg whites rise perfectly, use scrupulously clean utensils rinsed in cold water and thoroughly dried. Make sure that the whites contain no trace of yolk. If they are very fresh, add a pinch of salt to break them down. Begin by beating at medium speed to incorporate as much air as possible until the whites become frothy, then beat at the highest speed to firm them up. As soon as flecks of beaten egg appear around the edge of the bowl, add a little sugar to prevent them from becoming grainy. They will be firmer and more resistant, and therefore easier to mix and handle. This is most important when you are preparing both sweet and savory soufflés.

Unbeaten egg whites can be kept frozen in an airtight container for several weeks.

Egg yolks: To freeze, whisk lightly with 5–10% sugar, then freeze at −13°F/−25°C for no more than four weeks.

Egg yolks "burn" on contact with sugar or salt, so they must be beaten immediately with a whisk or spatula until completely homogeneous, otherwise they will form into hard little granules that are impossible to break up.

A cornucopia of glossy, ripe fruit. I always demand the highest quality from fresh ingredients.

Weighing eggs: A large egg weighing about 2 oz/60 g is made up of 1 oz/30 g white, ⅔ oz/20 g yolk, and ⅓ oz/10 g shell. 20 whole eggs, 32 egg whites, or 52 egg yolks = 1 quart/1 liter.

It is essential to note that I always use large eggs in my recipes. If a recipe calls for six eggs of 2 oz/60 g each, that makes a total weight of 12 oz/360 g. If you use 1¾ oz/50 g (medium) or 2¼ oz/70 g (jumbo) eggs, you will be using one-sixth less or more egg, which is not acceptable to achieve a perfect result.

Fondant: One of the classic icings for glazing choux puffs, éclairs, etc. Take care not to heat it above 100°F/37°C or it will craze and lose its gloss when cold. If it is too thick, thin it with a little sorbet syrup.

Gelatine: One gelatine leaf weighs ⅒ oz/3 g. It can be replaced by an equal weight of powdered unflavored gelatine, or 1⅛ teaspoons.

Glazing with eggwash: For a beautiful shiny finish, brush on two light coats of eggwash. A single, heavier coat is more likely to run.

Greasing: Use softened, clarified, or melted butter as appropriate. When greasing molds, tins, rings, and baking sheets, it is important to use the precise quantity of butter specified in the recipe. Too much may crinkle the pastry, too little may cause it to stick to the mold. Spray-on silicone coating can be used instead of butter.

Kiwi fruit: To peel, place in the freezer for about 10 minutes, drop in boiling water, and then in ice water, as if peeling a tomato. The skin can then be peeled off very easily without spoiling the oblong shape of the fruit, to give attractive, neat slices.

Marzipan or almond paste: If it is too crumbly or too firm, mix with fondant, liquid glucose or light corn syrup to soften it.

PASTRY: *Frozen pastry* should be left to thaw gradually in the refrigerator at 41°F/5°C until malleable.

Kneading leavened dough or puff pastry: The dough is sufficiently kneaded when all the ingredients are well incorporated and it comes away cleanly from the sides of the bowl or work surface. All the protein in the flour will be hydrated to make the dough very elastic.

Kneading and rising yeast-based dough: When kneading dough in a warm room, chill the liquid ingredients (milk, water, and eggs) in the refrigerator beforehand. After kneading, the temperature of the dough should not exceed 75°F/24°C.

After rising in a warm place, leave live yeast-based doughs (eg: brioches, Viennese pastries) at room temperature for a further 15 minutes before baking to obtain maximum volume during cooking.

Puff pastry: Transfer the rolled-out pastry to a baking sheet dampened with water. This prevents the pastry from slipping when you glaze it, and from shrinking during baking and thus spoiling the shape.

Refrigerating puff pastry: Puff pastry must be brought to room temperature before using so that the butter softens. Take it out of the refrigerator 3–5 minutes before rolling out to ensure that the layers of fat do not break, which would prevent the pastry from rising fully.

Rolled-out pastry and marzipan: To move it without spoiling the shape or breaking it, roll it up loosely around a pastry rolling pin, then unroll it onto the mold or baking sheet.

Removing desserts from their rings: To retain a perfect edge, place the gâteau in its dessert ring on an object about 4 in/10 cm high (eg: a can) and push the ring downward to release the gâteau. This is a delicate operation, but it gives perfect results.

Scales: Small electronic scales are very precise, and are useful for pâtisserie where only a few grams of certain ingredients may be required.

Sifting: This eliminates foreign bodies and lumps from ingredients such as flour, baking powder, ground almonds, cocoa powder, etc. It also aerates and homogenizes. Flour should always be sifted.

Staggered rows: Always arrange small pastries, macaroons, tartlet molds, brioches, etc. in staggered rows on the baking sheet to ensure more even cooking.

Syrup: If it contains impurities, clarify it by adding some beaten egg white and bubbling over low heat for a few minutes. Pass gently through a conical strainer and use as required. A 30° Beaumé sorbet syrup (1.2624 density) will keep in an airtight container in the refrigerator for two weeks.

CHAPTER ONE

PASTRY AND DOUGH

In pastry workshops, the *tourrier* is responsible for making all the dough and pastry, so basically almost all desserts begin with him. The precise weighing and measuring of the ingredients is vital; if the pastry is too salty, too soft, or too dry, the quality of the entire dessert will be compromised when it is baked.

Raw pastry has an agreeable smell that titillates the tastebuds. I find it a very sensual food; I love working it with my fingertips, kneading it carefully so that it remains firm but supple. I dust it with flour, then roll it out quickly and evenly to avoid bruising it. If I do not want to use it immediately, I can wrap it in plastic wrap and freeze it for future use.

BRIOCHE

THIS RICH, BUTTERY YEAST BREAD IS DELICIOUS SERVED FOR
BREAKFAST OR TEA.

INGREDIENTS:

½ oz/15 g compressed fresh
  yeast

6 tbsp warm milk

scant 1 tbsp/15 g salt

3½ cups/500 g flour, plus
  extra for dusting

6 eggs

12 oz (3 sticks)/350g
  softened butter

2 tbsp/30 g sugar

Eggwash (1 egg yolk beaten
  with 1 soup spoon milk
  and a pinch of salt)

Makes 2¾ lbs/1.2 kg
  dough, enough for 1 large
  brioche to serve 20, or
  16–20 individual
  brioches

Preparation time: 20
  minutes in an electric
  mixer, or 35 minutes by
  hand, plus resting and
  rising

Cooking time: 40–45
  minutes for a large
  brioche, 8 minutes for
  small brioches

MIXING THE DOUGH: Put the yeast and milk in a mixing bowl, whisk lightly, then add the salt. Add the flour and eggs and knead the dough with the dough hook of an electric mixer or by hand until it becomes smooth and elastic (this will take about 10 minutes in a mixer, 20 minutes by hand).

Beat the softened butter and sugar together, then, at low speed, add them to the dough a little at a time, making sure that they are completely amalgamated before adding more. Continue to mix for 5 minutes in a mixer or 15 minutes by hand, until the dough is perfectly smooth, shiny, and fairly elastic.

Cover the bowl with plastic wrap and leave at about 75°F/24°C for 2 hours, until the dough has doubled in volume.

PUNCHING DOWN THE DOUGH: Flip the dough over with your fingertips a couple of times to knock out the air. Cover with plastic wrap and refrigerate for several hours, but not more than 24 hours.

MOLDING THE BRIOCHE: Place the dough on a lightly floured surface and shape into a large ball. If you are using a saucepan, line it with buttered wax paper twice the height of the pan before putting in the dough. To make the brioche in a mold, cut off one-third of the dough to make the "head." Roll the larger piece into a ball and place in the mold. Make an indentation in the center with your fingertips. Holding your hand at an angle, roll the "head" into an elongated oval. Lightly flour your fingertips and gently press the narrow end of the oval into the indentation in the large ball.

Lightly brush the top of the brioche with eggwash, working from the outside inward and taking care not to let it run into the cracks in the dough or onto the edges of the mold, or the dough will not rise properly.

RISING: Leave the brioche to rise in a warm, draft-free place until it has almost doubled in bulk (about 20 minutes for the small brioches and 1½ hours for a large one).

BAKING: Preheat the oven to 425°F/220°C.

Lightly brush the top of the brioche again with eggwash. Slash the edge of the large brioche at intervals with scissors or a razor blade dipped in cold water. Do not slash the small brioches. Bake immediately in the hot oven, 40–45 minutes for the large brioche, 8 minutes for the small ones. Unmold the brioche immediately onto a wire rack and let cool.

SPECIAL EQUIPMENT:

1 large brioche mold,
  10 in/24 cm diam. at
  the top, 4 in/11 cm at
  the base, or a 7 in/18 cm
  copper saucepan, or 20
  small brioche molds,
  3¼ in/8 cm diam. at the
  top, 1½ in/4 cm at the
  base

NOTES:

Brioche dough can also be braided or shaped into a crown. Serve it sliced, sprinkled with confectioners' sugar, and glazed under a hot broiler, or warm with Chocolate Sauce (page 55).

The dough can be frozen, wrapped in plastic wrap, after the punching down stage. Thaw slowly in the refrigerator, for at least 4 hours or overnight, before molding, rising, and baking.

TART PASTRY
Pâte brisée

A LIGHT, CRUMBLY PASTRY THAT IS USED AS A CLASSIC BASE FOR MANY TARTS AND QUICHES.

INGREDIENTS:
1¾ cups/250 g flour
10 tbsp/150g butter,
   slightly softened
1 egg
A pinch of sugar
¾ tsp salt
1 tbsp milk

Makes about 1 lb/450 g
Preparation time: 15
   minutes

Sift the flour onto the work surface and make a well in the center. Cut the butter into small pieces and put them in the well with the egg, sugar, and salt. Mix all these ingredients with the fingertips of your left hand, then use your right hand to draw in the flour a little at a time. When everything is almost amalgamated, add the milk to make a paste. Knead with the heel of your hand two or three times until it is completely homogeneous. Wrap in plastic wrap and refrigerate for several hours before using.

NOTE:
The pastry can be kept a few days in the refrigerator, or frozen several weeks.

SWEET TART PASTRY
Pâte sucrée

THIS PASTRY IS MOSTLY USED FOR FRUIT TARTS. AS IT IS NOT TOO FRAGILE, IT IS SUITABLE FOR PICNIC DESSERTS.

INGREDIENTS:
1¾ cups/250 g flour
7 tbsp/100 g butter, diced
1 cup/100g confectioners'
   sugar, sifted
A small pinch of salt
2 eggs, at room temperature

Makes about
   1 lb 2 oz/520 g
Preparation time: 15
   minutes

Sift the flour onto the work surface and make a well in the center. Put in the butter and work it with your fingertips until very soft. Add the confectioners' sugar and salt, mix well, then add the eggs and mix again. Gradually draw the flour into the mixture to make a homogeneous paste. Knead the paste two or three times with the heel of your hand until very smooth. Roll it into a ball, flatten the top slightly, wrap in plastic wrap, and refrigerate for several hours before using.

NOTE:
This pastry keeps well in the refrigerator for several days or in the freezer 1 week.

SHORTBREAD PASTRY: RECIPE 1
Pâte sablée 1

THIS PASTRY IS EXTREMELY DELICATE, SO YOU MUST WORK VERY FAST AND MUST NOT OVERHANDLE IT, AS IT SOFTENS VERY QUICKLY.

INGREDIENTS:
1¾ cups/250 g flour
14 tbsp/200 g butter, diced
1 cup/100 g confectioners' sugar, sifted
A pinch of salt
2 egg yolks
Lemon or vanilla extract (optional)

Makes about 1 lb 6 oz/650 g
Preparation time: 15 minutes

Sift the flour onto the work surface and make a well in the center. Put in the butter and work it with your fingertips until very soft. Sprinkle the confectioners' sugar and salt onto the butter and work in. Add the egg yolks and mix thoroughly. Gradually draw in the flour, mixing until completely amalgamated, but taking care not to overwork the pastry or it will become too elastic. Add a drop of lemon or vanilla extract and knead the pastry two or three times with the heel of your hand. Roll the pastry into a ball and flatten it slightly. Wrap it in plastic wrap and refrigerate for several hours before using.

SHORTBREAD PASTRY: RECIPE 2
Pâte sablée 2

THIS RECIPE CONTAINS LESS BUTTER THAN RECIPE 1, WHICH MAKES IT EASIER TO PREPARE AND HANDLE, BUT LESS CRUMBLY AND RICH-TASTING.

INGREDIENTS:
6 tbsp/30 g ground almonds
1¾ cups/250 g flour
9½ tbsp/140 g butter, diced
1 cup/100 g confectioners' sugar, sifted
A pinch of salt
1 egg
Lemon or vanilla extract (optional)

Makes 1¼ lbs/600 g
Preparation time: 15 minutes

Sift the ground almonds and flour together onto the work surface and make a well in the center. Continue as for Recipe 1.

NOTE:
Both recipes will keep well in the refrigerator for several days or in the freezer 1 week.

FLAN OR LINING PASTRY
Pâte à foncer

ANOTHER PASTRY FOR FLANS AND TARTS.

INGREDIENTS:
1¾ cups/250 g flour
9 tbsp/125 g butter,
  softened
1 egg
1½ tsp sugar
¾ tsp salt
3 tbsp water

Makes about 1 lb/450 g
Preparation time: 15
  minutes

Sift the flour onto the work surface and make a well in the center. Cut the butter into small pieces and put them in the well with the egg, sugar, and salt. Mix these ingredients with the fingertips of your right hand, then use your left hand to draw in the flour a little at a time. When the dough is well mixed but still a little crumbly and not quite homogeneous, add the water. Knead the pastry two or three times with the heel of your hand until completely smooth. Wrap in plastic wrap and refrigerate for several hours before using.

NOTE:

This pastry will keep well several days in the refrigerator or several weeks in the freezer.

1. Large tart shell
2. Tartlet shell
3. Barquette or boat shells
4. Fluted tartlet shells
5. Mini-tartlet shells
6. Small brioches
7. Sliced brioche loaf
8. Unsliced brioche braid
9. Braided brioche basket
10. Sliced brioche braid

JEAN MILLET'S PUFF PASTRY
Feuilletage Jean Millet

MAKING PUFF PASTRY SHOULD HOLD NO TERRORS FOR THE HOME COOK. TRUE, IT IS A LENGTHY PROCESS, BUT IF YOU FOLLOW JEAN MILLET'S RECIPE, IT REALLY IS NOT AT ALL DIFFICULT.

INGREDIENTS:

3½ cups / 500 g flour, plus extra for turning

⅞ cup / 200 ml water

1¾ tsp salt

5 tsp white wine vinegar

4 tbsp / 50 g melted butter

14 oz (3½ sticks) / 400 g well-chilled butter

Makes 2¾ lbs / 1.2 kg

Preparation time: 1 hour 10 minutes, plus 5 hours resting

Work the pastry with the heel of your hand until it becomes completely homogeneous but not too firm (2). Roll it into a ball and cut a cross in the top to break the elasticity (3). Wrap in plastic wrap and refrigerate 2–3 hours.

MIXING THE PASTRY: Sift the flour onto the work surface or into a mixing bowl and make a well in the center. Put in the water, salt, vinegar, and melted butter and work the mixture with the fingertips of your right hand (1). Use your left hand to draw in the flour little by little, and mix well.

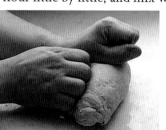

NOTES:

If you plan to store puff pastry, give it only 4 turns, then complete the 2 final turns and chill again for 30 minutes when you want to use it. It will keep up to 3 days in the refrigerator, or several weeks in the freezer.

INCORPORATING THE BUTTER: On a lightly floured surface, roll the edges of the pastry ball in four different places to form four "ears" around a small, round "head" (4). Beat the chilled butter several times with a rolling pin until supple but still firm and very cold. Lay the butter on top of the "head" to cover it without overhanging. Fold the four "ears" over the butter to enclose it completely (5). Refrigerate 20–30 minutes to bring the pastry and butter to the same temperature and therefore the same consistency. This process is vital.

TURNING THE PUFF PASTRY: On the lightly floured surface, roll the pastry away from you gently and gradually, to make a 27 × 16 in / 70 × 40 cm rectangle. Fold in the ends to make 3 layers (6). This is the first turn.

Rotate the pastry through 90 degrees and gradually roll it out again into a 27 × 16 in / 70 × 40 cm rectangle.

24

Fold in the ends to make 3 layers. This is the second turn. Wrap the pastry and refrigerate 30 minutes to rest and firm up.

Make two more turns as above and, after the fourth turn, wrap the pastry again and refrigerate another 30–60 minutes. Make two final turns, making a total of six. The puff pastry is now ready to roll and cut into shape. After cutting the pastry into your desired shape, refrigerate it for at least 30 minutes before baking, or it will shrink and distort the shape.

QUICK PUFF PASTRY
Feuilletage minute

THIS PASTRY WILL RISE ABOUT 30 PER CENT LESS THAN CLASSIC PUFF PASTRY, BUT IT HAS THE GREAT ADVANTAGE OF BEING VERY QUICK AND SIMPLE TO PREPARE.

INGREDIENTS:
3½ cups/500 g flour, plus extra for turning
1 lb 2 oz (4½ sticks)/500 g firm but not too hard butter (remove from the refrigerator 1 hour before using)
1 tsp salt
1 cup/250 ml ice water

Makes 2¾ lbs/1.2 kg
Preparation time: 20 minutes, plus 50 minutes chilling

Sift the flour onto the work surface or into a mixing bowl and make a well in the center. Cut the butter into small cubes and put it in the well with the salt. Using the fingertips of your right hand, work the ingredients together, gradually drawing in the flour with your left hand.

When the cubes of butter have become very small and the mixture is turning grainy, pour in the ice water and work it gradually into the pastry without kneading. Stop working the pastry as soon as it becomes almost homogeneous but still contains some small flakes of butter.

On the lightly floured surface, roll out the pastry away from you into a 16 × 8 in/40 × 20 cm rectangle. Fold in the ends to make three layers. Rotate the pastry through 90 degrees and roll it out again into a 16 × 8 in/40 × 20 cm rectangle. Fold again into three. These are the first two turns. Wrap the pastry in plastic wrap and refrigerate 30 minutes.

Make two more turns. The pastry is now ready to use. Wrap it and store, or roll it into the desired shape, place on a dampened baking sheet, and refrigerate for 20 minutes before using.

NOTE:
Quick puff pastry will keep only 2 days in the refrigerator or 1 week in the freezer.

CHOUX PASTE AND PUFFS
Pâte à choux

THIS VERSATILE PASTE FORMS THE BASIS OF MANY DESSERTS, INCLUDING MY
BLACK AND WHITE SAINT-HONORÉ (PAGE 106).

INGREDIENTS:

½ cup/125 ml water

½ cup/125 ml milk

7 tbsp/100 g butter, finely
diced

½ tsp fine salt

¾ tsp sugar

1 cup/150 g flour, sifted

4 eggs

Eggwash (1 egg yolk mixed
with 1 soup spoon milk
and a pinch of salt)
(optional)

Makes 22–25 small cream
puffs or éclairs

Preparation time: 20
minutes

Cooking time: 10–20
minutes, depending on the
size and shape of the puffs

MIXING THE CHOUX PASTE: Combine the water, milk, butter, salt, and sugar in a saucepan and boil over high heat for 1 minute (1). If any visible pieces of butter are left, boil for a few seconds more. Take the pan off the heat and quickly tip in the flour, stirring continuously to make a very smooth paste.

Return the pan to the heat and stir the paste with a spatula for 1 minute (2). This "drying out" process is vitally important for making a good choux paste. By now, some of the water will have evaporated. Take care not to let the paste dry out too much, or it will crack during cooking and spoil your choux puffs. Transfer the paste to a bowl and immediately use a spatula to beat in the eggs one by one (3). Beat until the paste is very smooth. It is now ready to use. If you do not wish to use it immediately, spread a little eggwash over the surface to prevent a crust from forming.

NOTE

Choux paste will keep in an airtight container 3 days in the refrigerator or 1 week in the freezer.

PIPING OUT THE CHOUX PASTE: Using a pastry bag with an appropriate tip, pipe the paste into your desired shapes or a flat base on a baking sheet lined with parchment or buttered wax paper (4). Brush with eggwash and press the top of the shapes lightly with the back of a fork, dipping it into the eggwash each time. This ensures that the choux puffs develop and rise evenly.

BAKING THE CHOUX PUFFS: Preheat the oven to 425°F/220°C. Bake the choux puffs for 4–5 minutes, then open the oven door a crack and leave it ajar. Continue to bake for another 5–15 minutes, depending on the size of the choux puffs.

Baked choux puffs on a
Saint-Honoré base

FRENCH PANCAKES
Crêpes

I USE CRÊPES IN MY COULIBIAC OF WINTER FRUITS (PAGE 98) AND
SOUFFLEED CHOCOLATE CRÊPES (PAGE 90).

INGREDIENTS:
1¼ cups/250 g flour
2 tbsp/30 g sugar
A pinch of salt
4 eggs
2⅔ cups/650 ml milk,
    boiled and cooled
⅞ cup/200 ml heavy cream
Flavoring of your choice
    (eg: vanilla, Grand
    Marnier, orange flower
    water, lemon zest)
2 tbsp/30 g clarified butter

Serves 10
Preparation time: 10
    minutes, plus resting
Cooking time: 1 minute per
    crêpe

MAKING THE BATTER: Combine the flour, sugar, and salt in a bowl, then add the eggs, two at a time, mixing well with a balloon whisk. Stir in ⅞ cup/200 ml milk to make a smooth batter. Add the cream and the rest of the milk, then let the batter rest in a cool place for at least 1 hour before using.

COOKING THE CRÊPES: Stir the batter and add your chosen flavoring. Brush a 12 in/30 cm frying pan with clarified butter and heat. Ladle in a little batter and cook the crêpe about 1 minute on each side, tossing it or turning it with a metal spatula.

SERVING: Roll or fold the crêpes and eat at once, either plain or sprinkled with sugar. They are also delicious filled with Apricot Jam with Almonds (page 58) or Apple Jelly (page 59).

NOTE:
Layer the cooked crêpes with bands of wax paper to prevent them from sticking together.

TULIP PASTE FOR BASKETS AND RIBBONS
Pâte à tulipe/ruban/caissette

THIS PASTE IS USED TO MAKE "CIGARETTES" FOR PETITS FOURS, AND LITTLE BASKETS
THAT YOU CAN FILL WITH ICE CREAM, SORBETS, OR FRESH FRUITS. SINCE IT IS VERY
MALLEABLE, I ALSO USE IT TO MAKE DECORATIONS SUCH AS RIBBONS (SEE PHOTO
PAGE 188) OR MULTI-COLORED BANDS TO ENCIRCLE A GATEAU.

INGREDIENTS:
7 tbsp/100 g softened
  butter
1 cup/100 g confectioners'
  sugar, sifted
6½ tbsp/100 g egg whites,
  at room temperature
½ cup/75 g flour, sifted
½ cup/40 g unsweetened
  cocoa powder, sifted
  (optional: see note
  opposite)

Makes 13 oz/375 g
Preparation time: 10
  minutes

Put the softened butter and confectioners' sugar in a bowl and mix
with a spatula, then add the egg whites, a little at a time. Finally stir
in the flour and cocoa to make a smooth, homogeneous paste. Cover
the bowl with plastic wrap and keep in the refrigerator for up to a
week.

Take the paste out of the refrigerator several hours before using and
let it soften at room temperature so that it becomes easier to work.

NOTES:
½ cup/40 g cocoa is
enough to color and flavor all
the paste. Like flour, it acts
as a binding agent, so you
will need to add an extra 4
tsp/ 20 g egg whites (½
cup/120 g in total). The
paste can also be flavored
with vanilla or a few drops
of lemon extract or orange
flower water.

Once baked, the paste is
delicate and loses its texture
after 24 hours, especially in
humid weather.

CIGARETTE PASTE FOR STRIPED COOKIES
Pâte à cigarette pour biscuit rayé

USE THIS PASTE TO GIVE AN ATTRACTIVE STRIPED EFFECT TO YOUR
SHOWPIECE DESSERTS AND GATEAUX.

INGREDIENTS:
7 tbsp/100 g softened
  butter
1 cup/100 g confectioners'
  sugar, sifted
7 tbsp/110 g egg whites
9 tbsp/80 g flour, sifted
Food coloring as appropriate
  (eg: green/red), or cocoa
  powder for chocolate
  brown

Makes about 14 oz/400 g
Preparation time: 15
  minutes

Cream the butter in a bowl. Work in the confectioners' sugar until
smooth, then add the egg whites, little by little. Finally add and mix
in the flour. When the paste is completely homogeneous, add a few
drops of food coloring to achieve your desired effect. The paste is
now ready to use.

Spread the paste onto parchment paper, in stripes or extremely thin
layers, using a metal spatula, icing comb, piping cone, or your
fingers, depending on the desired effect. Freeze for at least 10
minutes to harden the paste, then spread on a layer of Joconde or
Genoise sponge batter (pages 31 and 33), and bake according to the
recipe.

NOTE:
Cigarette paste can be kept in
an airtight container in the
refrigerator up to a week.
Bring it back to room
temperature and work with a
spatula to make it flexible
and malleable before using.

SPICED CAKE
Pain d'épices

THIS RECIPE WAS GIVEN TO ME BY MY FRIEND DENIS RUFFEL OF THE
PATISSERIE MILLET IN PARIS. I USE IT AS A BASE FOR MY LICORICE GATEAU
WITH A PEAR FAN (PAGE 116).

INGREDIENTS:
¾ cup/250 g highly
  perfumed honey
1 cup/125 g strong rye
  flour and ¾ cup + 2½
  tbsp/125 g all-purpose
  flour, sifted together
2 tbsp/20 g baking powder
½ cup/125 ml milk
3 eggs
¼ cup/50 g sugar
1 tsp ground cinnamon
A pinch of grated nutmeg
A pinch of aniseed, crushed
1 oz/30 g candied orange
  and lemon peel, minced
A few drops of vanilla or
  lemon extract

Serves 8
Preparation time: 20
  minutes
Cooking time: about 1 hour,
  depending on the size

THE CAKE BATTER: In a saucepan, warm the honey over low heat until completely liquid. Take off the heat and cool to about 77°F/25°C.

Put the sifted flours and baking powder in a bowl. Pour on the melted honey, then the milk, eggs, and sugar, whisking to obtain a smooth, creamy paste. Finally, add the cinnamon, nutmeg, aniseed, candied peel, and your chosen extract. The paste should be supple, smooth, and slightly elastic.

Preheat the oven to 320°F/160°C.

BAKING THE CAKE: Pour the batter into the prepared cake pan, place on a baking sheet, and bake in the preheated oven for 30 minutes. Slide a second baking sheet underneath the first after this time and bake the cake for a further 30 minutes. Let the cooked cake cool in the pan for 15 minutes, then unmold it onto a cooling rack and leave at room temperature.

PRESENTATION: Peel off the paper from the cold cake, slice it, and serve plain. I adore it served with a cup of tea or hot chocolate.

SPECIAL EQUIPMENT:
1 cake pan, 10 × 4 × 3¼
  in/24 × 10 × 8 cm, lined
  with parchment paper and
  greased
2 baking sheets

NOTES:
If you like, ice the cake when it comes out of the oven with a thin coating of apricot jam, then one of lemon icing (see Little Lemon Cakes, page 179).

This spiced cake keeps up to a week if stored in an airtight container at room temperature.

CHAPTER TWO

SPONGE
AND MERINGUE BASES

These sweet bases are of prime importance in the craft of pâtisserie. How elegantly they drape and support gâteaux, individual desserts, and small cakes! Soft, light, or crunchy, they range from the palest pastel blonde to golden brown. Their silken beauty can be enhanced by decoration, either applied by hand or piped.

They can be filled, covered, masked, or enrobed in mousse, cream, or ganache to delight the eye and palate. Remember, too, that they are delicious served on their own for a treat with tea or coffee.

These bases will keep well for two or three days if wrapped in plastic wrap and kept in a cool, dry place. They can also be successfully frozen for at least a week.

Light ladyfingers (see a recipe for these on page 32)

HAZELNUT OR COCONUT DACQUOISE

Dacquoise noisette ou coco

CRUNCHY OUTSIDE, SOFT INSIDE AND VERY SUGARY, A DACQUOISE RESEMBLES A TYPE OF MACAROON. I USE IT FOR MY COFFEE PARFAITS (PAGE 75).

INGREDIENTS:

¾ cup/60 g very finely ground almonds

2⅓ cups/180 g very finely ground hazelnuts, or 2 packed cups/160 g very finely grated coconut

2 cups/250 g confectioners' sugar, sifted

½ cup + 2 tbsp/150 g egg whites

½ cup/100 g superfine sugar

Makes one 24 × 16 in/60 × 40 cm sheet

Preparation time: 15 minutes

Cooking time: 15–18 minutes

PREPARATION: Mix the ground almonds, hazelnuts, or coconut and confectioners' sugar very thoroughly. Beat the egg whites until half-risen, then add the superfine sugar and continue to beat until very firm. Sprinkle the nut and sugar mixture onto the egg whites, folding it in delicately with a slotted spoon until well mixed, but taking care not to overwork the mixture.

SPREADING AND COOKING THE DACQUOISE: Preheat the oven to 350°F/180°C.

Line the baking sheet with the parchment or wax paper and spread on the dacquoise mixture to a thickness of about ⅜ in/7 mm. Bake immediately for 15–18 minutes; after 15 minutes, check the cooking by gently pressing the central part of the dacquoise with your fingertips. It should be fairly firm on top but still slightly soft in the middle.

Remove the dacquoise from the oven and immediately slide the paper onto a wire rack. Let cool at room temperature.

When the dacquoise is almost cold, peel it off the paper and use it at once.

SPECIAL EQUIPMENT:

24 × 16 in/60 × 40 cm baking sheet

Buttered and lightly floured wax or parchment paper

NOTE:

The dacquoise can be wrapped in plastic wrap and frozen for at least a week.

JOCONDE SPONGE

Biscuit joconde

THIS FINE, DELICATE SPONGE IS USED AS A BASE FOR MANY MOUSSE-BASED DESSERTS.

INGREDIENTS:

13 oz/375 g tant pour tant (equal weights of ground almonds and confectioners' sugar, sifted together, eg: 2½ cups nuts and 1½ cups sugar)

5 eggs, plus 5 extra whites

2 tbsp/25 g superfine sugar

3 tbsp/40 g butter, melted and cooled

⅓ cup/50 g flour

Makes one 24 × 16 in/60 × 40 cm sheet

Preparation time: 15 minutes

Cooking time: 2–3 minutes

Preheat the oven to 500°F/250°C.

Put the tant pour tant and whole eggs in a mixing bowl and beat at high speed to a ribbon consistency. Beat the egg whites until well-risen, then add the sugar and continue to beat at high speed until very firm. Using a skimmer, fold first the melted butter, then the flour into the whole egg mixture. Blend in one-third of the egg whites, then tip in the remainder and fold in very delicately until completely amalgamated. Take care not to overmix.

Use a metal spatula to spread the mixture over the parchment paper to a thickness of about ⅛ in/3 mm. Bake immediately for 2–3 minutes until the sponge is just firm to the touch, but still moist. Slide the cooked sponge on its paper onto a wire rack and let cool. Remove the paper immediately before using the sponge.

SPECIAL EQUIPMENT:

24 × 16 in/60 × 40 cm baking sheet, lined with parchment paper

NOTE:

It is not easy to achieve good results using less than the given quantities. If only half the quantity is required, I suggest that you make the whole recipe and freeze half the sponge for later use. Freeze it flat on the paper, or rolled up like a jelly roll.

SPONGE BATTER (FOR A JELLY ROLL)
Biscuits à la cuillère

USE THESE SPONGES AS THE BASE FOR A CHARLOTTE, OR LAYER THEM FILLED WITH CHANTILLY CREAM (PAGE 42).

INGREDIENTS:
4 eggs, plus 3 extra yolks
7 tbsp/85 g superfine sugar
¼ cup/35 g flour
5 tbsp/40 g potato flour
  (potato starch)

Makes one 24 × 16 in/
  60 × 40 cm sheet
Preparation time: 20
  minutes
Cooking time: about 6
  minutes, depending on the
  size of the sponge

THE BASIC MIXTURE: Separate the whole eggs and put the whites in one mixing bowl and all the yolks in another. Beat the yolks with two-thirds of the sugar to a ribbon consistency. Beat the whites until well-risen, then add the remaining sugar and continue to beat at high speed for 1 minute until very firm.

Using a skimmer, fold one-third of the egg whites into the yolks and blend thoroughly. Tip in the remaining whites all at once and delicately fold them into the mixture. Before it becomes completely homogeneous, sift in the flour and potato flour, mixing continuously. Stop mixing as soon as the batter becomes perfectly smooth, or it will lose its lightness.

Preheat the oven to 425°F/220°C.

JELLY ROLL: To make a jelly roll, spread the batter with a metal spatula on a sheet of parchment paper. Alternatively, use a pastry bag fitted with any size tip from ¼ in/5 mm to ⅝ in/15 mm, depending on the desired effect.

Slide the paper onto a baking sheet and bake in the oven for about 6 minutes if you used a ¼ in/5 mm tip, longer for a larger tip. Invert the cooked sponge onto a dish towel and immediately peel off the paper. Cool, then fill and roll the sponge.

SPECIAL EQUIPMENT:
24 × 16 in/60 × 40 cm
  baking sheet
A sheet of parchment paper.

SPONGE BATTER
(FOR LADYFINGERS OR DESSERT BASES)

INGREDIENTS:
6 eggs
1 cup/190 g superfine sugar
1¼ cups/180 g flour
¼ cup/30 g confectioners'
  sugar, for ladyfingers

Makes: about 1¼ lbs/600 g
Preparation time: 20
  minutes
Cooking time: 8 minutes for
  ladyfingers, 25 minutes
  for a dessert base

Prepare the batter as in the recipe above. Preheat the oven to 425°F/220°C. To make ladyfingers, use a pastry bag with a plain ⅝ in/15 mm tip to pipe 4 in/10 cm long fingers onto a baking sheet lined with parchment paper. Lightly dust them with confectioners' sugar, let rest for 5 minutes, then dust with confectioners' sugar again and bake in the oven for 8 minutes. Lift the fingers off the paper with a metal spatula before they have cooled completely, and place on a wire rack.

DESSERT BASE: To make a dessert base, pour the batter into a lightly greased and floured 9–10 in/23–25 cm cake pan and bake at 375°F/190°C for 20–25 minutes, depending on the thickness of the sponge. Invert it onto a wire rack as soon as it is cooked.

SPECIAL EQUIPMENT:
Baking sheet lined with
  parchment paper, or a
  9–10 in/23–25 cm
  diam. cake pan.

NOTE:
Use the sponge on the day it
is made, or it will lose its
delicious delicate taste.

A hollowed-out Genoise sponge filled with cherries in syrup

PLAIN GENOISE SPONGE
Génoise nature

INGREDIENTS:

1¼ cups/250 g sugar

8 eggs

1¾ cups/250 g flour

4 tbsp/50 g warm clarified butter (optional)

2 tbsp/25 g butter and a pinch of flour for the cake pans

Makes about 2¼ lbs/1 kg (two 8½ in/22 cm diam. sponges, or one 16 in/40 cm square sponge)

Preparation time: about 25 minutes

Cooking time: about 30 minutes

Preheat the oven to 375°F/190°C.

Beat the sugar and eggs in an electric mixer. Stand the bowl in a bain-marie and continue to beat until the mixture reaches 104°F/40°C. Remove the bowl from the bain-marie and beat the mixture for 5 minutes, until well risen, then reduce the speed of the mixer and beat for another 5 minutes, until the mixture has cooled and reached a ribbon consistency.

Sift in the flour and fold it gently into the mixture with a flat skimmer. Do not overwork it. Add the clarified butter now if you are using it. Divide the batter between two lightly greased and floured cake pans or one large pan, and bake immediately. The 8½ in/22 cm sponges will take 30 minutes; a very large cake will need about 50 minutes. To test whether it is ready, insert a skewer into the center; it should come out clean and dry.

As soon as the sponges are cooked, unmold onto a wire rack and let cool completely, giving them one quarter-turn every 15 minutes to prevent them from sticking to the rack.

CHOCOLATE GENOISE: Replace the 1¾ cups/250 g flour with 1¼ cups + 3 tbsp/200 g flour sifted with ¾ cup + 2 tbsp/75 g unsweetened cocoa powder, and proceed as above.

SPECIAL EQUIPMENT:

Two 8 in/22 cm diam. cake pans, or one 16 in/40 cm/square pan

NOTES:

It is best to bake the genoise sponges a day in advance, as they will hold their shape better when sliced. They can be wrapped in plastic wrap and kept in the refrigerator 3 days, or frozen up to 2 weeks.

If you plan to serve the cake plain, the addition of clarified butter will greatly improve the flavor.

It is also delicious hollowed out and filled with fruit.

33

WALNUT SPONGE
Biscuit aux noix

INGREDIENTS:
MIXTURE 1:
⅓ cup/80 g egg yolks mixed with 2 tbsp/30 g egg whites and 2 heaped tbsp/50 g clear honey

MERINGUE:
⅔ cup/150 g egg whites
¼ cup/50 g superfine sugar

MIXTURE 2:
½ cup/50 g walnut kernels, minced with a knife, mixed with 3 tbsp/10 g instant coffee and 7 tbsp/60 g flour

MIXTURE 1: Preheat the oven to 350°F/180°C. In an electric mixer, beat Mixture 1 to a ribbon consistency, then transfer to a wide-mouthed bowl.

THE MERINGUE: Beat the ⅔ cup/150 g egg whites in the electric mixer until half-risen, then add the sugar and continue to beat until stiff.

MIXING THE BATTER: Immediately sprinkle Mixture 2 onto Mixture 1, then delicately fold in the meringue without overworking the mixture, stopping as soon as it becomes homogeneous.

SPREADING AND BAKING THE SPONGE: Use a metal spatula to spread the batter over the whole surface of the paper, and bake in the preheated oven for 10 minutes.
Immediately slide the paper onto a cooling rack and leave at room temperature to cool completely.

SPECIAL EQUIPMENT:
24 × 16 in/60 × 40 cm baking sheet lined with lightly buttered and floured wax or parchment paper

NOTES:
Use the sponge immediately after it has cooled, or remove the paper, wrap the sponge in plastic wrap, roll up like a jelly roll, and freeze; it will keep at least a week.

Makes one 24 × 16 in/ 60 × 40 cm sheet
Preparation time: 10 minutes
Cooking time: 10 minutes

CHOCOLATE SPONGE
Biscuit chocolat

INGREDIENTS:
9 oz/240 g bitter couverture or best-quality bittersweet chocolate, chopped
4 tbsp/50 g butter, diced
¼ cup/60 g egg yolks
1 cup/250 g egg whites
7 tbsp/90 g superfine sugar

Makes one 24 × 16 in/60 × 40 cm sheet, or a 10 in/24 cm round sponge
Preparation time: 15 minutes
Cooking time: 8 minutes for a sheet, 35 minutes for a round sponge

THE SPONGE BATTER: Put the chocolate in a bowl, stand it in a bain-marie over medium heat, and melt it at 104°F/40°C. Add the diced butter and mix with a spatula.
Preheat the oven to 350°F/180°C.
Put the egg yolks in a bowl and cream with 1½ tbsp/20 g sugar until just pale. Beat the egg whites until semi-firm, then add the remaining sugar and beat until very firm, shiny, and smooth. Add the yolks, fold in delicately with a spatula, then gently mix in the chocolate.

BAKING THE SPONGE: Immediately, use a metal spatula to spread the batter onto the parchment paper to a thickness of ¼ in/5 mm, or pour it into the prepared ring. Bake the sheet in the preheated oven for 8 minutes, or the cake for 35 minutes. Place the cooked sponge on a cooling rack and use when cold.

SPECIAL EQUIPMENT:
Parchment paper, or a lightly greased dessert ring, 10 in/24 cm diam., 2 in/5 cm deep

NOTE:
This light sponge base contains no flour, which makes it extremely fragile and delicate.

Meringue Topping made with Egg Yolks
Meringage aux jaunes d'oeuf

This topping is often used to coat gateaux or ice creams, then glazed for 30 seconds under a salamander or with a blowtorch. I use it in my recipe for Souffleed Oranges with Caramel Sauce (page 84).

INGREDIENTS:

5 egg yolks, plus ½ cup/50 g confectioners' sugar

5 egg whites, plus 1 cup/100 g confectioners' sugar

Makes 14 oz/400 g
Preparation time: 15 minutes

With an electric mixer or by hand, whisk the egg yolks with ½ cup/50 g sugar to a ribbon consistency, then keep at room temperature.

As soon as you have whisked the yolks, beat the whites with the 1 cup/100 g sugar until very smooth and firm (this can be done in an electric mixer or by hand). Using a spatula, delicately fold the two mixtures together. The meringue is now ready and must be used immediately, or it will lose its lightness and volume.

NOTE:
The egg yolks for this meringue can be flavored with a little vanilla or a hint of instant coffee or cocoa powder.

Meringue Topping made with Egg Whites
Meringage aux blancs d'oeuf

Like the topping made with egg yolks, this is used to glaze patisserie and desserts, but its texture is less rich and soft. Use whichever type you prefer; it is purely a matter of taste.

INGREDIENTS:

5 egg whites
1¼ cups/250 g superfine sugar

Makes 14 oz/400 g
Preparation time: 7 minutes

With an electric mixer or by hand, beat the egg whites with half the sugar until risen and semi-firm. Add the remaining sugar and beat to a very firm, smooth, and shiny consistency. Use this meringue immediately.

NOTE:
The meringue topping is often piped onto the dessert with a decorative or plain tip to give an attractive finish.

ITALIAN MERINGUE
Meringue italienne

I USE THIS MERINGUE IN ALL MY MOUSSES AND IN CHIBOUST CREAM
(PAGE 39) AND BUTTERCREAM (PAGE 41).

INGREDIENTS:
6 tbsp water
1¼ cups/360 g sugar
1½ tbsp/30 g liquid glucose
    or light corn syrup
    (optional)
6 egg whites

Makes about 1½ lbs/650 g
Preparation time: 7 minutes
Cooking time: 15–20
    minutes

Pour the water into the pan and add the sugar and glucose. Bring to a boil over medium heat, stirring with a skimmer. Skim the surface and wash down the inside of the pan with a pastry brush dipped in cold water. Increase the heat and put in the candy thermometer.

When the sugar reaches 230°F/110°C, begin beating the egg whites in an electric mixer until firm. Keep an eye on the sugar and stop cooking as soon as it reaches 248°F/121°C.

When the egg whites are firm, set the mixer to its lowest speed and pour in the cooked sugar in a thin, steady stream, keeping it clear of the beaters. Continue to beat at low speed for about 15 minutes, until the mixture becomes tepid (about 86°F/30°C). The meringue is now ready to use.

SPECIAL EQUIPMENT:
Heavy-based sugar pan
Candy thermometer

NOTES:
Glucose prevents the formation of sugar crystals, but is not essential.

It is not really possible to make a successful Italian meringue using smaller quantities, but the mixture will keep in an airtight container in the refrigerator for several days

FRENCH MERINGUE
Meringue française

I USE THIS RECIPE IN MY MERINGUE PILLOWS WITH MARRONS GLACÉS (PAGE
74) AND IN VACHERINS OF ICE CREAM OR SORBETS.

INGREDIENTS:
7 tbsp/100 g egg whites
1½ cups/170 g
    confectioners' sugar, sifted

Makes 9 double meringues
    (about 10 oz/275 g)
Preparation time: 15
    minutes
Cooking time: 1 hour 50
    minutes

A stack of crisp French
meringues

THE MERINGUE MIXTURE: Using an electric mixer or a bowl and whisk, beat the egg whites with half the confectioners' sugar until semi-firm. Add the remaining sugar and beat to obtain a firm, shiny, homogeneous mixture.

Preheat the oven to 200°F/100°C.

PIPING THE MERINGUE: Pipe the meringue onto the paper, using the fluted tip to make eighteen 3¼ in/8 cm long meringues, or the plain tip to pipe eighteen 2 in/5 cm diam. balls.

COOKING THE MERINGUES: Slide the paper onto a baking sheet and cook the meringues in the oven for 1 hour 50 minutes. Let cool on the paper at room temperature, then peel off the meringues, place on a wire rack, and leave in a dry place.

CHOCOLATE MERINGUES: Use only 1½ cups/150 g confectioners' sugar and add ⅓ cup/30 g unsweetened cocoa powder for the last minute of beating.

SPECIAL EQUIPMENT:
Pastry bag with a fluted
    ⅝ in/14 mm tip or a
    plain ½ in/12 mm tip
Wax or parchment paper

NOTES:
The meringues will keep several days in an airtight container well away from any humidity.

A convection oven is best for making French meringues, which will emerge light and crisp on the outside and soft in the middle.

Chapter Three

CREAMS, MOUSSES, BAVAROIS, AND PARFAITS

These creamy confections, with their glowing or pastel colors, are used to garnish, fill, or mask cakes, gâteaux, and desserts. CREAMS are always used in fruit tarts. Often, different creams are mixed together (pastry cream with almond cream, for example). They are delicious and not too rich in calories. Most of my MOUSSES AND BAVAROIS are made from fruit, lightly whipped cream, and Italian meringue, with a little gelatine to keep their shape and consistency. Go easy on the gelatine; it is only there to hold the lightness between making the dessert and eating it. Too much will give the dessert an unpleasant rubbery texture. PARFAITS should always be served iced. A creamy marriage of mousses and ice creams, they are very rich, so are best served in small portions.

Creams, mousses, bavarois, and parfaits cannot successfully be made in small quantities, or they will lose their lightness and texture. They do, however, freeze very well.

Piping Chiboust Cream onto Princess Tart with Blueberries (see recipe page 132)

PASTRY CREAM
Crème pâtissière

INGREDIENTS:

6 egg yolks

½ cup + 2 tbsp/125 g
  sugar

4½ tbsp/40 g flour

2 cups/500 ml milk

1 vanilla bean, split

A little butter or
  confectioners' sugar, for
  cooling

Makes about
  1 lb 10 oz/750 g
Preparation time: 15
  minutes

In a bowl, whisk the egg yolks with about one-third of the sugar until pale and of a light ribbon consistency. Sift in the flour and mix it in thoroughly.

In a saucepan, bring the milk to a boil with the remaining sugar and the vanilla bean. As soon as it begins to bubble, pour about one-third onto the egg mixture, stirring continuously. Pour this custard back into the pan and bring to a boil over very gentle heat, stirring continuously. Bubble 2 minutes, then transfer to a bowl. Dot the surface with a few flakes of butter or dust lightly with confectioners' sugar to prevent a skin from forming as the pastry cream cools. To cool it more quickly, pour the pastry cream onto a marble work surface and keep turning it back onto itself with a metal spatula for 2 minutes.

COFFEE OR CHOCOLATE PASTRY CREAM: Substitute a little instant coffee or unsweetened cocoa powder for the vanilla. If you use cocoa, use a touch less flour and a little extra sugar.

NOTE:
Pastry cream can be stored in the refrigerator at 41°F/5°C for 36 hours.

CHIBOUST CREAM
Crème Chiboust

I USE THIS DELICATE CREAM FOR MY LOVE NESTS WIH RED-CURRANT PEARLS (PAGE 80) AND PRINCESS TART WITH BLUEBERRIES (PAGE 132)

INGREDIENTS:

6 egg yolks

6½ tbsp/80 g sugar

3½ tbsp/30 g custard
  powder

1½ cups/350 ml milk

½ vanilla bean, split

1 quantity freshly-made
  Italian Meringue (page
  37), cooled to tepid

2 gelatine leaves, soaked in
  cold water and well
  drained

3½ tbsp Curaçao, Grand
  Marnier, or rum

A little butter, for cooling

Makes 2 lbs 14 oz/1.3 kg
Preparation time: 25
  minutes

THE PASTRY CREAM: In a bowl, whisk the egg yolks with one-third of the sugar until pale and of a light ribbon consistency. Sift in the custard powder and mix well. In a saucepan, bring the milk to a boil with the remaining sugar and the vanilla. As soon as it starts to bubble, pour about one-third onto the egg mixture, stirring continuously. Pour the mixture back into the pan and bring to a boil over low heat, stirring all the time. Bubble 2 minutes, then take the pan off the heat. Warm the alcohol, dissolve the gelatine in it, and stir into the pastry cream. Transfer to a bowl, remove the vanilla bean, dot the surface with butter, and let cool until tepid (it should be at the same temperature as the meringue).

THE CHIBOUST CREAM: Using a whisk, fold one-third of the tepid meringue into the tepid pastry cream, then use a spatula to fold in the rest delicately until the cream is completely homogeneous. Do not overmix the cream or it will lose its lightness.

CHOCOLATE CHIBOUST CREAM: Add 3 oz/75 g melted dark couverture or bittersweet chocolate to the cooked pastry cream and use only 2½ tbsp/20 g custard powder.

NOTE:
Chiboust cream must be used as soon as you have mixed in the meringue, so have the base for your dessert ready before finishing the cream. The finished dessert can be frozen for 3–4 days.

CREME ANGLAISE

SERVE THIS DELICIOUS CUSTARD SAUCE WELL CHILLED AS AN
ACCOMPANIMENT TO CAKES OR BERRY FRUITS.

INGREDIENTS:
12 egg yolks
1¼ cups/250 g sugar
1 quart/1 liter milk
1 vanilla bean, split

Makes about 1½ quarts/1.5
liters
Preparation time: 15
minutes

In a bowl, whisk the egg yolks with one-third of the sugar to a ribbon consistency. Bring the milk to a boil with the remaining sugar and the vanilla and pour it onto the egg mixture, whisking continuously. Return the mixture to the pan and gently heat, stirring continuously, to 175°F/80°C, until the custard is just thick enough to coat the spoon. Do not let it boil.

Pass the custard through a conical strainer into a bowl and leave in a cool place until completely cold. Stir occasionally to prevent a skin from forming.

COFFEE OR CHOCOLATE CREME ANGLAISE: Replace the vanilla bean with 3 tbsp instant coffee powder or 4 oz/100 g melted bittersweet chocolate or couverture.

NOTES:
For a less rich custard, you can reduce the number of egg yolks, but you will need a minimum of 8 per 1 quart/1 liter milk.

The crème anglaise can be stored in the refrigerator at 41°F/5°C for 48 hours. Pass it again through a conical strainer before using.

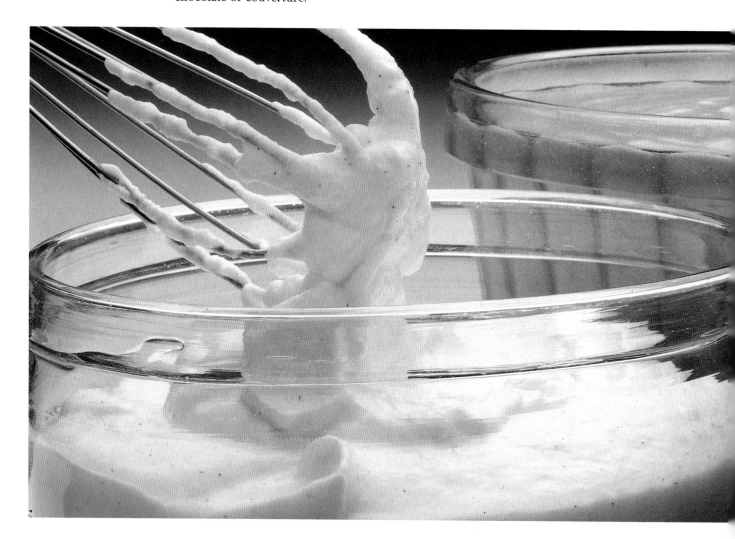

BUTTERCREAM
Crème au beurre

MY VERSION OF BUTTERCREAM IS NOT TOO RICH OR SICKLY, WHICH MAKES
IT EASILY DIGESTIBLE.

INGREDIENTS:
¾ cup/175 ml water
2¼ cups/450 g sugar
2 tbsp/40 g liquid glucose
  or light corn syrup
  (optional)
6 egg whites
1½ lbs/700 g butter, at
  room temperature, diced

Makes about 3½ lbs/1.6 kg
Preparation time: 20
  minutes

THE ITALIAN MERINGUE: First make an Italian meringue, following the method on page 37, and using all the ingredients except the butter. Leave in the mixer until almost cold.

THE BUTTERCREAM: Add the butter to the cooled meringue, a little at a time. Beat for 5 minutes until the buttercream is very smooth and homogeneous.

COFFEE BUTTERCREAM: Add instant coffee powder to taste, dissolved in a very little water.

NOTE:
Buttercream can be stored in an airtight container in the refrigerator for a week. Leave at room temperature for 1 hour before using, then stir well until smooth.

Left to right: Vanilla Chantilly cream; Caramel mousse; Dark chocolate mousse

MOUSSELINE CREAM
Crème mousseline

I USE THIS LIGHT CREAM AS A FILLING FOR TARTS AND TARTLETS, AND IN MY
MARZIPAN FIGS (PAGE 68).

INGREDIENTS:
PASTRY CREAM
4 eggs, plus 2 extra yolks
1 cup + 2 tbsp/220 g
    sugar
⅓ cup/50 g flour
2 cups/500 ml milk

9 oz (2 sticks + 2 tbsp)/
    250 g butter, at room
    temperature, finely diced
Flavoring of your choice
    (eg: caramel, chocolate,
    coffee, Grand Marnier)

Makes about 2 lbs 14 oz/
    1.3 kg
Preparation time: 30
    minutes

THE PASTRY CREAM: Follow the method on page 39 using all the
ingredients except the butter and flavoring.

THE MOUSSELINE CREAM: As soon as the pastry cream is cooked, take
the pan off the heat and beat in one-third of the diced butter. Transfer
to a bowl and keep in a cool place, stirring occasionally to prevent a
skin from forming and to cool the cream more quickly.

In an electric mixer, beat the remaining butter at low speed for
about 3 minutes, until fairly pale. Increase the speed to medium and
add the cooled pastry cream, a little at a time. Beat for 5 minutes, until
the mousseline is perfectly light and creamy. Use it plain, or add your
chosen flavoring.

NOTE:
Mousseline cream keeps well
in the refrigerator for up to 4
days. Store in an airtight
container or a bowl covered
with plastic wrap.

CHANTILLY CREAM
Crème Chantilly

I USE CHOCOLATE AND VANILLA FLAVORED CHANTILLY CREAMS IN MY BLACK
AND WHITE SAINT-HONORÉ (PAGE 106).

INGREDIENTS:
2 cups/500 ml well-chilled
    heavy cream
6½ tbsp/50 g confectioners'
    sugar, or 3½ tbsp Sorbet
    Syrup (page 144)
Vanilla powder or extract
    (optional)

Makes about 1¼ lbs/600 g
Preparation time: 8 minutes

Put the chilled cream, sugar or syrup, and vanilla in a chilled mixing
bowl and whip at medium speed for 1–2 minutes. Increase the speed
and whip for another 3–4 minutes, until the cream begins to thicken.
It should be a little firmer than a ribbon consistency. Do not overbeat,
or it may turn into butter.

CHOCOLATE CHANTILLY: Melt 5 oz/150 g dark couverture or best
quality bittersweet chocolate in a bain-marie to 113°F/45°C, stirring
continuously. Off the heat, whisk the melted chocolate into the
Chantilly cream, without beating over-vigorously.

COFFEE CHANTILLY. Dissolve 2 tbsp instant coffee powder in 1 tbsp hot
milk and add it when you whip the cream, or use 1 tbsp coffee
extract.

SPECIAL EQUIPMENT:
Chocolate thermometer

NOTE:
Chantilly cream is best used
as soon as it is made, but
can be kept in the
refrigerator at 41°F/5°C
for 24 hours.

FRANGIPANE OR ALMOND CREAM
Crème d'amandes

I USE THIS LOVELY ALMOND CREAM IN MY WALNUT PITHIVIERS (PAGE 100).

INGREDIENTS:

9 oz (2 sticks + 2 tbsp)/250 g butter, at room temperature

1 lb 2 oz/500 g tant pour tant (equal weights of ground almonds and confectioners' sugar, sifted together, eg: 3⅓ cups nuts and 2 cups sugar)

⅓ cup/50 g flour

5 eggs

3½ tbsp rum (optional)

Makes 2 lbs 10 oz/1.15 kg

Preparation time: 15 minutes

Beat the butter until very soft. Still beating, add the *tant pour tant* and flour, then the eggs, one at a time, beating well between each addition until the frangipane is light and homogeneous. Finally, stir in the rum.

NOTES:

Frangipane can be kept in the refrigerator at 41°F/5°C for up to a week. Store in an airtight container or a bowl covered with plastic wrap and remove from the refrigerator 30 minutes before using.

For a moister frangipane, stir in 20–30% extra pastry cream just before using.

Frangipane-Filled Walnut Pithiviers

CHESTNUT BAVAROIS
Bavaroise aux marrons

THIS MOUSSE MARRIES BRILLIANTLY WITH MERINGUES AND CHOCOLATE.

INGREDIENTS:

1¼ cups/300 ml milk

5 egg yolks

¼ cup/50 g sugar

4 gelatine leaves, soaked in cold water and well drained

14 oz/400 g canned sweetened chestnut purée

2 cups/500 ml heavy cream, whipped to a ribbon consistency

2 tbsp rum (optional)

Makes about 2 lbs 14 oz/1.3 kg

Preparation time: 10 minutes

THE CHESTNUT CUSTARD: In a saucepan, bring the milk to a boil. Put the egg yolks and sugar in a bowl and whisk until pale and of a ribbon consistency. Pour the boiling milk onto the mixture, whisking continuously, then pour the custard back into the pan and gently heat, stirring continuously with a wooden spatula, until the custard is thick enough to coat the spatula. Do not let it boil.

When the custard is ready, take the pan off the heat, stir in the gelatine and chestnut purée, then rub the mixture through a fine strainer into a bowl. Leave at room temperature, whisking from time to time, until the mixture is barely tepid.

MIXING THE BAVAROIS: Using a spatula, fold the cooled chestnut custard into the whipped cream without overworking the mixture, then stir in the rum. The bavarois is now ready to use, before the gelatine sets.

LICORICE BAVAROIS

Bavaroise à la réglisse

I USE THIS BAVAROIS IN MY LICORICE GATEAU WITH A PEAR FAN (PAGE 116). THE
FLAVOR OF LICORICE ALSO GOES WELL WITH LIGHTLY CARAMELIZED APPLES AND PEARS.

INGREDIENTS:

1¼ cups/300 ml milk

¼ cup/50 g sugar

5 egg yolks

3 gelatine leaves, soaked in
cold water and well
drained

1 oz/25 g licorice extract,
or 2 oz/50 g licorice
stick, cut into small pieces

7 oz/200 g freshly-made
Italian Meringue (page
37), cooled to tepid

⅔ cup/150 ml heavy
cream, whipped to a
ribbon consistency

3½ tbsp Armagnac
(optional)

Makes about 1¼ lbs/570 g

Preparation time: 15
minutes

THE LICORICE CUSTARD: Combine the milk and half the sugar in a saucepan and bring to a boil. If you are using a licorice stick, add the pieces now to dissolve them in the hot milk.

Meanwhile, in a bowl, whisk the egg yolks with the remaining sugar until pale and of a light ribbon consistency. Pour the boiling milk onto the mixture, whisking continuously, then return the custard to the pan and heat gently, stirring with a wooden spatula, until the custard is thick enough to coat the spatula. Do not let it boil.

When the custard is ready, take the pan off the heat, stir in the gelatine and licorice extract, and pass through a fine strainer into a bowl. Leave at room temperature, whisking from time to time, until barely tepid.

MIXING THE BAVAROIS: Pour the cooled custard onto the still tepid Italian meringue and mix it in delicately with a balloon whisk. Using a spatula, fold in the whipped cream (to which you have added the Armagnac) without overworking the mixture. The bavarois is now ready to use, before the gelatine sets.

APPLE BAVAROIS

Bavaroise aux pommes

I USE THIS DELICIOUSLY LIGHT BAVAROIS IN MY APPLE CHARLOTTE WITH APPLE CHIPS (PAGE 113).

INGREDIENTS:

1½ cups/350 ml apple cider

5 egg yolks

3 tbsp/35 g sugar, plus ½
cup/100 g for cooking
the apples

4 gelatine leaves, soaked in
cold water and well
drained

2 apples, total weight about
11 oz/300 g

THE APPLE CUSTARD: Pour the apple cider into a saucepan and boil to reduce by one-third. Meanwhile, in a bowl, whisk the egg yolks with 3 tbsp/35 g sugar until pale and of a ribbon consistency. Pour the boiling apple cider onto the mixure, whisking continuously. Pour the custard back into the pan and heat over low heat, stirring gently with a wooden spatula, until the custard is thick enough to coat the spatula. Do not let it boil.

When the custard is ready, take the pan off the heat, stir in the gelatine, then pass through a fine strainer into a bowl. Leave at room temperature until almost completely cold.

THE APPLES: Peel, core and cut into small dice and mix with the lemon

Juice of ½ lemon

4 tbsp/50 g butter

7 tbsp Calvados

6 tbsp/100 g apple purée

7 oz/200 g freshly-made Italian Meringue (page 37), cooled to tepid

2 cups/500 ml heavy cream, whipped to a ribbon consistency

Makes about 3½ lbs/1.65 kg
Preparation time: 30 minutes

juice. Heat the butter in a frying pan, toss in the diced apples, and cook over high heat for 2 minutes. Add the ½ cup/100 g sugar and cook briskly for another 2 minutes, stirring continuously. Pour in the half the Calvados and flame it, then immediately transfer the apples to a bowl and keep in a cool place.

MIXING THE BAVAROIS: Mix the cooled diced apples, apple purée, and the remaining Calvados into the almost cold, half-set custard. Using a spatula, delicately fold in the tepid Italian meringue and finally the whipped cream. Stop working the mixture as soon as it becomes smooth. The bavarois is now ready to use, before the gelatine sets.

PEAR BAVAROIS
Bavaroise aux poires

FOR A LOVELY LIGHT DESSERT, FOLD SOME DICED PEARS POACHED IN SYRUP INTO THE MOUSSE AND SANDWICH IT BETWEEN ROUNDS OF GENOISE OR JOCONDE SPONGE (PAGES 33 AND 31).

INGREDIENTS:

1½ cups/350 ml pear syrup, strongly flavored with vanilla (from freshly poached pears or from canned pears in syrup)

4½ tbsp/35 g milk powder

10 egg yolks

5 tbsp/60 g sugar

3 gelatine leaves, softened in cold water and well drained

4 oz/100 g freshly-made Italian Meringue (page 37), cooled to tepid

¼ cup/60 ml pear eau-de-vie (Poire Williams)

1¾ cups/400 ml heavy cream, lightly whipped to a ribbon consistency

Makes 2 lbs/950 g
Preparation time: 15 minutes

THE CUSTARD: Combine the syrup and powdered milk in a saucepan and, over a low heat, bring to a boil, whisking continuously.

Put the egg yolks and sugar in a bowl and whisk to a pale, light ribbon consistency. Pour the boiling syrup mixture onto the egg yolks and, whisking continuously, pour the mixture into the pan. Poach over low heat, stirring with a wooden spatula, taking care not to let the custard boil. When the custard is thick enough to coat the spatula, take the pan off the heat, stir in the gelatine, and pass the custard through a conical strainer into a bowl. Let it cool at room temperature until barely tepid, whisking from time to time.

MIXING THE BAVAROIS: Pour the pear custard over the tepid meringue, folding it in lightly with a balloon whisk, then add the pear eau-de-vie. Use a spatula to fold in the whipped cream, without overworking the mixture. The bavarois is now ready to use, before the gelatine sets.

NOTES:

This recipe makes enough bavarois to fill twenty-two 2⅜ in/6 cm diam., 1¼ in/3 cm deep dessert rings; serve on individual plates garnished with poached pear and a ribbon of coulis around the edge.

The bavarois can be kept frozen in the rings for at least a week.

CARAMEL MOUSSE
Mousse au caramel

I USE THIS RECIPE, WITH ITS RICH CARAMEL FLAVOR AND UNCTUOUS CREAMINESS, IN MANY CAKES AND DESSERTS, INCLUDING BANANA AND CARAMEL MOUSSE GATEAU (PAGE 110).

INGREDIENTS:

CARAMEL CREAM

1¾ cups/400 ml heavy cream

7 tbsp/150 g liquid glucose or light corn syrup

1 vanilla bean, split

1 cup/200 g sugar

4 tbsp/50 g butter

BOMBE MIXTURE:

⅓ cup/80 ml water

5 tbsp/60 g sugar

1½ tbsp/30 g liquid glucose or light corn syrup

¾ cup + 1 tbsp/200 g egg yolks

5 gelatine leaves, soaked in cold water and well drained

1 cup/220 ml heavy cream, whipped to a ribbon consistency

Makes about 2 lbs/900 g
Preparation time: 50 minutes

THE CARAMEL CREAM: Combine the cream, glucose, and vanilla in a saucepan and bring to a boil. Meanwhile, dissolve the sugar in a heavy casserole over low heat, stirring continuously with a spatula, until it turns to a nutty brown caramel. Do not let it become too dark, or it will taste bitter. Take the pan off the heat and pour the boiling cream mixture into the casserole to prevent the caramel from cooking further. Return the casserole to the heat and let the mixture bubble gently for 2 minutes. Take the pan off the heat again and whisk in the butter, then pass the caramel cream through a conical strainer into a bowl and let cool to about 75°F/24°C.

THE BOMBE MIXTURE: Put the water, sugar, and glucose in a saucepan and bring to a boil over low heat. Boil for 2 minutes, skimming the surface of the sugar to remove any impurities, and washing down the inside of the pan with a pastry brush dipped in cold water.

After 2 minutes, put the egg yolks in the bowl of an electric mixer and gently pour in the boiled sugar, whisking it in by hand. Stand the base of the bowl in a bain-marie of boiling water, set over medium heat, and poach the egg mixture, whisking continuously, until it reaches a temperature of about 158°F/70°C. Now beat the mixture with the electric mixer on low speed until it cools to about 75°F/24°C.

THE MOUSSE: Dissolve the gelatine in 2 tbsp of hot water and mix it into the caramel cream. With the caramel cream and the bombe mixture at the same temperature, mix the two together. Delicately fold in the whipped cream, then use the resulting caramel mousse immediately.

SPECIAL EQUIPMENT:
Candy thermometer

NOTES:
The quantities in this recipe will fill eighteen 2⅜ in/6 cm diam., 1¼ in/3 cm deep dessert rings; use a Walnut Sponge base (page 34).

This easily prepared dessert is particularly good in winter and can be frozen up to a week.

LIME MOUSSE
Mousse au citron vert

A MOUSSE FOR ALL SEASONS, WHICH IS SO REFRESHING THAT YOU WILL
NEVER TIRE OF IT. I USE IT IN MY JEWELED FRUIT GATEAU (PAGE 114), BUT
YOU COULD ALSO SERVE IT IN SMALL RAMEKINS, TOPPED WITH A FEW WILD
STRAWBERRIES OR RASPBERRIES.

INGREDIENTS:
1¼ cups/300 ml lime juice
¼ cup/50 g sugar
4 gelatine leaves, soaked in
    cold water and well
    drained
1 oz/30 g lime zests, finely
    sliced and blanched
11 oz/300 g freshly-made
    Italian Meringue (page
    37), cooled to tepid
2 cups/500 ml heavy
    cream, whipped to a
    ribbon consistency

Makes 2¾ lbs/1.25 kg
    (enough for 2 desserts for
    8 people)
Preparation time: 10
    minutes

PREPARATION: In a small saucepan, heat about one-third of the lime
juice with the sugar. As soon as the juice is warm and the sugar has
dissolved, take the pan off the heat, stir in the gelatine to dissolve it,
then add the remaining lime juice and the zests.

MIXING THE MOUSSE: Pour the lime juice mixture onto the meringue,
folding it in with a balloon whisk, without overworking it. With a
spatula, delicately fold in the whipped cream. Use the mousse at
once, before the gelatine begins to set.

SPECIAL EQUIPMENT:
2 dessert rings, 8½ in/22
    cm diam., 2 in/5 cm
    deep

NOTES:
To make individual desserts,
fill twenty-eight 2⅜ in/6
cm diam., 1¼ in/3 cm deep
dessert rings with the mousse
and decorate the plates with
a border of wild strawberries
and raspberries. Serve this
delectable dessert with or
without a fruit coulis.
    The mousses can be kept
frozen in the rings at least a
week.

Top to bottom:
Mint mousse
Raspberry parfait
Pear mousse
Dark chocolate mousse
Coffee parfait mousse
White chocolate mousse

47

BANANA MOUSSE
Mousse à la banane

INGREDIENTS:

9 oz/250 g very ripe
    bananas
Juice of 2 lemons
Juice of 1 orange
½ cup + 2 tbsp/125 g
    sugar
2 tbsp kirsch (optional), or
    2 tbsp water
3 gelatine leaves, soaked in
    cold water and well
    drained
1½ cups/350 ml heavy
    cream, whipped to a
    ribbon consistency

Makes about 1¾ lbs/820 g
Preparation time: 20
    minutes

Peel the bananas and cut them into chunks. Place in a blender with the lemon and orange juices and the sugar, and purée until very smooth, then transfer to a bowl. Warm the kirsch or water, then, off the heat, stir in and dissolve the gelatine and add it to the banana purée. Using a spatula, gradually and delicately fold the cream into the purée, without overworking the mixture. Use the mousse as soon as it becomes homogeneous, before the gelatine sets.

NOTES:

To make individual desserts, fill eighteen 2⅜ in/6 cm diam., 1¼ in/3 cm deep dessert rings with the mousse and serve on separate plates. The bottom of the rings can be lined with a Coconut Daquoise (page 31) for a wonderful marriage of flavors.

Like all mousses, this one freezes very well for up to a week

MINT MOUSSE
Mousse à la menthe

INGREDIENTS:

1 cup/250 ml milk
½ cup/100 g sugar
½ cup/25 g mint leaves
    (preferably spearmint),
    washed, drained and
    snipped
2 gelatine leaves, soaked in
    cold water and well
    drained
1 cup/250 ml heavy cream,
    whipped to a ribbon
    consistency
1 tbsp green peppermint eau-
    de-vie

Makes about 1½ lbs/650 g
Preparation time: 30
    minutes

In a saucepan, bring the milk and sugar to a boil, whisking all the time. As soon as it bubbles, toss in the snipped mint leaves, whisking continuously, then take the pan off the heat and put on the lid. Let infuse 20 minutes.

Dissolve the gelatine in the infused milk, then pass through a conical strainer into a bowl. Leave at room temperature and, as soon as the mixture is cold (but before the gelatine begins to set), stir in the whipped cream and eau-de-vie. Use the mousse immediately, before it sets.

GINGER MOUSSE

Mousse au gingembre

THIS FINE-FLAVORED MOUSSE IS PARTICULARLY DELICIOUS IN WINTER, AND IS SIMPLE TO PREPARE. I USE IT IN MY NOUGATINE BASKETS WITH YELLOW PEACHES (PAGE 76) AND MILLE-FEUILLE OF GINGER MOUSSE WITH CRUNCHY QUINCES (PAGE 118).

INGREDIENTS:

BOMBE MIXTURE

3½ tbsp water

¼ cup/50 g sugar

4 egg yolks

4 gelatine leaves, soaked in cold water and well drained

9 oz/250 g freshly made Italian Meringue (page 37), cooled to tepid

1¼ cups/400 ml heavy cream, whipped to a ribbon consistency

⅓ cup/80 g preserved ginger, finely diced

3½ tbsp ginger eau-de-vie

¼ cup/40 g slivers of Candied Grapefruit Peel (page 168), finely diced (optional)

Makes 2 lbs/900 g

Preparation time: 50 minutes

THE BOMBE MIXTURE: Pour the water into a small saucepan, add the sugar, and bring to a boil over low heat. Boil the syrup for 2 minutes, washing down the inside of the pan with a pastry brush dipped in cold water.

Meanwhile, put the egg yolks in a bowl and break them up with a whisk, then gently pour on the syrup, whisking continuously. Stand the base of the bowl in a bain-marie, set over medium heat, and whisk until the mixture reaches a ribbon consistency and a temperature of about 167°F/75°C. Take the bowl out of the bain-marie and continue to whisk until the temperature of the mixture reduces to about 75°F/24°C.

MAKING THE MOUSSE: Place the gelatine in a bowl and dissolve it in 2 soup spoons of hot water, then pour it into the bombe mixture, whisking continuously. Using a slotted spoon, fold the mixture into the tepid Italian meringue. Finally, delicately fold in the whipped cream, ginger, eau-de-vie, and the candied grapefruit peel. The mousse is now ready to use, before the gelatine begins to set.

SPECIAL EQUIPMENT:
Candy thermometer

NOTES:
To make individual desserts, fill twenty 2⅜ in/6 cm diam., 1¼ in/3 cm deep dessert rings with the mousse, using a Coconut Daquoise (page 31) for the base.

The mousse will freeze well for up to a week.

CHAPTER FOUR

COULIS, SAUCES, JELLIES, AND JAMS

COULIS: The choice of fruit is important when making a coulis to accompany a dessert. If the flavor is too strong, it will dominate the dessert, which it should not do. As a general rule, coulis should be light, with a pure flavor and not too much sweetness. Pour only a small amount onto the plate or in a ribbon around the dessert, but it may be wise to serve a little extra coulis separately in a sauceboat for greedy gourmets!

SAUCES: Sauces are always popular. They are richer and creamier than coulis and can be served hot or cold, depending on their composition and how they are intended to enhance and enrich the dessert.

JELLIES AND JAMS: The recipes in this chapter are among my favorites, particularly Apricot and Almond Jam. I adore this spread on crêpes or toast. A favorite childhood memory is of my mother buying the ripest fruits in season at the market and making them into jams. Each jar was meticulously labeled with the date of its creation, for jams are best eaten while still young and fresh.

Apricot Jam with Almonds
(see recipe page 58)

FRUIT COULIS
Coulis de fruits

YOU CAN MAKE A COULIS WITH ALMOST ANY SINGLE TYPE OF FRUIT,
DEPENDING ON THE DESSERT IT IS INTENDED TO ACCOMPANY, BUT DO NOT
USE A MIXTURE OF DIFFERENT FRUITS.

INGREDIENTS:
1¼ lbs/800 g fresh fruit
  (eg: berry fruits,
  pineapple, apricots,
  peaches, kiwis, etc.)
Juice of 1 lemon
1 cup/250 ml Sorbet Syrup
  (page 144)

Makes 1¾–2¼ lbs/800 g–1
  kg, depending on the
  texture and density of the
  fruit
Preparation time: 15
  minutes

Wash and drain, hull, peel, or core the fruit as appropriate. Purée in a blender or food processor with the lemon juice and syrup until smooth. Pass through a conical strainer and keep in the refrigerator until ready to use.

NOTES:
Fruit coulis can be made with canned or bottled fruits. Use only ½ cup/125 ml sorbet syrup and dilute it with the same quantity of water.

  All fruit coulis will keep in an airtight container in the refrigerator for several days. They also freeze well. Thaw and beat vigorously before serving.

STRAWBERRY JUICE
Jus de fraises

CHILDREN ADORE THIS LIGHT COULIS (YOU CAN ALSO USE OTHER RED FRUITS, SUCH AS
RASPBERRIES, WILD STRAWBERRIES, RED CURRANTS, AND CHERRIES). IT CAN ALSO BE USED AS
THE BASE FOR A VERY LIGHT, FRUITY SORBET. SIMPLY CHURN IT WITHOUT ADDING SYRUP.

INGREDIENTS:
1½ lbs/750 g best quality
  frozen strawberries
6 tbsp/75 g sugar
¼ lemon, roughly chopped

Makes about 3½ cups/850
  ml
Preparation time: 5 minutes
Cooking time: 3 hours

Put all the ingredients in a bowl and cover very tightly with plastic wrap. Stand the bowl in a bain-marie and poach at 194°–204°F/90°–95°C for 3 hours, taking great care that it does not boil.

  Lay the cheesecloth in a colander set over a bowl and pour in the poached juice and fruit pulp. Let drain for 30 minutes, then gather up the ends of the cheesecloth and press lightly to extract a little more juice; but do not squeeze or the juice will become cloudy. When it is cold, pour into an airtight container and refrigerate until ready to use. It will keep up to 2 weeks.

SPECIAL EQUIPMENT:
Cheesecloth
Cooking thermometer

NOTES:
A spoonful of strawberry juice added to a glass of champagne or sparkling white wine makes a delicious cocktail.

ORANGE SAUCE
Sauce à l'orange

THIS SAUCE MAKES AN EXCELLENT ACCOMPANIMENT TO MANY COLD DESSERTS
OR A CHOCOLATE MOUSSE. I USE IT WITH MY GRATINS OF RED CURRANTS
AND WILD STRAWBERRIES (PAGE 92).

INGREDIENTS:
2 eggs
¾ cup/150 g sugar
1 cup/250 ml orange juice
    (preferably freshly
    squeezed)

Serves 8
Cooking time: 8 minutes

Break the eggs into a bowl, add one-third of the sugar, and whisk to
a ribbon consistency. In a saucepan, boil the orange juice with the
remaining sugar, then pour the boiling juice onto the eggs, whisking
continuously. Pour the mixture back into the pan and cook over
medium heat for 2 minutes, whisking continuously. Pass the sauce
through a conical strainer into a bowl and let cool at room temperature, whisking from time to time. When the sauce is cold,
transfer it to a sealed container and refrigerate.

NOTE:
The sauce will keep in the
refrigerator for 3 days.

APPLE COULIS
Coulis de pommes

THIS VERSATILE COULIS MAKES A PERFECT ACCOMPANIMENT FOR MANY DESSERTS. IF IT
IS TOO THICK FOR YOUR TASTE, THIN IT WITH A LITTLE SORBET SYRUP (PAGE 144).

INGREDIENTS:
1 lb 2 oz/500 g apples,
    preferably Granny Smiths
1½ cups + 1 tbsp/375 ml
    water
6 tbsp/75 g sugar
Juice of 1 lemon
1 vanilla bean, split

Makes 2½ cups/600 ml
Preparation time: 10
    minutes

Wash the apples in cold water and cut each one into 6 or 8 segments.
Place in a saucepan with all the other ingredients, cover, and cook
gently until the apples have reduced almost to a purée. Remove the
vanilla bean, then purée the apples in a blender for 2 minutes, until
very liquid. Pass through a fine conical strainer and let cool at room
temperature.

NOTES:
Apple coulis keeps well in an
airtight container in the
refrigerator at 41°F/5°C
for up to a week.

    As with my apple sorbet,
I do not peel the fruit or
discard the cores, since they
contain so much flavor.

Sabayon with Raspberry Eau-de-Vie
Sabayon à l'alcool de framboises

I use this sabayon in many of my recipes, including Fresh Figs on a Sabayon Quilt (page 67). Or serve it plain in a bowl to accompany raspberries or wild strawberries or my Hazelnut Tuiles (page 172).

INGREDIENTS:

3 egg yolks

⅓ cup/65 g sugar

3½ tbsp water

5 tbsp rasberry eau-de-vie (framboise)

½ gelatine leaf (this is only necessary for a cold sabayon)

Serves 4 (makes about 1¾ cups/400 ml)

Preparation and cooking time: 15–20 minutes

Fresh Figs on a Sabayon Quilt

THE SABAYON: Half-fill a saucepan large enough to hold the base of a mixing bowl with warm water and heat gently to 95°–104°F/35°–40°C. Combine the egg yolks, sugar, water, and raspberry eau-de-vie in a bowl and stand it in the saucepan (bain-marie). Whisk continuously with a balloon whisk for 10–12 minutes, making sure that the water temperature does not rise above 194°F/90°C, or the sabayon may coagulate. If necessary, turn off the heat while you whisk the sabayon. It should swell into a ribbon consistency, like half-risen beaten egg whites, and the texture should be smooth, shiny, airy, and wonderfully rich, with an internal temperature of 122°F/50°C.

If you plan to eat the sabayon hot, it is best served immediately. For a cold sabayon, soak the ½ gelatine leaf in a soup spoon of warm water in a ramekin and as soon as it dissolves, whisk it into the sabayon.

PRESENTATION: Serve the sabayon in large burgundy glasses or champagne coupes, or in a glass bowl. If you plan to serve it cold, place the filled glasses or bowl in the freezer for 5 minutes, then chill in the refrigerator for an hour or two. Serve the sabayon cold and still trembling, not frozen.

SPECIAL EQUIPMENT:
Cooking thermometer

NOTES:
Other eaux-de-vie, such as pear or plum, can be substituted for the raspberry, or you could use a heavy sweet wine like a Banyuls or Marsala.

The sabayon can be kept in the bain-marie for 10–15 minutes before serving, but after that it will lose some of its lightness.

CHOCOLATE SAUCE
Sauce chocolat

INGREDIENTS:

7 oz/200 g best-quality
    bittersweet chocolate or
    couverture
⅔ cup/150 ml milk
2 tbsp heavy cream
2½ tbsp/30 g sugar
2 tbsp/30 g butter, diced

Makes about 1 lb/450 g
Preparation time: 10
    minutes

Melt the chocolate in a bain-marie set over medium heat, stirring from time to time. In a saucepan, bring to a boil the milk, cream, and sugar, stirring gently with a whisk. Pour this mixture onto the melted chocolate, stirring continuously. Return the sauce to the pan and let it bubble for 15 seconds.

Off the heat, beat in the butter, a little at a time, until the sauce is smooth and completely homogeneous. Pass through a conical strainer and serve warm.

NOTE:

The sauce will keep in the refrigerator for 3 days; store in an airtight container or a bowl covered with plastic wrap. Reheat gently before serving.

Left: Warm chocolate sauce ready for pouring

CARAMEL SAUCE
Sauce caramel

INGREDIENTS:

½ cup/100 g sugar
⅓ cup/80 ml water
2 cups/500 ml heavy cream
2 egg yolks, lightly beaten

Makes about 2⅞ cups/700
    ml
Preparation time: 5 minutes

In a large saucepan, dissolve the sugar with the water over low heat and bring to boiling point. Wash down the inside of the pan with a pastry brush dipped in cold water to prevent crystals from forming. Cook until the sugar turns to a deep amber color. Immediately turn off the heat and whisk in the cream.

Set the pan back over high heat and stir the sauce with the whisk. Let it bubble for 2 minutes, then turn off the heat. You can now strain the sauce and use it when cooled, or, for a richer, smoother sauce, pour a little of the caramel onto the egg yolks, then return the mixture to the pan and heat to 175°F/80°C, taking care that it does not boil. Pass the sauce through a conical strainer and keep in a cool place, stirring occasionally to prevent a skin from forming.

SPECIAL EQUIPMENT:
Cooking thermometer

NOTE:

The caramel sauce will keep in an airtight container in the refrigerator for 48 hours.

HONEY SAUCE
Sauce au miel

INGREDIENTS:

1 cup/250 ml clear honey
½ cup/125 ml Sorbet Syrup
    (page 144)
Juice of 3 limes

Makes 14 oz/400 g
Preparation time: 5 minutes

Mix all the ingredients with a spatula and keep the sauce in an airtight container until needed.

NOTES:

Use this very sweet sauce in small quantities. It can be flavored with vanilla, cinnamon, or cloves. For an orange or lemon honey sauce, add some thin slivers of blanched orange or lemon zest.

OLD BACHELOR'S BOTTLED FRUIT
Confiture de vieux garçon

ELDERLY GENTLEMEN LOVE SWEET THINGS AND HERE IS THE PERFECT SWEET TREAT. SOME MAY PREFER IT EVEN SWEETER, IN WHICH CASE INCREASE THE SUGAR BY 15–20%. I ADORE THIS BOTTLED FRUIT, WHICH LYN HALL KINDLY GAVE ME AS A CHRISTMAS GIFT MANY YEARS AGO AND WHICH I HAVE ENJOYED EVERY CHRISTMAS SINCE THEN. THE IDEAL TIME TO PREPARE THE FRUIT IS IN EARLY SUMMER. YOU SHOULD WAIT THREE MONTHS BEFORE EATING IT, BUT IT IMPROVES WITH KEEPING AND WILL TASTE EVEN BETTER AFTER SIX MONTHS — IF YOU CAN WAIT THAT LONG!

INGREDIENTS:

2¼ lbs / 1 kg soft fruit of your choice (eg: cherries, small strawberries, raspberries, black currants, red currants, seedless grapes)

3¾ cups / 750 g sugar

1 vanilla bean, split

2 small cinnamon sticks

2 small ginger roots, peeled with a potato peeler

A pinch of nutmeg

10 allspice berries (optional)

3 cups / 750 ml Cognac or white rum

Makes two 1-quart / 1-liter jars
Preparation time: 10 minutes

PREPARING THE FRUIT: Wash, drain, and dry on paper towels. Remove stems from the black currants, red currants, and grapes. Hull the strawberries and raspberries. Trim the cherry stems to ¾ in / 2 cm.

BOTTLING THE FRUIT: Sterilize the jars with boiling water and dry thoroughly. Place the fruit in the jars, layering it at intervals with the sugar and aromatics. Pour over your chosen alcohol and close the jars. If the fruit ferments after a few days, add a little more of the same alcohol and reseal the jars. You can add more fruit after two weeks, when the first fruits have shrunk.

SPECIAL EQUIPMENT:
2 wide-mouthed 1-quart / 1-liter canning jars

NOTE:
Serve the fruit in a liqueur glass after dinner, to be eaten with a coffee spoon or wooden toothpick, then drink the juice after your coffee. What a delight!

RHUBARB COMPOTE WITH SAUTERNES
Compote de rhubarbe au Sauternes

SERVE THIS SWEET FRUITY COMPOTE WITH SLICES OF BUTTERY BRIOCHE (PAGE 19).

INGREDIENTS:

1 lb / 450 g very tender young rhubarb, peeled

⅞ cup / 200 ml Sauternes or sweet dessert wine

¼ cup / 50 g sugar

Juice of 1 lemon

Serves 4
Preparation time: 5 minutes
Cooking time: 6 minutes

PREPARATION: Wash the rhubarb and cut into 1½ in / 4 cm lengths. Place in a saucepan with all the other ingredients and bring slowly to a boil. Lower the heat and poach gently for about 6 minutes, until the rhubarb is tender. Leave in the poaching liquid at room temperature until cold, then refrigerate for 2 hours before serving.

PRESENTATION. Serve the compote in a glass bowl or individual dishes.

A spoonful of Old Bachelor's Bottled Fruit

Apricot Jam with Almonds
Confiture d'abricots aux amandes

This jam is delectable spread on toast. I serve it to my guests at The Waterside Inn for breakfast during the summer.

INGREDIENTS:

1½ lbs/750 g very ripe
  apricots

5 tbsp water

2¾ cups/550 g sugar mixed
  with 1 tsp pectin
  (optional)

Juice of 1 lemon

½ cup/75 g whole almonds,
  skinned and soaked in
  milk for 2 hours (see
  note)

Makes 2¾ lbs/1.2 kg
Preparation time: 10
  minutes

Wash the apricots in cold water, halve them, and remove the pits.

Combine the water, sugar and pectin mixture, and the lemon juice in the preserving kettle and gently bring to a boil over low heat. Add the apricots and cook gently, skimming the surface occasionally. Drain the almonds, rinse in cold water, and add them to the pan after 45 minutes if the apricots are extremely ripe, or 1 hour if they are only just ripe, and cook for a further 3 minutes.

Let the jam cool in the pan and spoon into sterilized jars when it is still just warm. Cool completely, then seal the jars with cellophane covers.

SPECIAL EQUIPMENT:
Preserving kettle

NOTE:
When fresh almonds are in season, during June and July, substitute them for the semi-dried variety for an even better jam. It is not neccessary to soak fresh almonds in milk.

BLACKBERRY JELLY
Gelée de mûres

THIS WONDERFUL JELLY REMINDS ME VIVIDLY OF MY CHILDHOOD. FROM EARLY SEPTEMBER, I WOULD GATHER THEM FROM THE HEDGES IN THE VENDEE AND TAKE MY HARVEST BACK TO MOTHER. WITHIN A FEW HOURS, THE JELLY WAS PREPARED AND IN ITS JARS. WHAT A FANTASTIC MOTHER! THE FRUIT NEVER HAD TIME TO SPOIL, AND IT WAS A DELIGHT THE NEXT DAY TO EAT CREPES SPREAD WITH FRESH JELLY. NOT A SINGLE JAR EVER LASTED THROUGH THE WINTER IN OUR HOUSE!

INGREDIENTS:
2¼ lbs / 1 kg blackberries, preferably wild
⅞ cup / 200 ml water
1 lemon, washed and cut into large pieces
Sugar (the same quantity as the juice from the cooked blackberries)

Makes about 1½ lbs / 750 g
Preparation time: 15 minutes, plus draining the juice
Cooking time: about 7 minutes

PREPARING THE BLACKBERRIES: Wash and hull the fruit and place in a saucepan with the water and lemon. Bring to a boil over low heat, then bubble gently for 5 minutes. Remove the pieces of lemon, then rub the blackberries and juice through the mouli. Pour the pulp into the jelly bag or cheesecloth and let the juice drip through gently. After 30 minutes, squeeze very gently to extract as much juice as possible. Measure the juice and pour it into a preserving kettle with an equal amount of sugar.

COOKING THE JELLY: Cook gently, stirring with a spatula at first to dissolve the sugar completely. Bring to a boil, then start timing the cooking; the jelly will be ready in about 7 minutes. Skim the surface if necessary. Pour the blackberry jelly into sterilized jars and let cool before sealing with cellophane covers.

SPECIAL EQUIPMENT:
Vegetable mouli (food mill) with a coarse blade
Jelly bag or cheesecloth

NOTE:
Since the sugar and juice content of blackberries varies, it is difficult to give a precise quantity of sugar before they are cooked.

APPLE JELLY OR GLAZE
Gelée de pommes

THIS TRANSLUCENT JELLY MAKES AN EXCELLENT GLAZE FOR FRUIT TARTS AND GATEAUX.

INGREDIENTS:
2 cups / 500 ml water
1¼ cups / 250 g sugar
1 lb 2oz / 500 g firm tart-sweet apples
1 lemon
6 gelatine leaves soaked in cold water and well drained

Makes 2⅔ cups / 650 ml
Preparation time: 20 minutes
Cooking time: 15 minutes

In a saucepan, heat the water and sugar until the sugar has dissolved completely and the liquid begins to boil, stirring occasionally with a whisk and skimming the surface if necessary.

Wash the apples and lemon, but do not peel them. Coarsely chop the fruit, cores, seeds, and all, and put them into the boiling sugar syrup. Cover the pan and simmer for 10 minutes. Take the pan off the heat and push the fruit to one side to make room to put in the gelatine and dissolve it. When it has dissolved completely, pass the jelly carefully through a conical strainer or jelly bag set over a bowl. Use the jelly as a glaze when it is cold but not yet set.

SPECIAL EQUIPMENT:
Jelly bag or conical strainer

NOTE:
The jelly will keep in an airtight container in the refrigerator for 4 days. Reheat and let cool again before using.

Chapter Five

Cold Desserts

For over twenty years I have served my cold desserts ready assembled on the plate. The result is visually and gastronomically incomparable. To serve your desserts at home in this way, assemble them several hours or just a few minutes before serving and spoon a little coulis or sauce on the side or around the edge. Your guest can thus enjoy a delicate, individual dessert, specially prepared, presented and served at the ideal temperature. Specialist cookshops sell stacking rings for plates, which are perfect for this; once you have assembled the dessert on individual plates, place a ring around the edge, stack the plates into one or two piles, and refrigerate, all ready to serve.

Decorative feather patterns made on the plate with a combination of two or three coulis, sauces, or creams look attractive. Use the tip of a knife or a toothpick to swirl circles or ovals, but keep the decoration discreet. It should not detract from the main attraction, the dessert.

Red Fruit Tulip

APPLE FANTASY
L'Assiette de pommes

I ADORE THE CONTRASTING CRUNCHY AND SMOOTH TEXTURES OF THIS SIMPLE DESSERT. ALL THREE COMPONENTS CAN BE PREPARED IN ADVANCE AND ASSEMBLED AT THE LAST MINUTE..

INGREDIENTS: ❋
SYRUP:
1 cup/200 g sugar
½ vanilla bean, split
⅞ cup/200 ml water
Juice of 1 lemon

4 apples, not too ripe, about 7 oz/200 g each
4 oz/100 g Pastry Cream (page 39)
½ quantity Apple Sorbet (page 146)
3 tbsp/20 g confectioners' sugar (optional)

Serves 4
Preparation time: 25 minutes
Cooking time: 20 minutes

THE SYRUP: Combine the sugar, vanilla, water, and lemon juice in a saucepan and heat gently until the syrup starts to bubble.

THE APPLE GAUFRETTES: Peel and core the fruit with an apple corer. Adjust the rippled blade of the mandoline to a thickish setting and cut a ridged slice from one side of an apple. Discard this first slice, and cut 8 latticed slices (gaufrettes) from the sides of three of the apples (discarding all the first slices), giving the fruit one-quarter turn each time, so that they resemble latticed potato chips. Drop the gaufrettes at once into the boiling syrup and immediately remove from the heat. Let them cool in the syrup.
Preheat the oven to 310°F/160°C.

THE LACY APPLE CRISPS: Finely dice the remaining apple. spread on a nonstick baking sheet, and cook in the preheated oven for 20 minutes. Let cool at room temperature.
Increase the oven temperature to 350°F/180°C.
Lay the template on a nonstick baking sheet or parchment paper, put in a little pastry cream, and smooth with a metal spatula. Move the template sideways and make 16 disks of pastry cream in this way. Place the cooked diced apples in the center of the pastry cream disks and cook in the preheated oven for 3 minutes, until pale golden. Carefully lift off the disks with a metal spatula and crinkle them slightly with your fingertips. Place the lacy apple crisps on a cooling rack and dust with confectioners' sugar if you wish.

PRESENTATION: Place a large scoop of apple sorbet in the middle of four chilled deep plates. Stick four lacy apple crisps in each ball of sorbet. Arrange the gaufrettes around the edge and spoon a little of the poaching syrup over them. Serve at once.

SPECIAL EQUIPMENT:
Mandoline
2 nonstick baking sheets, or parchment paper
2⅜ in/6 cm diam. template, 1/24 in/1 mm thick

Red Fruit Tulips
Tulipes de fruits rouges

THESE CRISP, MELT-IN-THE-MOUTH PASTRY TULIPS ADD AN EXTRA DIMENSION
TO SERVING RED FRUITS.

INGREDIENTS: ❄

1 quantity *Tulip Paste*
  (page 28) (to be made 24
  hours in advance)
2 tbsp/10 g unsweetened
  cocoa powder, sifted
2¼ lbs/1 kg assorted berry
  fruits in season (eg:
  blackberries, cultivated
  and wild strawberries, red
  currants, blueberries)
⅔ cup/150 ml *Peach*
  Coulis (see Fruit Coulis,
  page 51), mixed with the
  juice of 1 orange and
  ½ lemon

Serves 6
Preparation time: 40
  minutes

Cooking time: about 12
  minutes

THE TULIP PASTE: Follow the recipe on page 28. When the paste is ready, place one-quarter in a bowl and mix in the cocoa to color and flavor it.

SHAPING THE TULIPS: Lay the largest stencil on a corner of a baking sheet and spread a very thin layer of the plain tulip paste in the center, using a metal spatula to spread it flat across the template (1). Move the template along and repeat the operation five times to make six wafer-thin, very even round shapes. Use the smaller templates to make six 5 in/13 cm and six 4 in/10 cm circles.

    Preheat the oven to 350°F/180°C.

DECORATING AND COOKING THE TULIPS: Fill the paper piping cone with the chocolate tulip paste. Snip off the end of the cone with scissors and decorate the pastry circles with spirals (2). Then, with the tip of a knife, lightly mark out rays, alternately starting from the center of the spiral drawing outward (3), then from the outside inward to make an attractive wavy effect, like the fondant icing on a mille-feuille.

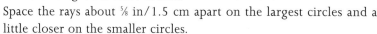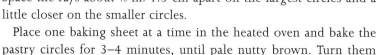

Space the rays about ⅝ in/1.5 cm apart on the largest circles and a little closer on the smaller circles.

    Place one baking sheet at a time in the heated oven and bake the pastry circles for 3–4 minutes, until pale nutty brown. Turn them over on the baking sheet, then roll them one at a time around the

foil-covered cone, starting at the opposite side from the center of the spiral (4). Press the tulip into shape, lightly at first, then a little more firmly, until it is stable enough to be removed from the cone. Place the shaped tulips on a cooling rack and leave in a dry place until needed.

SPECIAL EQUIPMENT:
3 wafer-thin templates,
  6 in/16 cm diam.,
  5 in/13 cm diam.,
  4 in/10 cm diam.
Paper piping cone
Foil-covered cardboard cone,
  for shaping the cooked
  tulips
3 lightly greased 24 × 16 in/
  60 × 40 cm baking sheets

NOTE:
The tulips can be made a day
in advance, but it is essential
to keep them in an airtight
container in a dry place.

PRESENTATION: Wash all the fruits except the wild strawberries, drain well, hull, and mix them together. Arrange one tulip of each size on each serving plate and delicately fill them with the fruits, allowing some to spill out seductively. Pour a ribbon of peach coulis around the tulips and a little in between them, and serve at once.

Red Berries with Lightly Candied Orange Beads

L'Assiette de baies rouges aux pustules d'oranges mi-confites

LAVENDER FLOWERS ARE HIGHLY PERFUMED. IT IS BEST TO USE THEM AS THEY FIRST COME INTO FLOWER, WHEN THEIR SCENT IS NOT TOO POWERFUL. THEY LOOK VERY PRETTY WHEN LIGHTLY CANDIED, AND ADD A FLAVOR OF SUMMER. A FEW STEMS MARRY WELL WITH THE ORANGES, CARAMEL SAUCE, AND RED BERRIES — BUT DON'T EAT THEM ALL.

INGREDIENTS: ❄

1½ cups/350 ml Sorbet Syrup (page 144), plus an extra ⅔ cup/150 ml if you are using lavender

½ cup/100 g sugar

20 small stems of lavender, newly come into flower (optional)

14 oz/400 g chilled mixed red berries, according to the season (equal quantities, or in whichever proportion you prefer), eg: small strawberries. raspberries, wild strawberries, red currants, blackberries, black currants, blueberries

Serves 4

Preparation time: 25 minutes

Cooking time: 2½ hours (for the orange peel)

PREPARING THE ORANGES: Use the tip of a small knife to incise the orange peel into 4 quarters, then, with your thumb, carefully remove the quartered peel without damaging it. Place the peel in a saucepan, cover with cold water, bring to a boil, and blanch for 2 minutes, then refresh and drain.

Pour 1½ cups/350 ml sorbet syrup into another saucepan, bring to a boil, then drop in the orange peel, and simmer over low heat for 1 hour (see photo). Let the peel cool in the syrup at room temperature. When it is cold, bring the syrup back to a boil and simmer for another hour. If the syrup becomes too thick, add a little cold water. When the peel is lightly candied, leave it in the syrup at room temperature until cold. Drain the peel and cut each piece into round beads with small, different-sized cookie cutters, then place in a bowl. The trimmings can be cut into large dice, rolled in sugar, and served as little sweetmeats with coffee.

THE ORANGE CARAMEL SAUCE: Separate the peeled oranges into quarters, remove any seeds, and purée the fruit in a blender for 2–3 minutes. Pass the purée through a cheesecloth-lined fine strainer set over a saucepan, pressing to extract as much juice as possible (you should have about ⅔ cup/150 ml). Heat the juice gently.

Put the sugar into another saucepan and dissolve it over very low heat, stirring continuously until it becomes a pale caramel. Pour on the warm orange juice, little by little, stirring all the time, then reduce the sauce over medium heat for 3 or 4 minutes. Let it cool at room temperature, then refrigerate.

THE LAVENDER: Bring the ⅔ cup/150 ml sorbet syrup to a boil and drop in the lavender flowers. Simmer very gently for 2 minutes, then let the lavender cool in the syrup at room temperature. Drain it just before serving.

PRESENTATION: Arrange your chosen well-chilled fruits in four deep plates. Dot the candied orange beads among the berries and add five sprigs of lavender to each plate. Pour on some chilled orange caramel sauce, and serve.

NOTE:

All the elements of this dessert can be prepared in advance, even the day before if you wish; you will need just 5 minutes to arrange all the ingredients on the plates when you are ready to serve.

Fresh Figs on a Sabayon Quilt
La coupe de figues sur douillet de sabayon

THIS CREAMY AND DELICIOUS AUTUMN DESSERT IS EXCEPTIONALLY EASY TO MAKE AND CAN BE PREPARED A DAY IN ADVANCE. IT IS A GREAT FAVORITE WITH BOTH YOUNG AND OLD.

INGREDIENTS: ❀
Double quantity Sabayon (page 53), made with Marsala or Sauternes
5 or 6 very ripe figs, preferably 2 types, black and green

Serves 6–8
Preparation time: 5 minutes

THE SABAYON: Before starting, chill a glass bowl until very cold.

Follow the sabayon recipe on page 53, substituting Marsala or Sauternes for the raspberry eau-de-vie. Since the sabayon is to be served cold, you will need to add the gelatine.

Pour the sabayon into the chilled bowl and chill in the freezer for 10 minutes, then in the refrigerator for at least 2 hours.

PRESENTATION: Just before serving, cut the figs into segments and arrange them around the edge and in the center of the bowl, alternating the black and green segments. Serve immediately.

Pistachio Creme Brulee
Crème brûlée pistache

I ADORE PISTACHIOS AND MY FAVORITE VERSIONS OF CREME BRULEE ARE THOSE WITH PISTACHIOS OR WILD STRAWBERRIES. A VANILLA ICE CREAM (PAGE 137) SERVED SEPARATELY IN A GLASS OR COUPE WILL FURTHER ENHANCE THE PISTACHIO FLAVOR.

INGREDIENTS:
2 cups/500 ml milk
2 cups/500 ml heavy cream
2 oz/60 g pistachio paste
1¼ cups/260 g sugar
¾ cup + 1 tbsp/200 g egg yolks
¼ cup/30 g skinned pistachios

Serves 6
Preparation time: 10 minutes
Cooking time: 30 minutes

Fresh figs on a Sabayon Quilt

SPECIAL EQUIPMENT:
Six 15 cm/6 in diam. gratin dishes
Blowtorch (optional)

NOTES:
The sugar topping will soften within an hour or two, depending on the humidity, so I would recommend that you caramelize the crème brûlées only a short time before serving.

If you cannot buy commercially-made pistachio paste, make your own by pounding freshly skinned pistachios in a small mortar to make a very smooth purée.

THE CUSTARD: Heat the milk, cream, pistachio paste, and 7 tbsp/90 g of the sugar in a saucepan, whisking continuously at first.

In a bowl, lightly whisk the egg yolks with 5 tbsp/60 g sugar until slightly pale. As soon as the milk comes to a boil, pour it onto the eggs, little by little, whisking all the time.

COOKING THE CUSTARDS: Preheat the oven to 200°F/100°C.

Ladle the custard into the gratin dishes and cook in the warm oven for 30 minutes. Remove from the oven and carefully slide the dishes onto a wire rack. Once the custards are completely cold, transfer them to the refrigerator.

PRESENTATION: Just before serving, sprinkle the tops of the crèmes brûlées with ⅓ cup/70 g sugar and caramelize them with a blowtorch, or under a very hot broiler, to make a thin, pale nut-brown topping.

Heat a small frying pan, then toss in the pistachios, sprinkle them with the remaining sugar, and stir vigorously for 1 minute, so that they are well coated with the sugar. Tip them onto a plate, separate the pistachios with a fork, and arrange about 8 pistachios on top of each crème brûlée. Serve immediately.

MARZIPAN FIGS
Figues au parfum d'amandes

YOUR CHILDREN WILL BE INTRIGUED BY THE PREPARATION OF THIS SIMPLE,
IMAGINATIVE DESSERT. THEY MIGHT EVEN HELP YOU TO MAKE THE MOCK FIGS!

INGREDIENTS: ❊
½ quantity Choux Paste
   (page 26)
2 very ripe black or green
   figs
½ quantity Mousseline
   Cream (page 42)
2 tbsp kirsch (optional)
1 lb 2 oz–1 lb 10 oz/
   500–750 g marzipan
   (depending on your taste
   and artistry)
Food colorings: mauve, red,
   green, yellow (depending
   on the desired effect)
½ cup/50 g confectioners'
   sugar for dusting

Serves 6
Preparation time: 45
   minutes
Cooking time: 20 minutes

PIPING AND BAKING THE CHOUX "FIGS": Preheat the oven to
400°F/200°C.

Using the pastry bag with the ¼ in/5 mm tip, pipe about twelve 1¼
in/3 cm diam. choux puffs onto a baking sheet. They need not be
uniformly sized; after all, not all figs are the same size. Bake in the
oven for 20 minutes, then pierce the bases of the puffs with the tip
of a sharp knife, transfer to a cooling rack, and let cool at room temperature.

FILLING THE CHOUX "FIGS": Finely dice the fresh figs, mix them
delicately into the mousseline cream, and add the kirsch. Using the
pastry bag with the ½ in/1 cm tip, generously fill the choux buns
with this mixture through the incision in the bases.

PREPARING THE MARZIPAN AND WRAPPING THE FIGS: Put the marzipan on
the work surface and, using your hands, color two-thirds with
mauve-toned coloring and the rest with greener tones. Use your own
artistic judgment to decide the precise shades.

Dust the work surface with confectioners' sugar and roll out
2–3 oz/50–70 g marzipan into a small disk, about ⅛ in/3 mm thick,
lightly blending the two colors to achieve a marbled effect. Lay a
choux puff on the disk and gather up the marzipan over the puff.
Pinch the edges together to form a stem and voilà! there is your "fig."
Mark it with the modeling tool or the back of a knife blade to
resemble a real fig, and lightly dab on a little confectioners' sugar
here and there with your fingertips (see photo, opposite). Wrap and
decorate all the choux puffs in the same way.

PRESENTATION: Serve the marzipan figs on a china plate or, for a more
rustic effect, in the wooden crate in which the real figs were sold.

SPECIAL EQUIPMENT:
Plastic modeling tool (eg: for
   Playdoh) (optional)
Pastry bag with a plain
   ¼ in/5 mm tip
Pastry bag with a plain
   ½ in/1 cm tip

NOTE:
For a picnic, transport the
figs in their wooden crate.
They should be eaten within
24 hours, as the mousseline
cream will sour if kept
longer.

ANGEL'S HAIR IN A LIGHT SAUTERNES JELLY

Cheveux d'ange en gelée de Sauternes mi-prise

THIS ORIGINAL, REFRESHING DESSERT IS THE PERFECT ENDING FOR AN
ELEGANT SUMMER MEAL.

INGREDIENTS: ❊

½ bottle sweet white wine,
  preferably Sauternes
2 gelatine leaves, soaked in
  cold water and well
  drained
⅞ cup/200 ml Sorbet Syrup
  (page 144)
8 egg yolks, strained
6 kumquats
1 small pomegranate

Serves 6

Preparation time: 30
  minutes, plus setting
Cooking time: 10 minutes
  for the kumquats

THE SAUTERNES JELLY: Heat 3½ tbsp of the Sauternes in a small
saucepan. Off the heat, add and dissolve the gelatine, then stir in the
remaining wine, without overmixing. Refrigerate for about 1 hour,
until the jelly is lightly set.

THE ANGEL'S HAIR: Heat the syrup in a deep roasting
pan. As soon as it starts to tremble, fill a paper piping
cone with 2 egg yolks, and snip off the end to make a
tiny opening. Move the cone backward and forward
across the roasting pan about 2 in/5 cm above the
surface of the syrup, letting the yolks escape through
the hole into the syrup (see photo, right). Poach for
about 1 minute until they form strands like angel's hair.
Remove with a flat slotted spoon and place in a bowl of
cold water. Repeat until you have used all the yolks.
Leave the angel's hair in the cold water for 5 minutes,
then drain, place in a bowl, and refrigerate.

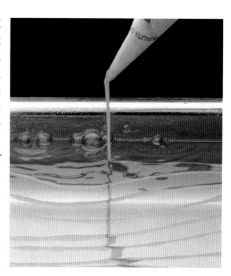

THE KUMQUATS: Blanch in a small saucepan of boiling
water, refresh, and drain. Pour the poaching syrup

NOTE:

The dessert can be prepared a
day in advance and assembled
just before serving.

from the angel's hair into the same pan and bring to a boil. Put in the kumquats and poach for 10 minutes, keeping the syrup at a gentle simmer. Let cool in the syrup at room temperature, then refrigerate them.

THE POMEGRANATE: Peel, scoop the seeds into a bowl, and refrigerate.

PRESENTATION: Arrange the angel's hair in the center of six balloon glasses or shallow glass bowls. Put a kumquat in the middle and the pomegranate seeds around the edge. Lightly whisk the Sauternes jelly just to loosen it, then pour it into the bowls to cover the angel's hair, kumquats, and pomegranate seeds. Serve with a spoon and fork.

SPECIAL EQUIPMENT: Paper piping cone

PALM TREES WITH EXOTIC FRUIT
Le cocotier et ses fruits exotiques

THE PERFECT DESSERT FOR A CHILDREN'S PARTY. THEY WILL LOVE THE COMBINATION OF FRUIT AND CRISP PASTRY.

INGREDIENTS: ❋
1¼ lbs/600 g Jean Millet's Puff Pastry (page 24), or Quick Puff Pastry (page 25)
Flour for dusting
Eggwash (1 egg yolk mixed with 1 tbsp milk and a pinch of salt)
Confectioners' sugar for dusting
1 very ripe mango, about 11 oz/300 g
5 tbsp Sorbet Syrup (page 144)
5 tbsp water
1 coconut

Serves 4
Preparation time: 30 minutes
Cooking time: 10 minutes

THE PASTRY PALM TREES: On a lightly floured surface, roll out the pastry into a 24 × 6 in/60 × 14 cm rectangle, ½2 in/2 mm thick. Lay the template on one side of the rectangle and, using the tip of a small sharp knife, cut the pastry into the shape of a palm tree. Invert the template, trunk upward, leaves toward you, so as to waste as little pastry as possible. Cut out a second palm tree, then repeat the operation to make four trees in all.

Delicately transfer the trees to a lightly dampened baking sheet, taking care not to spoil the shape. Brush with eggwash and refrigerate for 20 minutes.

Preheat the oven to 350°F/180°C.

BAKING THE PALM TREES: Brush the trees again with eggwash and bake in the preheated oven for 10 minutes. 1 minute before removing them from the oven, dust with confectioners' sugar and bake for the final minute to glaze them.

THE MANGO COULIS: Peel the mango, cut off the flesh from around the pit, and purée in a blender with the syrup and water for 1 minute, to make a smooth coulis.

THE COCONUT: Remove the shell and break the flesh into small pieces.

PRESENTATION: Arrange the palm trees on four plates. Pour the mango coulis around each one and place little heaps of coconut at the base.

SPECIAL EQUIPMENT: Homemade cardboard template of a double palm tree, about 5 in/12 cm high (see page 188 for a photo of the pastry palm tree)

NOTE: You can use sweet tart pastry (page 20) instead of puff pastry. Roll it out to a thickness of ⅛ in/3 mm and do not glaze with confectioners' sugar.

ANISEED PARFAIT WITH BLACKBERRY COULIS
Parfait à l'anis et son coulis de mûres

THE COMBINATION OF BLACKBERRIES WITH ANISEED AND THE RICHNESS OF
THE PARFAIT IS SURPRISING AND IMMENSELY POPULAR. THIS DESSERT IS A
GREAT SUMMER AND AUTUMN FAVORITE AT THE WATERSIDE INN.

INGREDIENTS: ❅
½ quantity Joconde Sponge
    batter (page 31)
4½ oz/140 g Nougatine
    (page 189)

BLACKBERRY COULIS
12 oz/350 g blackberries
1 tbsp Pastis or Ricard
½ cup/120 ml Sorbet Syrup
    (page 144)

BOMBE MIXTURE
½ cup/100 g sugar
Juice of ½ lemon
4 egg yolks
3 tbsp Pastis or Ricard
1 gelatine leaf, soaked in
    cold water and well
    drained
1¼ cups/300 ml heavy
    cream, whipped to a
    ribbon consistency

GARNISH
36 blackberries, washed and
    hulled
8 small sprigs of mint

SERVES 8
Preparation time: 45
    minutes

THE SPONGE BASES: Cut out eight sponge circles with a plain 2⅜ in/6
cm cookie cutter. Arrange the dessert rings on a small baking sheet
and line the bases with the sponge circles, then refrigerate.

THE BLACKBERRY COULIS: Wash and hull the blackberries, and purée in
a food processor with the Pastis or Ricard and the sorbet syrup for 2
minutes. Pass the coulis through a cheesecloth-lined conical strainer
and refrigerate.

THE NOUGATINE BASES: Roll out the nougatine until wafer-thin and cut
out eight 3¼ in/8 cm rounds. Keep in a dry place.

THE BOMBE MIXTURE: Combine 2 tbsp water, the sugar, and lemon juice
in a small, heavy-based saucepan and bring to a boil. Wash down the
inside of the pan with a pastry brush dipped in cold water. Put the
candy thermometer in the syrup and cook gently until it reaches
240°F/115°C. Now start creaming the egg yolks in an electric mixer or
by hand. As soon as the sugar temperature reaches 250°F/121°C,
remove from the heat and let the syrup bubble down for 1 minute.
   Start pouring the syrup onto the egg yolks in a thin stream, still
beating, but more slowly. When all the syrup is incorporated into the
yolks, continue to beat until completely cold. Warm the Pastis or
Ricard and dissolve the gelatine in it, then let cool for a few minutes
before folding it delicately into the whipped cream.
   Use a whisk to fold one-third of the whipped cream into the
bombe mixture, then delicately fold in the rest with a spatula.

ASSEMBLING THE PARFAITS: Fill a pastry bag with the parfait mixture and
pipe it into the dessert rings. Smooth the surface with a metal spatula
and freeze for at least 2 hours.

PRESENTATION: Use a coffee spoon to hollow out a small ¾ in/2 cm
deep cavity in the center of each parfait. Lift the rings off the parfaits
by heating the outsides very gently with a blowtorch, or by sliding a
knife blade dipped in hot water between the parfaits and the rings.
   Arrange each parfait on a nougatine round and place on individual
plates. Halve the 12 largest blackberries lengthwise. Place three whole
blackberries in the cavity of each parfait, then arrange three halved
berries on the plate, along with a sprig of mint. Pour a little of the
light blackberry coulis onto the whole berries and a little onto the
plates, and serve at once.

SPECIAL EQUIPMENT:
Candy thermometer
8 dessert rings, 2⅜ in/6 cm
    diam., 1¼ in/3 cm deep
Pastry bag with a plain
    2¾ in/7 cm tip
Blowtorch (optional)

NOTE:
This iced dessert will keep
well in the freezer for at least
a week.

MERINGUE PILLOWS WITH MARRONS GLACÉS
Douillets de meringue aux marrons glacés

FOR AN EXTRA TREAT, SERVE A COULIS OR WARM CHOCOLATE SAUCE (PAGE 55) WITH
THIS DIVINE DESSERT.

INGREDIENTS: ❄

½ quantity French Meringue
(page 37)

3 heaped tbsp/30 g
almonds, lightly toasted
and cut into slivers

½ tsp poppy seeds (optional)

7 oz/200 g Chocolate
Chantilly Cream (page
42)

⅓ quantity Chestnut
Bavarois (page 43),
prepared in advance and
refrigerated

7 oz/200 g marrons glacés,
or chestnuts in syrup
(whole or pieces)

Serves 6

Preparation time: 35
minutes, plus 1 hour for
the meringues

THE MERINGUE BASES: Preheat the oven to 200°F/100°C. Make the meringue according to the method on page 37. Using the template, make a round of meringue on the baking sheet or parchment, and smooth with a metal spatula. Move the template along and make seventeen more meringue bases in the same way (see pictures, right). Scatter the almonds and poppy seeds over six of them. Cook the meringues for 1 hour, remove from the oven, and let cool on the baking sheet. When they are almost cold, use a metal spatula to transfer them to a wire rack. Once they are completely cold, keep in a very dry place.

ASSEMBLING THE PILLOWS: Prepare the chocolate Chantilly cream and put it into the pastry bag. Pipe a border three rings high onto all the plain meringue bases, giving a height of about ½ in/1 cm. Refrigerate the pillows for 5 minutes to harden the cream.

SPECIAL EQUIPMENT:
1 template 3 in/7.5 cm
diam., ⅙ in/4 mm thick
Pastry bag with a plain
⅛ in/3 mm tip
1 nonstick baking sheet, or
parchment paper

NOTES:
Apart from the Chantilly cream which must be made at the last moment, all the other elements of this dessert can be made the day before. The chestnut bavarois should be firm so that it does not soften the meringue, which should remain crunchy outside and a little gooey inside.

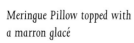

Meringue Pillow topped with
a marron glacé

PRESENTATION: Reserve 6 of the best marron pieces for decoration. Spoon the chestnut bavarois into the center of the 12 pillows with borders and arrange 2 or 3 small pieces of marrons glacés on the mousse. Double up the bases by placing one on top of another and finish with an almond and poppy seed base. Use a metal spatula to slide the pillows onto serving plates. Decorate each with an attractive marron piece or half and serve without delay.

COFFEE PARFAITS
Parfaits au café

KEEP THE DECORATION RESTRAINED ON THESE PARFAITS: A LIGHT CHOCOLATE COATING OR A FEW COFFEE OR CHOCOLATE BEANS ARRANGED ON TOP ARE ENOUGH TO ENHANCE THE PRESENTATION.

INGREDIENTS:
½ quantity baked Hazelnut Dacquoise (page 31)
1 tbsp water
6 tbsp/75 g sugar
4 egg yolks
1 gelatine leaf, soaked in cold water and well drained
2 soup spoons instant coffee, dissolved in 2 soup spoons warm water
1 cup/250 ml heavy cream, whipped to a ribbon consistency

Serves 10
Preparation time: 40 minutes

THE DACQUOISE BASES: Cut out ten dacquoise circles the size of the dessert rings. Place the rings on a baking sheet, line them with the dacquoise bases, and refrigerate.

THE BOMBE MIXTURE: Put the water into a small, heavy-based saucepan, add the sugar, and set over low heat. Bring to a boil, washing down the inside of the pan with a pastry brush dipped in cold water. Put the thermometer into the syrup and cook until the temperature reaches 240°F/115°C. Now start whisking the egg yolks in an electric mixer or by hand. As soon as the syrup reaches 250°F/121°C, remove from the heat and let the syrup bubble down for 1 minute. Pour the syrup onto the yolks in a thin stream, whisking continuously but slowly. When the syrup is well amalgamated with the yolks, stir in the well-drained gelatine and whisk until the mixture is completely cold. Stir the dissolved coffee into the mixture, then using a spatula, delicately fold in the whipped cream.

ASSEMBLING THE PARFAITS: Pipe the coffee bombe mixture into the lined rings and smooth the surfaces with a metal spatula. Place the parfaits in the freezer.

PRESENTATION: To remove the rings, heat the outsides very lightly with a blowtorch, or run a knife blade dipped in hot water between the parfaits and the rings and lift them off. Place each parfait on a plate and serve frozen like an ice cream. Serve them just as they are or pour a ribbon of coffee Crème Anglaise (page 40) around the edge.

SPECIAL EQUIPMENT:
Candy thermometer
Pastry bag with a plain ⅜ in/7 mm tip
10 dessert rings, 2⅜ in/6 cm diam., 1¼ in/3 cm deep
Blowtorch (optional)

NOTES:
The parfaits keep well in the freezer up to a week, so this recipe may make enough for two meals, depending on how many guests you are entertaining and how greedy you are.

NOUGATINE BASKETS WITH YELLOW PEACHES

La coupelle de nougatine aux pêches jaunes

AN ELEGANT AND DELICATE DESSERT FOR A GRAND OCCASION OR A CANDLELIT
DINNER, WHICH REQUIRES SOME DEXTERITY. SINCE THIS IS A WINTER DESSERT,
I USE CANNED PEACHES IN SYRUP, WHICH TASTE DELICIOUS AND WHOSE COLOR
AND FLAVOR GO WONDERFULLY WELL WITH THE NOUGATINE.

INGREDIENTS: ❊

1¾ lbs/840 g freshly-made
 Nougatine (page 189)
2 tbsp peanut oil, for
 greasing
2 tbsp Royal Icing (page
 181)
¼ cup/50 g sugar
½ quantity Ginger Mousse
 (page 49), to be prepared
 at least 2 hours in advance
 and kept in the refrigerator
6 yellow peach halves in
 syrup (about 11½ oz/
 320 g, drained weight)
48 pine nuts, sprinkled with
 confectioners' sugar and
 glazed under a very hot
 broiler

Serves 6
Preparation time: 1 hour 15
 minutes

THE NOUGATINE BASES: Preheat the oven to 320°F/160°C. On a warmed but not very hot greased baking sheet, roll out half the nougatine to

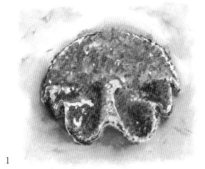

a thickness of ½ in/2 mm. It should be freshly made, and therefore still malleable. If it is too hard, place the baking sheet with the nougatine in the warm oven for a few seconds, but do not overheat the nougatine or it will stick to the baking sheet.

Cut out six nougatine rounds with a plain 6 in/15 cm diam. cookie cutter, then quickly pleat each one into five waves with your fingers. Give one wave at the front a more pronounced shape (1). Place the bases on a wire rack.

THE NOUGATINE BASKETS: Heat the blade of a small, very sharp knife over a gas flame. Gently warm the hemispherical mold in the oven.

Roll out the remaining nougatine in the same way as before and cut out another six rounds. Use the very hot knife blade to cut an incision from the center of each round out to the edge, heating the blade again if necessary. Shape these rounds by molding them one at a time around the warmed mold. Roll over the nougatine at the point

where you made the incision and press it into two small curls (2), taking care that the entire shape of the basket is neatly formed. Throughout this operation the nougatine should remain malleable but not too soft.

Place the nougatine shapes on the wire rack and use a piping cone to decorate the edges with royal icing.

Put ¼ cup/50 g caster sugar in a small saucepan and dissolve it over very low heat without water, stirring continuously. As soon as it dissolves into a caramel, use a teaspoon to dab a little of the caramel onto the bottom of one basket and immediately stick this onto a nougatine base. Assemble all the baskets in this way.

SPECIAL EQUIPMENT:

1 hemispherical stainless
 steel dome, 1¾ in/4.5 cm
 high, 3½ in/9 cm diam.
Heavy wooden or special
 metal rolling pin for
 nougatine
Lightly greased baking sheet
Paper piping cone
Pastry bag with a plain ⅝
 in/15 mm tip

NOTES:

To ensure that the nougatine
is malleable when you are
rolling it out or shaping the
waves, warm it whenever
necessary for a few seconds
in a microwave oven, or for
2 or 3 minutes in a
conventional oven at
320°F/160°C.

The nougatine baskets can
be made two or three days in
advance. Keep them in a very
dry place and do not fill
with mousse more than 2
hours before the meal.

THE GINGER MOUSSE: The mousse should have been prepared at least 2 hours in advance and refrigerated, so that it has set. Put in the pastry bag and pipe it into the baskets, without filling them right to the top. The baskets can now be kept in the refrigerator up to 2 hours.

PRESENTATION: Drain and pat dry the peach halves. Thinly slice each half and arrange one on the mousse in each basket, fanning out the slices into a flower shape. Scatter on the pine nuts and place the nougatine baskets on plates that complement their shape. Serve cold but not chilled.

INDIVIDUAL KOUGLOFS
Kouglof à ma façon

THIS IS MY VERSION OF A WONDERFUL WINTER DESSERT. THE KOUGLOFS ARE
SLIGHTLY REMINISCENT OF BREAD PUDDING, BUT MORE DELICATE AND ATTRACTIVE. IF
YOU DO NOT HAVE SMALL KOUGLOF MOLDS, MAKE ONE LARGE DESSERT, SOAKING IT
FOR LONGER AND BASTING REGULARLY WITH THE SYRUP.

INGREDIENTS:

KOUGLOF DOUGH:

½ oz/12 g compressed fresh
   yeast
¼ cup/60 ml milk, boiled
   and cooled to tepid
1 heaped tsp/7 g fine salt
1¾ cups/250 g flour
3 eggs
6 oz (1½ sticks)/175 g
   softened butter
3 tbsp/35 g sugar
Flour for dusting
⅔ cup/100 g golden raisins,
   plus about ⅓ cup/50 g
   for the garnish, soaked in
   3½ tbsp rum

90 blanched almonds, split
   (ie: 180 halves)
1 egg white
2 cups/500 ml Sorbet
   Syrup (page 144)
11 oz/300 g Chantilly
   Cream (page 42)
15 small mint sprigs
3 cups/750 ml Crème
   Anglaise (page 40)

Makes 15 individual
   kouglofs, or 1 large
   kouglof
Preparation time: 50
   minutes, plus 45 minutes
   proving and 24 hours
   resting
Cooking time: 25 minutes

THE KOUGLOF DOUGH: Follow the method for Brioche dough on page
19 and let the dough rest in the refrigerator for 24 hours.

MOLDING THE KOUGLOFS: Mix the ⅔ cup/100g raisins into the dough.
Divide it into fifteen small 2 oz/50 g pieces and, on a lightly floured
surface, use the hollow of your hand to roll these into balls, shaping
them one at a time. Press one ball into a kouglof mold, making sure
that it follows the contours of the mold. Fill the rest of the molds in
the same way.

Moisten the flat side of the almond halves with a little egg white
and press the flat side onto the dough in each of the indentations in
the molds. Let the
kouglofs rise in a warm,
draft-free place for about
45 minutes.

Preheat the oven to
400°F/200°C.

BAKING THE KOUGLOFS:
Bake in the preheated oven
for 25 minutes. Carefully
unmold the kouglofs,
taking care not to dislodge
the almonds. Place them
on a wire rack and let cool
at room temperature.

SOAKING THE KOUGLOFS: Bring the sorbet syrup to a boil with
1 cup/250 ml water, then let cool to about 104°F/40°C. Arrange the
kouglofs in one or two deep dishes and spoon over the syrup. Let
steep for about 20 minutes, then drain on a wire rack.

When the kouglofs are cold, pipe the Chantilly cream into the
cavities and decorate with a sprig of mint.

PRESENTATION: Place a kouglof in the center of each plate. Pour a
ribbon of crème anglaise around the edge and sprinkle on the
reserved raisins. Serve at room temperature.

SPECIAL EQUIPMENT:
15 small kouglof
   (kugelhopf) molds,
   1½ in/4 cm diam. at the
   base, 3½ in/9 cm at the
   top, 2 in/5 cm deep,
   greased with 4 tbsp/50 g
   butter
Pastry bag with a fluted
   ½ in/1 cm tip

NOTE:
It is not possible to make a
smaller quantity of dough
without adversely affecting
the quality of these cakes,
but you could keep some of
the unsoaked kouglofs in an
airtight container in a dry
place for several days, or
freeze them for up to 8 days.
Soak them in syrup just
before serving.

Love Nests with Red-currant Pearls

Puits d'amour aux perles de groseille

The perfect dessert for a special occasion, such as a Valentine's day celebration or a wedding anniversary. It is also delicious served with a Red Fruit Coulis (page 51).

INGREDIENTS: ❋

9 oz/250 g trimmings of Quick Puff Pastry (page 25) or Flan pastry (page 22)

A pinch of flour

Eggwash (1 egg yolk mixed with 1 soup spoon milk and a pinch of salt)

½ quantity Choux paste (page 26)

Butter for greasing

1 cup/200 g sugar

½ quantity warm Chiboust Cream (page 39), freshly made without alcohol

7 oz/200 g red currants, plus a few sprays for decoration

Serves 8

Preparation time: 25 minutes

Cooking time: 25 minutes

PREPARING THE BASES: On a lightly floured surface, roll out the pastry trimmings to a thickness of ⅛ in/3 mm. Cut out 8 rounds with the cookie cutter and transfer to a baking sheet, without damaging the shape. Prick several times with a fork. Refrigerate for 20 minutes.

BAKING THE NESTS: Preheat the oven to 425°F/220°C.

Brush the inner border of each pastry circle with eggwash. Fill the pastry bag fitted with the plain tip with choux paste and pipe a neat sausage of paste over the eggwashed area. Next pipe a spiral of choux paste in the center of each base, holding the tip very close to the base, to make a coil of half-squashed and therefore thinner paste than the outer border. Brush the edges of the choux paste with eggwash and bake the nests in the hot oven for 10 minutes. Now lower the temperature to 350°F/180°C and bake for a further 7 or 8 minutes. Remove the nests from the oven and slide them onto a wire rack.

THE CHOUX PASTE HEARTS: Fill a paper piping cone with choux paste and snip off the pointed end with scissors to make a tiny opening. Onto a lightly greased baking sheet, pipe out eight hearts, approximately 1½ x 1½ in/4 × 4 cm, and eight smaller hearts of about 1 × 1 in/2.5 × 2.5 cm. Bake these in the oven at 350°F/180°C for 8 minutes, then place them on the wire rack with the nests.

THE CARAMEL: In a small saucepan, dissolve the sugar over low heat, stirring continuously to make a very pale blond caramel. Immediately take the pan off the heat. Dip the base, sides, and borders of all the choux nests in the caramel, one at a time, taking care to coat only a little of the pastry and not its entire thickness with the caramel. This operation should be done by hand. Using tweezers, dip one half of each heart in the caramel, so that only half the thickness is coated. Place the hearts on a wire rack. If during this process the caramel cools and hardens, warm it over a very low heat for 30–60 seconds to keep it liquid and not coat the choux pastry too thickly.

ASSEMBLING THE LOVE NESTS: Fill the pastry bag fitted with the star tip with the freshly-made, warm Chiboust cream. Pipe a generous rosette of Chiboust cream into the hollow of each nest. On top of each border of choux pastry, arrange a necklace of red-currant pearls. Place a large and a small heart in the cream, then finish each Love Nest with a small spray of red currants.

SPECIAL EQUIPMENT:

1 plain 4 in/10 cm cookie cutter

2 pastry bags, one with a ½ in/1 cm plain tip, one with a ⅝ in/15 mm star tip

Tweezers

NOTES:

The completed Love Nests can be frozen, but it is better to decorate them with the red currants after they come out of the freezer.

Although you will need only a quarter quantity of Chiboust cream to fill the nests, you must make at least a half quantity for a successful recipe. Serve the remainder in glasses with some diced fruit on the following day.

HOT DESSERTS

Hot or warm desserts are particularly welcome in autumn and winter. They usually involve a certain amount of advance preparation, and must be cooked during or just at the end of the meal. However, if you keep the situation under control, it is not difficult to make a successful hot dessert.

As you will see from the number of hot soufflés featured in this chapter, they never fail to thrill me. There is no dessert as delicate, light, melting, and tempting as a soufflé. They are the consecration of a meal, the royal seal on a missive. Soufflés are not merely for eating – they are for savoring. They are delicious served with a coulis, a very light sauce, or an ice cream. The three golden rules for successful soufflés are:

1. The desire to succeed

2. Good organization

3. Serve them the moment they are ready. As the saying goes: "You can wait for a soufflé, but a soufflé will not wait for you."

Pouring raspberry sauce into the center of the soufflé

Candied Fruit Soufflés

Soufflés aux fruits candis

WE HAVE SERVED THESE MELTINGLY SWEET, FRUITY SOUFFLÉS AT THE WATERSIDE INN FOR
MANY YEARS AND OUR REGULAR CLIENTS NEVER SEEM TO TIRE OF THEM. A FRESHLY CHURNED
HONEY ICE CREAM MAKES A DELIGHTFUL ACCOMPANIMENT, BUT IS NOT ESSENTIAL.

INGREDIENTS:

2 tbsp/30 g softened butter

6½ tbsp/80 g sugar, plus
2½ tbsp/30 g for the
dishes

4 oz/100 g mixed candied
fruits, in equal quantities
(cherries, angelica, orange
or lemon, apricots)

¼ cup/60 ml milk

1 vanilla bean, split, or 1
coffee spoon vanilla extract

6 oz/180 g Pastry Cream
(page 39)

1 tbsp/20 g clear honey

7 egg whites

8 vanilla-flavored macaroons
(optional)

2 tbsp/15 g confectioners'
sugar

Serves 4

Preparation time: 25
minutes

Cooking time: 6–7 minutes

PREPARING THE SOUFFLÉ DISHES: Brush the insides of the dishes with the softened butter. Put 2½ tbsp/30 g sugar into one dish and rotate it so that the inside is well coated with sugar. Tip the excess sugar into the next dish and repeat the operation to coat all the dishes.

Preheat the oven to 425°F/220°C and place a baking sheet in the oven to heat.

ASSEMBLING THE SOUFFLÉS: Chop the candied fruits very finely. Put the milk in a bowl and mix in the fruits with a spoon. Scrape out the inside of the vanilla bean with the tip of a knife and stir it or the vanilla extract into the mixture.

Place the pastry cream in a wide-mouthed bowl and warm it to tepid in a microwave oven, or in a bain-marie. Now add the fruit mixture and the honey.

Beat the egg whites in an electric mixer or by hand until half-risen, then add the remaining sugar and continue to beat until stiff. Use a whisk to fold one-third of the egg whites into the pastry cream, then add the rest and fold them in with a spatula. Fill the soufflé dishes up to one-third with the mixture, sprinkle two lightly crushed macaroons over each one, then fill up the dishes, and smooth the surface with a metal spatula. Ease the mixture away from the edge of the dishes with the tip of a knife.

COOKING THE SOUFFLÉS: Place the soufflé dishes on the hot baking sheet and bake in the hot oven for 6–7 minutes.

PRESENTATION: As soon as the soufflés come out of the oven, dust them with a light veil of confectioners' sugar, place on individual plates lined with a paper doily, and serve at once.

SPECIAL EQUIPMENT:

4 soufflé dishes, 4 in/
10 cm diam., 2⅜ in/
6 cm deep

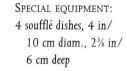

Souffléed Oranges with Caramel Sauce

Oranges soufflées, sauce caramel

THIS DELICIOUS DESSERT IS DELICATE, AND CANNOT BE KEPT WAITING. THIS IS TRUE OF ALL SOUFFLÉS, BUT PARTICULARLY SO IN THIS CASE, SINCE THE FRAGILE MIXTURE CONTAINS NO FLOUR. THE CONTRAST BETWEEN THE WARM, MELTING SOUFFLÉ AND THE COLD CHOCOLATE SORBET IS DIVINE.

INGREDIENTS:

12 oranges, about
   11 oz/300 g each

6 tbsp/75 g sugar

2 quantities freshly-made
   Orange Caramel Sauce
   (see Red Berries with
   Lightly Candied Orange
   Beads, page 64)

3½ tbsp Grand Marnier
   (optional)

½ quantity Chocolate Sorbet
   (page 148), churned
   several hours in advance,
   and very firm

4 tsp/20 g softened butter

48 small fresh lemon
   verbena or mint leaves

1 quantity Meringue
   Topping made with Egg
   Yolks (page 35)

1 vanilla bean, split

Serves 8

Preparation time: 45
   minutes

Cooking time: 7–8 minutes

THE CANDIED ORANGE ZESTS: Wash the oranges in cold water and dry them. Use a potato peeler to pare off the zests from two of the oranges. Cut the zests into thin slivers with a sharp knife. Place in a small saucepan, cover with cold water, and bring to a boil over high heat. Refresh and drain. Return the zests to the pan with the sugar and enough cold water to cover. Cook gently until almost all the liquid has evaporated, leaving only about 1 soup spoon of syrup. Tip the candied zests into a colander and let drain until needed.

THE ORANGE SECTIONS: Take four oranges, including the two from which you removed the zests. Peel them with a fine knife, removing all the pith and membrane, and cut out the sections, sliding the knife between the membrane and flesh. Reserve the sections in a bowl. Holding them over the bowl, squeeze the orange pulp and membranes with your hands to extract all the juices. Keep at room temperature.

THE ORANGE CARAMEL SAUCE: Keeping the more stable end of the remaining oranges as the base, slice one-third off the tops in a zig-zag. Use a soup spoon to scoop out the pulp into a bowl, taking care not to damage the orange skins. Discard the small top parts of the orange skins.

Place the orange skin containers in the refrigerator. Extract the juice from the pulp in a food processor, then prepare the orange caramel sauce following the method on page 64, adding the Grand Marnier if desired. Keep the cooked sauce at room temperature.

THE ORANGE CONTAINERS: Preheat the oven to 325°F/170°C.

Using a pastry brush, very lightly brush the edges of the zigzags with softened butter. Divide the chocolate sorbet among the orange containers. Freeze for at least 20 minutes.

THE SERVING PLATES: Meanwhile, prepare the serving plates. (It is essential to do this before assembling and cooking the souffléed oranges.) Arrange six orange sections in a rosette on each plate, leaving a space in the center for the souffléed orange. Place a lemon verbena or mint leaf between each section, and pour a little sauce onto the plates.

ASSEMBLING AND COOKING THE SOUFFLÉED ORANGES: Make the meringue topping, following the method on page 35. Scrape out the seeds from

SPECIAL EQUIPMENT:

Pastry bag with a fluted
   ⅝ in/15 mm tip

Ice cubes or coarsely crushed
   ice

NOTE:

As the ice cubes in the
roasting pan will be almost
completely melted, be careful
not to spill water everywhere
when you take the pan out of
the oven.

84

the vanilla bean with the tip of a knife to flavor the meringue.

Place the ice in a 1½–2 in/4–5 cm deep roasting pan large enough to hold all 8 oranges, and put in the sorbet-filled oranges. Pipe in the meringue to within ¾ in/2 cm of the top of the zigzags. Immediately cook in the preheated oven for 7–8 minutes.

PRESENTATION: The instant the oranges are ready, place one in the center of each plate. Arrange the candied zests on top and serve without delay.

Passion Fruit Soufflés

Soufflés aux fruits de la passion

The perfect dessert: a sharp-flavored soufflé that is easy to prepare.

INGREDIENTS:

2 tbsp/30 g softened butter

½ cup + 2 tbsp/120 g
   superfine sugar, plus 2½
   tbsp/30 g for the dishes

9 oz/250 g Pastry Cream
   (page 39)

12 passion fruit (about
   9 oz/240 g)

8 egg whites

Serves 4

Preparation time: 15
   minutes

Cooking time: 7–8 minutes

PREPARING THE SOUFFLÉ DISHES: Brush the insides of the dishes with softened butter. Put 2½ tbsp/30 g sugar into one dish and rotate to coat the whole surface with sugar. Tip the excess sugar into the next dish and repeat to coat all the dishes.

Preheat the oven to 375°F/190°C and put in a baking sheet to heat.

ASSEMBLING THE SOUFFLÉS: Put the pastry cream in a wide-mouthed bowl and reheat it to tepid in a microwave oven, or by standing the base in a bain-marie set over medium heat. Halve the passion fruit and use a teaspoon to scrape the seeds from ten of them into the goblet of a blender. Reserve the seeds from the remaining two fruits for the garnish.

Blend the seeds for several seconds to break them up slightly, then add them to the pastry cream.

In an electric mixer or by hand, beat the egg whites until half-risen. Add the remaining sugar and continue to beat into semi-firm peaks. Use a whisk to mix one-third of the egg whites into the pastry cream, then delicately fold in the rest with a spatula. Pour the mixture into the prepared dishes and smooth the surface with a metal spatula. With the tip of a knife, ease the mixture away from the edge of the dishes.

SPECIAL EQUIPMENT:

4 soufflé dishes, 4 in/
   10 cm diam.,
   2⅜ in/6 cm deep

COOKING THE SOUFFLÉS: Place the dishes on the hot baking sheet and cook the soufflés in the preheated oven for 7–8 minutes.

PRESENTATION: As soon as the soufflés come out of the oven, spoon a few of the reserved passion fruit seeds on the top of each one and spread them gently over the center. Place the soufflés on serving plates each lined with a paper doily and serve immediately.

CHOCOLATE SOUFFLÉS
Soufflés chocolat

THESE SOUFFLÉS ARE VERY EASY TO MAKE. IF YOU LIKE, ACCOMPANY THEM WITH A VELVETY FRESHLY-CHURNED VANILLA ICE CREAM (PAGE 137) OR SOME HEAVY CREAM AND LET YOUR GUESTS ADD A SPOONFUL TO THEIR SOUFFLÉ.

INGREDIENTS:
2 tbsp/30 g softened butter
¾ cup/150 g superfine sugar, plus 2½ tbsp/30 g for the dishes
11 oz/300 g Pastry Cream (page 39)
¾ cup/65 g unsweetened cocoa powder, sifted
8 egg whites
2 soup spoons confectioners' sugar

Serves 4
Preparation time: 20 minutes
Cooking time: 7–8 minutes

SPECIAL EQUIPMENT:
4 soufflé dishes,
4 in/10 cm diam.,
2⅜ in/6 cm deep

PREPARING THE SOUFFLE DISHES: Brush the insides of the dishes with softened butter. Put 2½ tbsp/30 g sugar into one dish and rotate it so that the inside is well coated with sugar. Tip the excess sugar into the next dish and repeat to coat all the dishes in this way.

Preheat the oven to 375°F/190°C and place a baking sheet on the middle shelf to heat.

ASSEMBLING THE SOUFFLÉS: Put the pastry cream into a wide-mouthed bowl and reheat it to tepid in a microwave oven, or stand the base of the bowl in a bain-marie set over medium heat. When the cream is warm, whisk in the cocoa.

Beat the egg whites in an electric mixer or by hand until half-risen. Add the remaining superfine sugar and beat into semi-firm peaks. With a whisk, fold one-third of the egg whites into the chocolate pastry cream, then delicately fold in the remainder with a spatula. Pour the mixture into the dishes and smooth the surface with a metal spatula. Ease the mixture away from the edge of the dishes with the tip of a knife.

COOKING THE SOUFFLÉS: Place the dishes on the hot baking sheet and cook the soufflés in the hot oven for 7–8 minutes.

PRESENTATION: As soon as the soufflés come out of the oven, dust them with confectioners' sugar, place each one on a plate lined with a paper doily, and serve at once.

Marbled Peppermint and Chocolate Soufflés

Soufflés à la menthe marbré au chocolat

THESE REFRESHING SOUFFLÉS ARE REALLY OUT OF THE ORDINARY. THE MARRIAGE OF
MINT WITH THE POCKETS OF MELTED CHOCOLATE IS SURPRISING AND UNUSUAL.

INGREDIENTS:

2 tbsp/30 g softened butter

¾ cup/150 g superfine
  sugar, plus 2½ tbsp/30 g
  for the dishes

11 oz/300 g Pastry Cream
  (page 39)

3½ tbsp green peppermint
  liqueur

8 egg whites

3 oz/80 g bitter couverture
  or best-quality bittersweet
  chocolate, chopped

4 sprigs of mint

2 tbsp/15 g confectioners'
  sugar

Serves 4

Preparation time: 20
  minutes

Cooking time: 7–8 minutes

PREPARING THE SOUFFLÉ DISHES: Brush the insides of the dishes with
softened butter. Put 2½ tbsp/30 g sugar into one dish and rotate it to
coat the surface completely with sugar. Tip the excess sugar into the
next dish and repeat until all the dishes are coated.

Preheat the oven to 375°F/190°C and put in a baking sheet to heat.

ASSEMBLING THE SOUFFLÉS: Put the pastry cream into a wide-mouthed
bowl and warm to tepid in a microwave, or stand the base of the bowl
in a bain-marie set over medium heat. Stir in the peppermint liqueur.

Beat the egg whites until half-risen, then add the remaining
superfine sugar and beat into semi-firm peaks. Use a whisk to mix
one-third of the beaten egg whites into the pastry cream, then
delicately fold in the rest with a spatula. Scatter in the chopped
chocolate. Pour the mixture into the prepared dishes and smooth the
surface with a metal spatula. Use the tip of a knife to ease the mixture
away from the edge of the dishes.

COOKING THE SOUFFLÉS: Place the soufflé dishes on the hot baking
sheet and cook in the hot oven for 7–8 minutes.

PRESENTATION: As soon as the soufflés come out of the oven, place a
mint sprig on each one and dust with a light veil of confectioners'
sugar. Place each dish on a plate lined with a paper doily, and serve
immediately.

SPECIAL EQUIPMENT:
4 soufflé dishes,
  4 in/10 cm diam.,
  2⅜ in/6 cm deep

*Marbled Peppermint and
Chocolate Soufflés*

SOUFFLÉED CHOCOLATE CREPES
Crêpes soufflées au chocolat

HERE TRULY IS A DESSERT FOR CHOCOHOLICS: CHOCOLATE CREPES,
CHOCOLATE SOUFFLÉ, AND CHOCOLATE SAUCE IF YOU FANCY THAT AS WELL,
ALL DELECTABLE AND CREAMY.

INGREDIENTS:
½ cup/40 g unsweetened
   cocoa powder
1 tbsp confectioners' sugar,
   plus 2 pinches for dusting
2 tbsp/20 g flour
2 eggs, plus 1 egg yolk
5 tbsp heavy cream
½ cup milk
3 tbsp/45 g clarified butter
1 quantity Chocolate Soufflé
   mixture (page 87)
½ quantity Chocolate Sauce
   (page 55) (optional)

Makes 12 crêpes (to serve 6)
Preparation time: 20
   minutes, plus 30 minutes
   resting
Cooking time: 27 minutes

THE CREPE BATTER: Combine the cocoa, 1 tbsp confectioners' sugar, the flour, whole eggs and extra yolk, and the cream in a bowl. Mix with a whisk, without overworking the mixture, then pour in the milk, stirring as you go. Cover the bowl with plastic wrap and let the batter rest at room temperature for 30 minutes.

COOKING THE CREPES: Place the non-stick frying pan on the heat and brush the bottom with clarified butter. When the pan is very hot, ladle in enough batter to cover the bottom (1). Cook the crêpe for 1 minute, then carefully turn it over with a metal spatula and cook for another minute. Transfer the cooked crêpe to a plate and lay a band of wax paper on top to prevent the next crêpe from sticking to the first and so on. Cook and stack all the crêpes in this way, brushing the pan with melted butter after every two crêpes. Let them cool at room temperature and, when they are cold, trim each crêpe into a 5½ in/14 cm circle using a sharp knife or cookie cutter (2).

SPECIAL EQUIPMENT:
Nonstick 6½ in/16 cm
   frying pan
11 narrow strips of wax
   paper

NOTE:
Souffléed crêpes will tolerate waiting even less than a soufflé, so it is essential to serve them the moment they are ready.

BAKING AND FILLING THE CREPES: Preheat the oven to 400°F/200°C and heat six serving plates.

Lay six crêpes on a baking sheet and fill the center of each one with 2 generous soup spoons of soufflé mixture. Fold the crêpes in half with a metal spatula, without pressing them (3). Do the same with the remaining crêpes and immediately bake them in the hot oven for 3 minutes (4). As soon as they are ready, dust with confectioners' sugar, slide a metal spatula under one crêpe at a time and transfer to heated plates, allowing two per person. Serve at once.

PRESENTATION: If you like, pour a little chocolate sauce around the crêpes on one side of each plate.

GRATINS OF RED CURRANTS AND WILD STRAWBERRIES
Gratins de perles de groseilles et fraises des bois

THESE MOIST, DELICATE GRATINS CAN BE PREPARED SEVERAL DAYS IN
ADVANCE AND COOKED AT THE LAST MOMENT.

INGREDIENTS: ✽
Italian Meringue (page 37),
    made with 5 egg whites
    and ¾ cup/160 g
    superfine sugar
½ cup/125 ml lemon juice
½ cup/125 ml heavy cream
6 egg yolks
5 tbsp/60 g sugar
3 tbsp/25 g flour
2 gelatine leaves, soaked in
    cold water and well
    drained
1 tbsp finely grated lemon
    zest, blanched
4½ oz/125 g wild
    strawberries and 4½ oz/
    125 g red currants, or
    9 oz/250 g of one variety
¼ cup/30 g confectioners'
    sugar
½ quantity Orange Sauce
    (page 52), chilled, for
    serving

Serves 10
Preparation time: 35
    minutes, plus 2–3 hours
    freezing
Cooking time: 8 minutes

THE ITALIAN MERINGUE: Make the meringue according to the recipe on page 37. Place in a bowl, cover with plastic wrap and keep at room temperature until tepid.

THE LEMON PASTRY CREAM: Heat the lemon juice and cream in a saucepan. Place the egg yolks and 5 tbsp/60 g sugar in a bowl, and whisk to a light ribbon consistency. Add the flour and work until smooth. Pour the boiling lemon and cream onto the eggs, whisking continuously. Return the mixture to the pan and bubble over high heat for 2 minutes, whisking all the time. Take the pan off the heat and stir in the drained gelatine. Let cool.

THE GRATIN MIXTURE: Using a whisk, fold half the tepid Italian meringue into the tepid pastry cream, then delicately fold in the rest with a spatula, and shower in the lemon zest like rain. Stop working the mixture as soon as it becomes homogeneous.

ASSEMBLING THE GRATINS: Reserve one-third of the best fruits for decoration. Line a baking sheet with wax paper and arrange the tartlet rings on it. Using a metal spatula or a pastry bag fitted with a plain ½ in/1 cm tip, fill the bottom of the rings up to one-third and coat the sides with the tepid gratin mixture. Scatter on the remaining strawberries and red currants, then fill up the rings with the rest of the gratin mixture and smooth the surface with a metal spatula. Freeze for several hours.

COOKING THE GRATINS: Preheat the oven to 425°F/220°C.
    Remove the gratins from the freezer. Dip the tip of a small knife in boiling water, then slide it between the inside of each tartlet ring and the mixture, and lift off the rings. Sprinkle the gratins generously with confectioners' sugar. Slide a metal spatula under each gratin and place one in each buttered dish. Cook in the hot oven for about 8 minutes, until the gratins puff up and are lightly colored. They should still be soft and slightly runny in the center (see photo, right).

PRESENTATION: As soon as the gratins come out of the oven, pour a ribbon of orange sauce around each one. Arrange the reserved wild strawberries on the sauce and top the gratins with a small cluster of red currants. Serve at once.

SPECIAL EQUIPMENT:
10 tartlet rings, 3¼ in/
    8 cm diam., ¾ in/2 cm
    deep
10 round gratin dishes,
    5½ in/14 cm diam., very
    lightly buttered in the
    middle 3¼ in/8 cm

NOTE:
The prepared gratins can be frozen up to a week; just cover with plastic wrap as soon as the mixture is frozen. You could make several batches of this dessert to serve at different meals.

CITRUS RAVIOLI WITH PEACH GRATIN
Ravioles au citrus et gratin de pêches

THIS MULTI-FACETED THREE-STAR DESSERT REQUIRES PATIENCE AND SOME
DEXTERITY, SO I HAVE GIVEN YOU STEP-BY-STEP INSTRUCTIONS TO FOLLOW.
I ASSURE YOU THAT IT IS WORTH THE EFFORT.

INGREDIENTS:

LEMON FILLING
3 tbsp lemon juice
Zest of ½ lemon
2½ tbsp/30 g sugar
A large pinch of cornstarch
1 egg yolk
1 tbsp/15 g egg white

RAVIOLI DOUGH:
1 tbsp/15 g lard, at room
    temperature
½ cup/75 g flour, plus extra
    for dusting the work
    surface
2 tbsp water
A tiny pinch of fine salt
Eggwash (1 egg yolk mixed
    with 1 soup spoon milk
    and a pinch of salt)
2½ tbsp/30 g sugar
5 mint leaves

ORANGE AND PASSION
FRUIT SAUCE:
⅔ cup/150 ml orange juice
2½ tbsp/30 g sugar
3 passion fruit

6 bananas
⅓ cup/60 g raw brown
    sugar (turbinado)
½ quantity freshly made
    Sabayon (page 53), made
    with Sorbet Syrup (page
    144) instead of alcohol
3 peaches, preferably white-
    fleshed, peeled and lightly
    rubbed with lemon juice
½ quantity Vanilla Ice
    Cream (page 137)

THE LEMON FILLING: Combine all the ingredients for the filling in a
small saucepan and bring to a boil over low heat, whisking continuously. As soon as the mixture starts to bubble, transfer it to a bowl
and let cool at room temperature. When it is cold, cover with plastic
wrap and refrigerate.

THE RAVIOLI DOUGH: Put the first four ingredients in a bowl and work
to a smooth dough with your fingertips. Cover with plastic wrap and
refrigerate for 30 minutes.

THE ORANGE AND PASSION FRUIT SAUCE: Put the orange juice and sugar in
a small saucepan and reduce by one-third over low heat. Transfer to a
bowl, let cool, then halve the passion fruit, and scoop out the seeds
with a teaspoon into the orange sauce. Keep at room temperature.

FILLING THE RAVIOLI: Divide the
dough into two pieces, one 45%
of the dough, the other 55%.

On a lightly floured surface,
roll the smaller piece of dough
into a ½ in/2 mm thick 11 ×
7½ in/28 × 19 cm rectangle,
using a pasta machine or
rolling pin. Fill the pastry
bag with the lemon filling and pipe eighteen small balls onto
the sheet of dough in staggered rows, six along the longer
side, and three along the shorter side (1). Brush the dough
around the balls with eggwash.

Roll out the remaining dough into a thin 12 × 8½ in/30 ×
21 cm rectangle and lay this over the first sheet of dough.
Using your fingertips, very delicately press down around the
balls of filling.

Using the non-cutting edge of the 1¼ in/3 cm cookie
cutter, press lightly around the balls of filling. Cut out the
eighteen ravioli with the larger, fluted cutter (2) and lay
them on a very lightly floured sheet of wax paper.

THE BANANAS: Peel and cut each into eighteen diagonal slices,
then arrange them in threes on a baking sheet. Sprinkle with
raw brown sugar and caramelize the little heaps of banana
with a blowtorch (3).

SPECIAL EQUIPMENT:
Plain 1¼ in/3 cm cookie
    cutter
Fluted 2 in/5 cm cookie
    cutter
Pastry bag with a plain
    ¼ in/5 mm tip
Blowtorch
Pasta machine or a rolling
    pin

Serves 6
Preparation time: 1 hour 20
    minutes
Cooking time: 7 minutes

NOTE:
During the winter, substitute
very ripe pears for the
peaches.

4

THE SABAYON: Prepare this not more than half an hour in advance. Keep the sabayon in a bain-marie for the shortest possible time until ready to use.

COOKING THE RAVIOLI: Bring 1 quart/1 liter water to the boil with 2½ tbsp/30 g sugar, drop in the ravioli and mint leaves, and cook over low heat for 7 minutes. Meanwhile, heat the serving plates.

PRESENTATION: Halve the peaches. Slice each half very thinly and arrange one sliced half in a rosette in the center of each heated plate, leaving a gap in the middle for the ice cream.

Place three ravioli at the edge of each plate, then three heaps of caramelized bananas. Spoon a little orange and passion fruit sauce over the ravioli. Coat the sliced peaches with sabayon (4) and glaze to a hazelnut color with the blowtorch (5). Top the peaches with a scoop of ice cream and serve immediately.

5

BAKED APPLE IN A GOLDEN CAGE WITH CRUNCHY APPLE PEARLS

Pomme en cage dans sa croûte dorée et ses perles croquantes

A RUSTIC DESSERT, FULL OF AUTUMNAL FLAVORS. YOU CAN OMIT THE GOLDEN CAGES, BUT THEY DO ADD AN ARTISTIC DIMENSION TO A SIMPLE AND INEXPENSIVE DISH, AND ARE NOT AT ALL DIFFICULT TO MAKE.

INGREDIENTS:

5 oz/150 g trimmings of Jean Millet's or Quick Puff Pastry (pages 24 and 25), or Flan Pastry (page 22)

Flour for dusting

Eggwash (1 egg yolk mixed with 1 soup spoon milk and a pinch of salt)

6 firm, tart-sweet apples, each about 5 oz/150 g

4 tbsp/50 g butter

4 oz/100 g dried apricots, finely diced

3 tbsp/60 g clear honey

¾ cup/80 g toasted sliced almonds

1¼ cups/250 g sugar

1 cup/250 ml Apricot Coulis (see Fruit Coulis, page 51)

SERVES 4

Preparation time: 50 minutes

Cooking time: 30 minutes

THE GOLDEN CAGES: On a lightly floured surface, roll out the pastry trimmings into a square about ½ in/2 mm thick. Roll the lattice rolling pin over the pastry in one direction only (1). Using a chef's knife, cut the pastry square into 4 smaller squares. Drape one square over a hemispherical mold, teasing the pastry lightly with your fingertips to give a latticed effect (2). Cut off the excess pastry around the base of the mold with the cookie cutter. Prepare three more pastry cages in this way and refrigerate for 20 minutes.

Meanwhile, preheat the oven to 350°F/180°C.

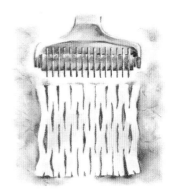

1

2

BAKING THE CAGES: Brush the pastry cages with eggwash, taking care not to let it drip onto the molds. Bake in the preheated oven for 7–8 minutes, then let cool at room temperature. When the cages are almost cold, lift them carefully off the molds.

THE BAKED APPLES: Reduce the oven temperature to 300°F/150°C.

Wash four apples in cold water, wipe dry, and, using the tip of a knife, make an incision all around the middle to ensure even cooking. Remove the cores with an apple corer, then arrange the apples in a roasting pan greased with all the butter.

In a bowl, mix the diced apricots, honey, and half of the sliced almonds. Divide this filling among the cavities in the apples and pile up the excess in a dome on top of the fruit. Bake for 30 minutes, basting the apples every 10 minutes with the cooking juices and butter from the roasting pan. Keep the cooked apples warm in the pan.

THE CRUNCHY APPLE PEARLS: Peel the remaining two apples with a vegetable peeler. Use the melon baller to scoop out twenty-four balls of apple. In a small, heavy-based saucepan, cook the sugar without water, stirring continuously. As

SPECIAL EQUIPMENT:

4 hemispherical molds, 3½ in/9 cm diam., 1¾ in/4.5 cm deep, lightly greased on the outside and chilled

Lattice rolling pin

4 in/10 cm plain cookie cutter

⅜ in/7 mm melon baller

soon as it turns to a very pale caramel, take the pan off the heat.

Spread the remaining sliced almonds on a baking sheet. Quickly dip the apple balls one at a time in the caramel, then lay them on the almonds. With your fingertips, bring up the almonds slightly around the apple balls, taking care not to touch the barely set caramel coating (see photo, opposite). Keep at room temperature.

PRESENTATION: Place a baked apple in the center of each serving plate and moisten with the cooking juices from the pan. Pour the cold apricot coulis around the edge, and make a border of six crunchy apple pearls. Carefully place the pastry cages over the apples and serve at once.

Coulibiac of Winter Fruits
Coulibiac aux fruits d'hiver

ALTHOUGH THIS DESSERT MAY NOT LOOK AS SPECTACULAR AS SOME, IT HAS
A WONDERFUL FLAVOR, AND THE SCENT OF THE FRUITS THAT PERVADES THE
ROOM AS YOU CUT IT OPEN AT THE TABLE IS A KNOCKOUT.

INGREDIENTS: ✲
9 oz/250 g rhubarb
1 cup/190 g sugar
2 bananas
6 tbsp/80 g butter
Juice of 1 lemon
2 firm, tart-sweet apples,
 about 7 oz/200 g each
A pinch of ground cinnamon
14 oz/400 g Brioche dough
 (page 19)
Flour for dusting
4 crêpes, 7 in/18 cm
 diam., made with
 ½ quantity Crêpe batter
 (page 27)
4 oz/100 g moist dried
 apricots, coarsely diced
5 tbsp/100 g apricot jam,
 mixed with the pulp of 2
 passion fruit
Eggwash (1 egg yolk mixed
 with 1 soup spoon milk
 and a pinch of salt)

Serves 6
Preparation time: 40
 minutes
Cooking time: 35 minutes

SPECIAL EQUIPMENT:
Apple corer

NOTE:
*To gild the lily, serve a
kirsch-scented Sabayon (page
53) with the coulibiac, but
this is not really necessary.*

THE RHUBARB: Peel the stems and cut into 2⅜ in/6 cm lengths. Rinse in cold water and place in a saucepan with ½ cup/110 g sugar and ½ cup/100 ml water. Bring to a boil and remove from the heat as soon as the liquid bubbles. Let the rhubarb cool in the poaching syrup and drain when cold.

THE BANANAS: Peel, then, starting from one end, run your thumb downward to divide them lengthwise into their three segments. In a frying pan, brown the bananas over high heat for a few seconds with 3 tbsp/40 g each of butter and sugar, but do not cook them. Place on a plate.

THE APPLES: Peel and core, and use the apple corer to cut as many tubes as possible from the apple flesh. In the frying pan, brown the tubes over high heat for 1 minute with 3 tbsp/40 g each butter and sugar. Sprinkle with cinnamon and lemon juice and place on a plate.

ASSEMBLING THE COULIBIAC: On a lightly floured surface, carefully roll out the brioche dough into a 12 × 8 in/30 × 20 cm rectangle. Cover this with the cold crêpes (1). Down the middle, lay an 8 in/20 cm line of half of the bananas, rhubarb, apples, and diced apricots (2). Use a spoon to spread half the apricot jam and passion fruit mixture over the fruits, then lay on the remaining fruits and spread over the rest of the jam. Fold the crêpes over the fruits and brush the four edges of the brioche dough with eggwash (3).

Fold one of the longer sides of the dough over the crêpe-wrapped fruits. Brush the top of the dough with eggwash, then bring the other side up over the first side (4). With a rolling pin, lightly flatten the two ends of the dough (5), trim off a little of the excess, brush with eggwash, and fold up the ends. Turn the coulibiac over onto a baking sheet and refrigerate for 20 minutes.

Meanwhile, preheat the oven to 350°F/180°C.

BAKING THE COULIBIAC: Brush the coulibiac with eggwash. With the tip of a sharp knife, score a pattern of sunray lines over the surface (6). Use the tip of the knife to cut two little chimneys in the top of the coulibiac. Bake in the preheated oven for 35 minutes.

PRESENTATION: Serve the piping hot coulibiac whole at the table and slice with a very sharp knife.

WALNUT PITHIVIERS WITH PISTACHIO COULIS
Pithiviers aux noix, coulis à la pistache

I ADORE THIS DIVINE AUTUMN OR WINTER DESSERT. FRESH WALNUTS ARE
IN SEASON FROM OCTOBER TO NOVEMBER, GIVING TWO MONTHS PLEASURE.

INGREDIENTS: ❊
1½ lbs/750 g Jean Millet's
  Puff Pastry (page 24)
A pinch of flour
24 walnuts, preferably fresh,
  skinned and quartered
6 oz/180 g Frangipane
  (page 43)
Eggwash (1 egg yolk mixed
  with 1 soup spoon milk
  and a pinch of salt)
2½ tbsp/20 g confectioners'
  sugar
1¼ cups/250 g sugar
Oil, for greasing
1 cup/120 g pistachios,
  skinned
1¼ cups/300 ml Crème
  Anglaise (page 40)

Serves 6
Preparation time: 35
  minutes
Cooking time: about 15
  minutes

ASSEMBLING THE PITHIVIERS: 20 minutes before baking the pithiviers, preheat the oven to 425°F/220°C.

On a lightly floured surface, roll out 40% of the pastry into a 12 × 8 in/30 × 20 cm rectangle. Cut the rectangle in half lengthwise, then into three widthwise to make six small, regular squares. Place on a dampened baking sheet. Reserve twenty-four of the best walnut quarters for caramelizing, and mix the remainder into the frangipane cream. Heap this mixture in the middle of each pastry square and brush the edges of the pastry around the mixture with a little eggwash.

Roll out the remaining pastry into an 18 × 12 in/45 × 30 cm rectangle and cut into six regular squares. Invert these onto the top of the filled squares and press the edges with your fingertips to seal them thoroughly.

CUTTING OUT AND DECORATING THE PITHIVIERS: Press the non-cutting edge of the cookie cutter onto one of the Pithiviers (1). Using a small, very sharp knife, cut the pastry outside the cutter into twelve to fifteen little "ears," making three of them slightly more pronounced (2). Lift off the cookie cutter and repeat the operation with the other five Pithiviers.

Brush the top of the Pithiviers with eggwash. With the tip of a knife, trace criss-cross lines on the little "ears." Use the knife tip to score curved rays like the arcs of a circle from the center to the outer edges of the Pithiviers (3).

BAKING THE PITHIVIERS: Bake in the hot oven for 14 minutes, reducing the oven temperature to 375°F/190°C after 10 minutes. Remove the Pithiviers from the oven and increase the temperature to 475°F/240°. Dust the tops of the Pithiviers with a veil of confectioners' sugar and return them to the hot oven for a minute or two, until they have an attractive glaze, like a varnish. Remove from the oven and transfer them with a metal spatula to a wire rack.

SPECIAL EQUIPMENT:
3¼ in/8 cm diam. cookie
  cutter

NOTES:
All the elements of this dessert can be prepared the day before. Bake the Pithiviers just before the meal and keep near a heat source, taking care that they do not dry out, until ready to serve.

1

2

The uncooked Pithiviers can be frozen for at least a week. Glaze and decorate them after thawing.

3

CARAMELIZING THE WALNUTS: Put the sugar in a small, heavy-based saucepan, and dissolve over low heat, stirring continuously with a wooden spatula. As soon as the sugar has dissolved, take the pan off the heat and use a fork to dip the reserved walnuts one at a time into the sugar. Place on a lightly-oiled baking sheet.

THE PISTACHIO COULIS: Put ⅔ cup/80 g of the pistachios in a food processor with the crème anglaise and process for 3 minutes, then pass through a fine strainer and put into a sauceboat. Use a chef's knife to chop the remaining pistachios.

PRESENTATION: Place the warm Pithiviers on individual serving plates. Pour a ribbon of pistachio coulis around them, scatter on little heaps of chopped pistachios, and arrange four caramelized walnut quarters on each plate. Serve at once.

CHAPTER SEVEN

LARGE DESSERTS AND GATEAUX

These convivial, imposing desserts are often served on special occasions, such as a feast day, a family reunion, or a gathering of friends. They are presented in all their glory and served at the table.

They are made on a base of light sponge cake, meringue, or puff pastry and filled with a variety of delectable fruit mousses. They should always be served chilled, either just as they are or with a fruit coulis.

Since these gâteaux can be successfully frozen for several days, you might like to make two at a time. Then if unexpected guests arrive, with a wave of your magic wand, you can conjure up an astonishing homemade dessert from the freezer. They also make the most wonderful gifts to take to friends.

Glazing the Cardinal Gâteau

CARDINAL GATEAU
Entremets Cardinal

SILKY-SMOOTH, RICH, FRUITY, AND GLORIOUS, THIS DESSERT IS A GREAT
FAVORITE OF MY CLIENTS AT THE WATERSIDE INN — AND OF MINE, TOO. IT
MAY EVEN SERVE TEN PEOPLE IF YOUR GUESTS ARE NOT TOO GREEDY!

INGREDIENTS:

RASPBERRY PARFAIT

7 oz/200 g bitter couverture
or best-quality bittersweet
chocolate, chopped

½ cup/100 g sugar

1 whole egg

2 egg yolks

2 gelatine leaves, separately
soaked in cold water and
well drained

1 cup/250 ml raspberry
purée, strained

1¼ cups/300 ml heavy
cream, whipped to a
ribbon consistency

an 8 in/20 cm round
chocolate Genoise Sponge
(page 33), cut into a disk
⅛-¼ in/3–5 mm thick

1½ lbs/650 g raspberries
(reserve 7 oz/200 g of
the best for decoration)

GLAZE

3½ tbsp grenadine syrup

3½ tbsp raspberry jam,
strained

Serves 8–10

Preparation time: 45
minutes, plus 2–6 hours
chilling

THE RASPBERRY PARFAIT: Put the chocolate in a bowl and set it in a bain-
marie over medium heat to melt. Put 2 tbsp of water and the sugar in
a small saucepan and bring to a boil over low heat, skimming the
surface and brushing down the inside of the pan from time to time
with a pastry brush dipped in cold water. When the syrup has boiled
for a couple of minutes, put in the candy thermometer. When the
temperature reaches 240°F/116°C, place the whole egg and the yolks
in the bowl of the electric mixer and begin to whisk at low speed. As
soon as the syrup reaches 250°F/121°C, take the pan off the heat.
Wait for a minute, until the syrup stops bubbling, then pour it onto
the eggs in a thin stream, mixing all the time. Add 1 gelatine leaf and
leave the mixer running
on low speed for 5
minutes. Still at low
speed, whisk in the
melted chocolate, mix
for a minute or two
until you have a
homogeneous mixture,
then stop the motor.

With a wire whisk,
delicately fold ⅞ cup/
200 ml of the raspberry
purée into the whipped
cream. Using a spatula,
fold the raspberry-
flavored cream into the
egg and chocolate mixture. Do not overwork this raspberry parfait,
which must be used immediately.

ASSEMBLING THE GATEAU: Lay the chocolate sponge on the cake board.
Place the ring around the sponge, then half-fill it with raspberry
parfait. On top, arrange 1 lb/450 g of the raspberries in a single layer,
packing them tightly together without crushing them, then fill the
ring with the remaining parfait. Smooth the surface with a metal
spatula. Transfer the gâteau to the freezer and freeze for 2–3 hours,
or refrigerate for 5–6 hours.

THE GLAZE: Combine the grenadine, jam, and the remaining raspberry
purée in a small saucepan and boil for 2 or 3 minutes. Take the pan
off the heat and add the remaining gelatine leaf, then gently pass this

SPECIAL EQUIPMENT:

1 dessert ring, 8½ in/22 cm
diam., 1½ in/4 cm deep

Rigid cake board,
8½ in/22 cm diam.

Candy thermometer

Blowtorch (optional)

NOTES:

The unglazed gâteau can be
frozen for a week; glaze it
just before serving, or a few
hours in advance.

I do not moisten the
chocolate sponge with syrup
in this dessert, as the
raspberry parfait is so
creamy that the sponge
would be saturated.
Like all parfaits, this should
be served ice cold.

jelly through a cheesecloth-lined strainer and keep at room temperature.

Just as the glaze becomes almost cold, it will begin to thicken without solidifying. This is the moment to use it to glaze the gâteau. Leave the ring on during this process.

If the gâteau is in the freezer, take it out and leave at room temperature for about 20 minutes. If it is in the refrigerator, you can glaze it immediately. Pour half the glaze over the top of the gâteau, smooth with a metal spatula, then return the gâteau to the refrigerator for 5 minutes. As soon as the glaze has set, pour on the remainder and keep the dessert in the refrigerator until ready to serve.

PRESENTATION: To remove the dessert ring, run a blowtorch briefly around the edge of the ring, or slide a knife blade dipped in hot water between the edge of the gâteau and the ring. Lift off the ring by rotating it upward, or place the dessert on a can and slide the ring downward (see page 17). Place the gâteau on a pretty round serving plate. Arrange the reserved raspberries in attractive semi-circles around the top to delineate the individual portions, and serve at once.

CHOCOLATE MINT SNAILS
Le colimaçon chocolat menthe

THIS EASY AND QUICK TO MAKE DESSERT IS A PERFECT TREAT FOR CHILDREN OR ADULTS. FOR ADDED EFFECT, TOP WITH CHOCOLATE CURLS (PAGE 154) AND SERVE WITH A COFFEE-FLAVORED CREME ANGLAISE (PAGE 40).

INGREDIENTS: ❋
¾ quantity chocolate Genoise Sponge batter (page 33)
1 quantity Mint Mousse (page 48)
Confectioners' sugar for dusting

Makes 3 gâteaux, each serving 4
Preparation time: 20 minutes
Cooking time: 8 minutes

THE CHOCOLATE SPONGE: Preheat the oven to 400°F/200°C.

Make the chocolate genoise sponge batter following the method on page 33. Spread the batter evenly onto the lined baking sheet, smoothing it with a metal spatula. Bake the sponge in the preheated oven for 8 minutes.

Slide the paper onto a cooling rack and leave the sponge until cold. Lay a dish towel, then another rack over the cold sponge and invert it. Peel off the paper and use a serrated knife to trim off about ¼ in/5 mm from the edges of the sponge.

Spread the half-set mint mousse over the sponge, leaving an empty ¾ in/2 cm border all around. Refrigerate for 30 minutes, then roll up the shorter side of the sponge like a jelly roll, using the dish towel to help you. Refrigerate for at least 2 hours before serving.

PRESENTATION: Using a serrated knife, cut the roll into three equal pieces. Stand the pieces upright on a plate like snail shells and dust with confectioners' sugar. Serve well chilled and slice the "snails" at the table.

SPECIAL EQUIPMENT:
24 × 16 in/60 × 40 cm baking sheet lined with parchment paper

NOTE:
The "snails" can be frozen for a week, so if you prefer, serve only one or two and freeze the rest. Thaw in the refrigerator for 3 hours before serving.

Black and White Saint-Honoré

Saint-Honoré noir et blanc

Since my youth, I have always regarded a Saint-Honore as the ultimate gastronomic and visually appealing dessert. In this black and white version, the combination of the vanilla and chocolate Chantilly creams is sublime and a testament to the cook's dexterity.

Ingredients: ❋

7 oz/200 g trimmings of Jean Millet's or Quick Puff Pastry (pages 24 and 25)

Flour for dusting

1 quantity Choux Paste (page 26)

1 cup/200 g sugar

Eggwash (1 egg yolk mixed with 1 soup spoon milk and a pinch of salt)

Vanilla Chantilly cream

2½ cups/600 ml well-chilled heavy cream

½ cup/60 g confectioners' sugar

1 vanilla bean, split

Chocolate Chantilly cream

1 cup/250 ml well-chilled heavy cream

5 oz/150 g bitter couverture or best-quality bittersweet chocolate, heated to 122°F/50°C

Serves 8

Preparation time: 50 minutes, plus 1 hour chilling

Cooking time: 35 minutes

The pastry base: On a lightly floured surface, roll out the pastry into a neat circle ½ in/2 mm thick. Roll this over the rolling pin, then unroll it onto a baking sheet dampened with cold water. Lay the ring on the pastry and, using the tip of a knife, cut around it to make a 9½ in/24 cm pastry circle. Prick with a fork and refrigerate for 20 minutes.

Piping out the choux paste: Preheat the oven to 400°F/200°C.

Fill the pastry bag fitted with the ½ in/12 mm tip with choux paste. Starting from the center of the pastry base and working outward, pipe out a spiral, holding the tip fractionally above the base. Stop piping 1¼ in/3 cm from the edge of the pastry to leave a clear border. Brush this border with eggwash, then pipe on a raised circle of choux paste, holding the tip well above the pastry. Brush the choux circle with eggwash and bake the base in the preheated oven for 35 minutes.

Using the pastry bag fitted with the ¼ in/5 mm tip, pipe seventeen small ¾ in/2 cm choux puffs onto the lightly-greased baking sheet. Brush with eggwash and press the puffs lightly with the back of a fork. Bake in the oven with the pastry base for 20 minutes. Make a small hole in the bottom of the choux puffs with the tip of a small knife, place them and the pastry base on a cooling rack, and leave at room temperature until cold.

Making the caramel: Put 3½ tbsp water in a small, heavy-based saucepan and add the 1 cup/200 g sugar. Bring to a boil over low heat, skim the surface, then wash down the inside of the pan with a pastry brush dipped in cold water. Remove from the heat as soon as the sugar becomes a pale amber caramel. Pierce one side of the choux puffs with the tip of a small knife, and dip the tops one at a time into the caramel (1). Place the puffs on a baking sheet.

The vanilla and chocolate chantilly creams: Put the 2½ cups/600 ml heavy cream and confectioners' sugar in a bowl and scrape in the inside of the vanilla bean. Whip to a ribbon consistency.

In another bowl, whip the 1 cup/250 ml heavy cream to a ribbon consistency, then whisk in the melted chocolate, without beating over-vigorously.

Assembling the saint-honoré: Using the pastry bag with the ¼ in/5 mm tip, fill the choux puffs with the vanilla

Special equipment:

2 baking sheets, 1 lightly greased

1 dessert ring, 9½ in/24 cm diam.

Pastry bag with a plain ½ in/12 mm tip

Pastry bag with a plain ¼ in/5 mm tip

2 pastry bags, each fitted with a Saint-Honoré tip

Chantilly cream. Stick them onto the choux pastry crown, attaching them on one by one with a little caramel (2). Fill the Saint-Honoré base with a ⅝ in / 1.5 cm deep layer of vanilla Chantilly cream.

3

4

Fill one of the pastry bags fitted with a Saint-Honoré tip with vanilla Chantilly and the other with chocolate Chantilly. Pipe in staggered bands of chocolate Chantilly, interlacing them evenly with bands of vanilla Chantilly (3 and 4). Refrigerate the Saint-Honoré for 1 hour before serving.

PRESENTATION: Place the Saint-Honoré on a round serving plate and slice it with a very sharp knife.

FLOATING ISLAND WITH DATES

Ile flottante aux dattes

I DREAMT UP THIS DESSERT DURING MY TIME IN NORTH AFRICA. THE DELICIOUS DATES THAT GROW
ALL OVER THE REGION WERE THE INSPIRATION FOR THIS VARIATION ON THE CLASSIC FLOATING
ISLAND WITH ALMONDS OR PRALINES. IT IS A WONDERFUL AUTUMN OR WINTER DISH.

INGREDIENTS:
½ cup/120 g sugar
4 tsp/20 g softened butter
6 dates, pitted and halved
    lengthwise
6 dates, finely diced
A tiny pinch of ground star
    anise
¼ quantity *Crème Anglaise*
    flavored with vanilla (page
    40)

MERINGUE
4 egg whites
7 tbsp/85 g superfine sugar

Serves 4
Preparation time: 20
    minutes
Cooking time: 20 minutes

PREPARING THE BASIN OR MOLD: Butter the inside of the mold with the
softened butter and arrange the twelve halved dates side by side to
within about ⅝ in/1.5 cm of the top of the mold, placing the uncut
surface against the mold.

PREPARING THE MERINGUE: Preheat the oven to 275°F/140°C.

Using a bowl and whisk or an electric mixer, beat the egg whites
until half-risen. Add the sugar and continue to beat until very stiff
and well-risen. Add the diced dates and star anise and whisk for just
a few seconds more.

Pour the meringue into the mold and gently smooth the surface.

COOKING THE FLOATING ISLAND: Place on a baking sheet and cook in the
warm oven for 20 minutes. Insert a fine metal skewer into the center
of the floating island to check whether it is cooked; the skewer should
come out shiny and clean. Cook for a few minutes more if necessary.
Let the cooked floating island cool at room temperature in the basin
or mold for 30 seconds before unmolding.

PRESENTATION: Using a dish towel to hold the mold, unmold the hot
but not scalding floating island by inverting it a few centimeters
above a round, shallow serving plate. Pour the chilled crème anglaise
all around the floating island.

In a small, heavy-based saucepan set over low heat, dissolve the
sugar without water, stirring continuously with a wooden spatula
until it turns to an attractive caramel color.

Spoon an even coating of warm caramel over the top of the dessert
and refrigerate for 15–20 minutes.

The floating island can be served as soon as the caramel has set,
about 15 minutes after coating. Let your guests help themselves with
a spoon to the dessert and the accompanying crème anglaise.

SPECIAL EQUIPMENT:
Round heatproof basin, or a
    stainless steel
    hemispherical mold,
    6½ in/16 cm diam. at
    the opening, 3¼ in/8 cm
    deep

NOTES:
*After its final coating of
caramel, the dessert can if
necessary be kept in the
refrigerator for an hour
before serving without
affecting the crunchiness of
the caramel.*

BANANA AND CARAMEL MOUSSE GATEAU
Entremets mousse bananes et caramel

THE COMBINATION OF THE TWO MOUSSES AND DELICATE SPONGE WITH THE LIGHTLY CARAMELIZED BANANAS MAKES THE TIME SPENT IN PREPARING THIS DESSERT WELL WORTHWHILE.

INGREDIENTS: ✳

4½ oz/140 g chocolate Cigarette Paste (page 28)

1 quantity Joconde Sponge batter (page 31)

8 bananas, about 7 oz/ 200 g each

4 tbsp/60 g butter

½ cup /100 g sugar

⅔ quantity (1 lb 6 oz/ 600 g) Caramel Mousse (page 46)

1 quantity Banana Mousse (page 48)

½ cup/100 ml Apple Jelly (page 59)

Makes 2 gâteaux, each serving 8

Preparation time: 40 minutes, plus about 1½ hours freezing

THE PATTERNED SPONGE: Preheat the oven to 500°F/250°C.

Using a metal spatula, spread the cigarette paste all over the sheet of parchment paper as thinly and evenly as possible. With the tip of your index finger, mark out small banana-shaped arcs ¾ in/2 cm long all over the surface of the paste, spacing them ¾ in/2 cm apart. Freeze for about 10 minutes to harden the paste.

Spread the joconde sponge batter over the cigarette paste, smooth with a metal spatula, then bake in the very hot oven for 2–3 minutes until just firm but still moist. Let the cooked sponge cool slightly for 10 minutes, then invert it onto a cooling rack and remove the parchment paper. Keep at room temperature.

CARAMELIZING THE BANANAS: Peel the bananas and cut them diagonally into ½ in/1 cm thick rounds. In a nonstick frying pan, sauté half the bananas over high heat for 2 minutes with half the butter and half the sugar, then transfer to a plate. Sauté the remaining bananas in the same way.

Reserve the sixteen best lightly-caramelized banana rounds for decorating the top of the dessert. Place the two flan rings on a baking sheet lined with plastic wrap and arrange the rest of the bananas inside. Freeze for 30 minutes.

ASSEMBLING THE GATEAUX: Cut three 1½ in/4 cm wide strips from the length of the sponge and two 8 in/20 cm disks from the rest. Place the two dessert rings on the cake bases and line the rings with the bands of rodoïde or acetate. Press on the bands of sponge, patterned-side against the acetate, cutting and splicing to line the inside of the rings completely.

Place the sponge disks in the bottom of the rings. Divide the caramel mousse between the rings. Unmold the frozen sliced bananas and place them on the mousse, without pressing them down. Chill the half-assembled gâteaux in the freezer for 30 minutes.

Finish by filling the rings with banana mousse. Smooth the surface with a metal spatula and freeze again for 30 minutes.

PRESENTATION: At least 4 hours before serving, transfer the gâteaux to the refrigerator to thaw for 2 hours, then glaze with apple jelly and refrigerate 2 more hours. Remove the dessert rings and bands of rodoïde or acetate. Arrange the reserved banana rounds in an arc on one side of each gâteau. Place the desserts on serving plates and keep in the refrigerator until ready to serve. They should be served well chilled.

SPECIAL EQUIPMENT:

24 × 16 in. 60 × 40 cm baking sheet lined with parchment paper

2 dessert rings, 8½ in/ 22 cm diam., 2 in/5 cm deep

2 bands of rodoïde or acetate, 28 × 2 in/ 72 × 5 cm

2 rigid cardboard cake bases, 9½ in/24 cm diam.

2 flan rings, 6½ in/16 cm diam., ⅝ in/1.5 cm deep

NOTES:

It is impossible to make this dessert successfully if you reduce the quantities, hence the necessity to make two gâteaux. One can be frozen for another occasion. They freeze well, unglazed, for up to a week; glaze them a few hours before serving.

YELLOW PEACH SOUVERAIN
Souverain aux pêches jaunes

THIS ATTRACTIVE DESSERT IS EASY TO MAKE. IF POSSIBLE, USE FRESHLY POACHED PEACHES IN SEASON; CANNED PEACHES ARE OF EXCELLENT QUALITY AND SIMPLIFY THE PREPARATION. IF YOU WISH, SERVE THE SOUVERAIN WITH A STRAWBERRY COULIS (PAGE 51)

INGREDIENTS: ❋

8 oz/220 g yellow peaches in syrup (drained weight)

1 Genoise Sponge (page 33), 8½ in/22 cm diam., 2 in/5 cm thick

1 lb 3 oz/550 g Mousseline Cream (page 42)

⅞ cup/200 ml Sorbet Syrup (page 144), mixed with 3½ tbsp kirsch (optional)

1 quantity Italian Meringue (page 37), freshly made with 6 egg whites, and cooled

⅔ cup/60 g sliced almonds, toasted

Serves 8

Preparation time: 25 minutes

PREPARATION: Reserve one attractive peach half to decorate the dessert; finely dice the rest and mix them into the mousseline cream.

Slice the genoise sponge horizontally into three ⅝ in/1.5 cm thick disks (1) and brush with the kirsch-flavored sorbet syrup (2).

ASSEMBLING THE SOUVERAIN: Lay one sponge disk on the cake base and spread over half the mousseline cream with a metal spatula. Top with a second sponge disk and spread with the remaining mousseline cream (3). Finish with the third disk and press lightly with your fingertips.

Using a metal spatula, coat the top and sides of the dessert with a ¼ in/5 mm thick layer of meringue (4). Take a handful of sliced almonds in your right hand and, holding the dessert with your left hand, press the almonds all around the sides (5).

Fill the pastry bag fitted with a Saint-Honoré tip with Italian meringue and, starting from the center of the dessert, swirl on curved arcs of meringue all over the surface to make a daisy effect (6). Brown the edges lightly with a blowtorch, or place briefly under a salamander or very hot broiler. Place the peach half in the center of the dessert and refrigerate for at least an hour.

PRESENTATION: Place the souverain on a round serving plate and slice it at the table.

SPECIAL EQUIPMENT:

8½ in/22 cm round cardboard cake base

Pastry bag with a Saint-Honoré tip

Blowtorch or salamander

APPLE CHARLOTTE WITH APPLE CHIPS
Charlotte aux pommes et ses chips

THIS DESSERT NEEDS NO ACCOMPANYING SAUCE OR COULIS. THE
CRUNCHY APPLE CHIPS MAKE A MARVELOUS CONTRAST WITH THE
SMOOTH, CREAMY BAVAROIS.

INGREDIENTS: ❊

3 firm, tart-sweet apples,
    total weight about
    1 lb 2 oz/500 g

6½ tbsp/80 g sugar
1 quantity Apple Bavarois
    (page 44)
12 × 8 in/30 × 20 cm
    sheet of Hazelnut
    Dacquoise (page 31)
1 tbsp Decorating Chocolate
    (page 186) (optional)

APPLE JELLY
All the apple trimmings,
    including the cores and seeds
½ cup + 2 tbsp/125 g
    sugar
½ lemon, chopped
1 split vanilla bean
3 gelatine leaves, soaked in
    cold water and well
    drained
1 cup/250 ml water

Makes 2 charlottes, each
    serving 8
Preparation time: 1 hour 15
    minutes

THE APPLE CHIPS AND SLICES FOR DECORATION: Preheat the oven to
350°F/180°C.

Wash but do not peel the apples, wipe them dry, and halve them.
Cut four wafer-thin slices from the middle of the two best halves, lay
them on a lightly greased baking sheet, sprinkle with
about 1 tsp sugar, and cook in the oven for 6 minutes.
Turn over the apple slices and cook for another 4
minutes. Place on a plate and let cool at room temperature.

Lay the six apple halves flat side-
down. Cut out a tube from each (see
left) and cut the tubes into wafer-thin
slices (see right), discarding the core
end. Arrange these on the second
baking sheet and sprinkle with the
remaining sugar. Cook in the oven for
10–15 minutes, until pale golden.
Let cool on the baking sheet. When the chips are
cold, lift them off with a metal spatula and keep in
an extremely dry place so that they remain crunchy.

THE APPLE JELLY: Make the jelly using the listed ingredients, following
the method on page 59, then let the jelly cool.

ASSEMBLING THE CHARLOTTE: Place the cake pan or cardboard mold on
the parchment paper. Slide this onto a baking sheet and arrange two
apple slices at each end of the rectangle. Make the bavarois following
the method on page 44 and pour it into the mold as soon as it begins
to set. Trim the edges of the hazelnut dacquoise to fit the mold, then
lay it over the mousse, press lightly with your fingertips, and chill the
charlotte in the freezer for at least 1 hour or in the refrigerator for at
least 3 hours.

PRESENTATION: Invert the mold containing the charlotte onto the work
surface. Remove the parchment paper, then slide a small knife blade
between the bavarois and mold and lift off the mold. Cut the charlotte
in half widthwise to make two desserts. Glaze the two charlottes with
half-set apple jelly. If you like, pipe on the words "Apples" or
"Pommes" with the decorating chocolate. Lightly press the apple
chips all 'around the edges of the charlottes, place one or both on a
serving plate, and serve well chilled.

NOTE:
Once you have removed the
mold and divided the
charlotte, you can return one
half to the freezer before
glazing with apple jelly. It
will keep well for up to a
week.

SPECIAL EQUIPMENT:
Rectangular cake pan,
    12 × 8 × 1½ in/
    30 × 20 × 4 cm, or a
    cardboard mold of the
    same dimensions covered
    with plastic wrap
1½ in/4 cm cookie cutter
2 nonstick baking sheets,
    1 lightly greased
Parchment paper

Jeweled Fruit Gateau

Diamant de fruits, mousse au citron vert

As it is difficult to make a satisfactory citrus mousse in small quantities, you will need to prepare two of these wonderfully refreshing gateaux — a good excuse for a little greedy indulgence!

Ingredients: ❊

4 oz/100 g red currants

5 oz/150 g strawberries

5 oz/150 g kiwi fruit

1 plain Genoise Sponge (page 33), 8 in/20 cm diam., 2 in/5 cm thick

⅔ cup/150 ml Sorbet Syrup (page 144)

2 tbsp kirsch

1 quantity Lime Mousse (page 47)

2 soup spoons Decorating Chocolate (page 186)

½ cup/100 ml Apple Jelly (page 59)

Makes 2 gâteaux, each serving 8

Preparation time: 35 minutes, plus 2 hours freezing or 6 hours chilling

PREPARING THE FRUIT: Use a fork to strip the red currants from their stems without damaging the fruit, and place in a bowl. Hull the strawberries, cut them into ¼ in/5 mm dice, and place in another bowl. Peel the kiwi fruit and cut 8 attractive slices from the middle, then halve these; dice the rest of the kiwi like the strawberries. Place in a bowl, cover with plastic wrap and refrigerate all the fruit.

THE GENOISE SPONGE: Mix the sorbet syrup with the kirsch. Use a serrated knife to cut two ¼ in/5 mm thick rounds from the sponge. Brush these with the kirsch-flavored syrup.

ASSEMBLING THE GATEAUX: Cover the cardboard cake bases with plastic wrap. Place a dessert ring over each base and arrange 8 kiwi semi-circles against the plastic wrap to make a border inside the rings. Scatter one-third of the diced strawberries and kiwi and half the red currants into the rings (1), then cover the fruit with a layer of lime mousse (2).

Mix the remaining fruit into the rest of the lime mousse and fill up the rings to within ¼ in/5 mm of the top. Lay a circle of sponge over each gâteau, syrup-side down (3). Press lightly with your fingertips, then cover the gâteaux with plastic wrap and chill in the freezer for at least 2 hours, or in the refrigerator for at least 6 hours.

GLAZING THE GATEAUX: Remove the plastic wrap, invert the gâteaux onto the work surface, sponge-side down, and remove the cake bases. Glaze with the almost set apple jelly (4) and spread with a metal spatula (5). Fill a paper piping cone with the decorating chocolate and pipe on a modern geometric design(6). Return the gâteaux to the refrigerator until ready to serve.

PRESENTATION: Briefly run a blowtorch around the outside of the rings, or slide the tip of a knife dipped in hot water between the inside of the rings and the desserts. Lift off the rings, rotating them slightly, or place the gâteaux on a can and slide the rings downward (see page 17). Serve immediately, or freeze.

SPECIAL EQUIPMENT:

2 cardboard cake bases, 10 in/24 cm diam.

2 dessert rings, 8½ in/ 22 cm diam., 2 in/5 cm deep

Blowtorch (optional)

NOTE:

The gâteaux can be frozen for up to a week. Freeze them unglazed and glaze just a few hours before serving.

LICORICE GATEAU WITH A PEAR FAN
Délice à la réglisse, éventail de poires

THIS UNUSUAL LICORICE-SCENTED DESSERT IS VERY SIMPLE TO PREPARE. THE
COMBINATION OF THE TWO FLAVORS IS EXCEPTIONALLY GOOD.

INGREDIENTS: ❊

1 quantity Spiced Cake
batter (page 29)

2 pears, about 7 oz/200 g
each, peeled, halved, and
poached in syrup

1 quantity Licorice Bavarois
(page 44)

1 pear, about 4 oz/120 g,
peeled, but with a small
collar of skin left on near
the stem, poached whole
in syrup

¼ cup/60 ml Apple Jelly
(page 59)

Serves 8

Preparation time: 30
minutes, plus 1 hour
freezing

THE SPICED CAKE BASE: Bake the spiced cake in the greased dessert ring,
following the method on page 29. Bake for only 40 minutes, then
leave on a cooling rack at room temperature.

ASSEMBLING THE GATEAU: Place the second dessert ring on the cardboard
cake base and line the inside with the band of rodoïde. With a small
sharp knife, cut three of the pear halves into ¼ in/5 mm thick slices.
Delicately dab them dry, then arrange them in a rosette all over the
cake base and up against the band of rodoïde.

Pour one-third of the licorice bavarois over the pears in the ring
and chill in the freezer for 10 minutes.

Finely dice the fourth pear half and mix it into the remaining
bavarois, then pour this mixture into the dessert ring. With a serrated
knife, slice the spiced cake into a disk of an even thickness of about
½ in/1 cm. Lay the cake disk over the bavarois in the ring, pressing
down lightly with your fingertips. Freeze for at least 1 hour.

PRESENTATION: At least 2 hours before serving the dessert, invert it,
remove the cardboard cake
base, and place it under the
gâteau on a serving plate.
Refrigerate for 1 hour, then
glaze with the apple jelly.
Remove the dessert ring and
band of rodoïde.

Pat dry the whole poached
pear and use a small sharp
knife to cut out the core from
the bottom of the fruit
without spoiling the shape.
With the same knife, slice
down and all around the pear
from the bottom of the collar
at ¼ in/5 mm intervals, press
lightly to fan it out, then
arrange it on the center of the dessert. Brush lightly with apple jelly
and refrigerate until ready to serve. Serve the gâteau very cold.

SPECIAL EQUIPMENT:

2 dessert rings, 8½ in/22 cm
diam., 2 in/5 cm deep,
1 lightly greased

1 band of rodoïde or acetate,
30 × 2 in/75 × 5 cm

1 rigid cardboard cake base,
9½ in/24 cm diam.,
covered in plastic wrap

Parchment paper

NOTES:

The gâteau keeps well in the
freezer for up to a week.
Glaze it and decorate with
the pear fan several hours
before serving.

If you prefer, a Chocolate
Sponge base (page 34) makes
an excellent substitute for the
spiced cake. Bake a sheet and
cut out two rounds to make
a double thickness to form
the base of the gâteau.

Press the sliced pear lightly
to make it into a fan

MILLE-FEUILLE OF GINGER MOUSSE WITH CRUNCHY QUINCES

Mille-feuille, mousse gingembre et croquants de coings

COOKED QUINCES ARE DELICIOUS, ESPECIALLY WHEN THEY ARE STILL SLIGHTLY CRUNCHY. THE GRENADINE ENHANCES THE FLAVOR OF THIS LOVELY FRUIT.

INGREDIENTS: ❋
14 oz/400 g Quick Puff
  Pastry (page 25)
Flour for dusting
2 cups/500 ml Sorbet
  Syrup (page 144)
2 quinces, total weight about
  14 oz/400 g
Juice of 1 lemon
½ cup/125 ml grenadine
½ quantity freshly-made
  Ginger Mousse (page 49)
¼ cup/30 g confectioners'
  sugar

Serves 8
Preparation time: 45
  minutes, plus 45 minutes
  chilling

PREPARING THE PASTRY: On a lightly floured work surface, roll out the pastry into a 24 × 16 in/60 × 40 cm rectangle, ½₂ in/2 mm thick. Roll the pastry around the rolling pin, then unroll it onto a baking sheet lined with parchment paper. Refrigerate for at least 30 minutes.

POACHING THE QUINCES: Put the syrup in a saucepan and bring to a boil. Peel the quinces and rub them with lemon juice. Poach in the syrup for 15 minutes if they are very ripe, or for 30 minutes if they are hard and slightly unripe. Add the grenadine a few minutes before the cooking time is up, then let the quinces cool in the poaching syrup at room temperature. Refrigerate them once they are completely cold.
  Preheat the oven to 350°F/180°C.

BAKING THE PASTRY: Prick the pastry with a fork, cover it with a sheet of parchment paper, and lay the second baking sheet on top. This will prevent the pastry from rising too unevenly during cooking.
  Bake in the preheated oven for 8 minutes until the pastry is pale golden. Remove the top baking sheet and parchment paper, slide the pastry sheet onto a cooling rack, and leave at room temperature.

SPECIAL EQUIPMENT:
1 dessert ring, 7 in/18 cm
  diam., 1½ in/4 cm deep
  (optional)
1 band of rodoïde or acetate,
  22 × 1½ in/57 × 4 cm
2 baking sheets, 24 × 16 in/
  60 × 40 cm
1 cardboard cake base,
  7 in/18 cm diam.
Metal skewer, for decorating
  the mille-feuille

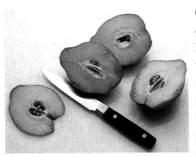

CUTTING THE QUINCES: Cut one quince into ten even segments. Halve the second quince lengthwise and cut off one ⅛ in/3 mm slice (see photo, left). Finely dice the rest of the fruit and put half in a sauceboat with some of the poaching syrup. Put the segments and slice of quince in a bowl and keep in the refrigerator.

NOTE:
This crisp and creamy dessert freezes very well inside the rodoïde band. Let it thaw slowly for 3 hours in the refrigerator before the final stages of presentation.

ASSEMBLING THE MILLE-FEUILLE: Prepare the ginger mousse, following the method on page 49. As soon as it begins to set, add the remaining diced quinces and start assembling the mille-feuille. Remove the paper from underneath the pastry, then place the dessert ring on the pastry and cut around it with a small, sharp knife to make four circles.

Lay one pastry circle on the cake base. Encircle it with the band of rodoïde or acetate and secure the band with sticky tape. Pour one-third of the ginger mousse over the pastry base and smooth with a soup spoon. Lay a second pastry circle on top and repeat the operation twice more, finishing with the fourth pastry circle. Leave to set in the refrigerator for at least 2 hours, or in the freezer for 45 minutes.

PRESENTATION: Heat the metal skewer along two-thirds of its length over a gas flame.

Remove the band of rodoïde or acetate from around the mille-feuille and sprinkle the top generously with confectioners' sugar. When the skewer is red-hot, lay it across the surface of the mille-feuille at ¾ in/2 cm intervals to mark out caramelized but not burnt lines. Reheat the skewer as often as necessary and mark out another set of lines to make a regular diamond pattern.

Place the mille-feuille on a serving plate, and arrange the quince slice in the center and the segments around the base. Serve the mille-feuille chilled but not frozen, and serve the diced quinces in syrup separately in the sauceboat.

Chapter Eight

Tarts and Tartlets

Whichever type of pastry you use as a tart shell, it should always be very thin, well-cooked, and crisp. Ideally, tarts should be filled with very ripe fresh fruits, sun-ripened and bursting with sugar. They are delicious served warm or cold, but should never be chilled. They are appetizing even when you are not hungry, and children adore them.

Tarts are simple and inexpensive to make. Whether they be rustic or elegant, with their glowing colors, they are always alluring and mouth-wateringly good. Delicately spread between the pastry and the fruit are wonderful soft pillows of cream, which make these tarts into the undisputed champions of desserts.

Almost all uncooked tarts can be frozen for several days. Bake them just an hour or two before serving and be patient enough to let them cool a little before sinking in your teeth . . . .

Adding rhubarb to the cream-filled tartlet

RHUBARB TARTLETS
Tartelettes à la rhubarbe

IF YOU PREFER, MAKE ONE LARGE TART INSTEAD OF THE SMALL
TARTLETS.

INGREDIENTS: ❋
1¼ lbs/600 g tender young
    rhubarb
⅞ cup/200 ml sweet white
    wine, preferably Sauternes
2 tbsp water
¾ cup/150 g sugar
1½ tbsp grenadine syrup
Flour for dusting
9 oz/250 g Sweet Tart
    Pastry (page 20)
⅞ cup/200 ml heavy
    cream, whipped to a
    ribbon consistency with 2
    tbsp/25 g sugar
4 oz/100 g Pastry Cream
    (page 39)

Serves 8
Preparation time: 30
    minutes
Cooking time: 7 minutes

PREPARING THE RHUBARB: Scrape the stems, removing any fibrous threads. Cut the rhubarb into 2–2⅜ in/5–6 cm chunks. Choose the two most tender chunks and cut them into julienne.

Put the wine, water, sugar, and grenadine into a shallow pan and bring to a boil. Drop in the rhubarb julienne and simmer for 30 seconds, then lift them out with a slotted spoon, and place in a bowl with a couple of spoons of the cooking syrup.

With the syrup still boiling in the pan, add the rhubarb chunks, then lower the heat, and poach gently for about 30 minutes. Let the rhubarb cool in the syrup and, when it is cold, drain in a strainer for 30 minutes. Do not discard the syrup, which can be used to make a sorbet or champagne cocktail.

Meanwhile, preheat the oven to 350°F/180°C.

THE TARTLET SHELLS: On a lightly floured work surface, roll out the pastry to a thickness of ⅛ in/3 mm. Cut out eight circles with the cookie cutter and use these to line the tartlet molds. Crimp the pastry edges with your fingertips to make a border slightly higher than the top of the molds. Refrigerate the pastry shells for 10 minutes.

BAKING THE TARTLET SHELLS: Prick the bottoms with a fork and bake in the preheated oven for 7 minutes. Leave in the molds to cool slightly, then carefully unmold the pastry shells onto a wire rack.

FILLING THE TARTLETS AND PRESENTATION: Use a whisk to mix the whipped cream with the pastry cream, and divide the mixture among the tartlet shells. Spoon in the poached rhubarb and scatter the barely-cooked rhubarb julienne over the top. Serve the tartlets on individual plates at room temperature.

SPECIAL EQUIPMENT:
8 nonstick or lightly
    buttered tartlet molds,
    4 in/10 cm diam.,
    ¾ in/2 cm deep
4 in/10 cm plain cookie
    cutter

NOTES:
All the components of this
dessert can be prepared in
advance; the tartlets will
take only 8 minutes to fill at
the last moment, or at most
1 hour before serving. If you
fill them any earlier, the
pastry will become soggy. Do
not refrigerate these tartlets,
or the rhubarb will lose its
flavor.

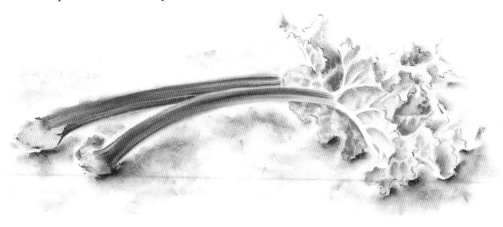

121

FRUIT TARTLETS WITH GLAZED FIVE-SPICE SABAYON

Grandes tartelettes aux fruits, gratinées aux cinq épices

THE WARMTH OF THE SABAYON AND THE HEAT OF THE BROILER DEVELOP
THE SCENT OF THE FRUITS IN A SPECTACULAR WAY, AND THE FIVE SPICES ADD
A MUSKY FLAVOR TO THE SABAYON — A TRULY HEADY COMBINATION.

INGREDIENTS:

14 oz/420 g Tart Pastry
(page 20), or Quick Puff
Pastry trimmings (page
25)

Flour for dusting

1½ lbs/720 g assorted
fruits (eg: bananas,
blueberries, raspberries, red
currants, blackberries),
according to your taste
and the season

1 quantity Sabayon (page
53)

½ tsp five spice powder

18 wild strawberries for
decoration (optional)

6 small mint sprigs

Serves 6

Preparation time: 20
minutes

Cooking time: 11 minutes

PREPARING THE PASTRY SHELLS: On a lightly floured surface, roll out the pastry to a thickness of ½ in/2 mm. Cut out six circles with the cookie cutter and line the tartlet molds lightly pinching up the edges of the pastry to make a border slightly higher than the molds. Refrigerate for 10 minutes.

Meanwhile, preheat the oven to 350°F/180°C.

BAKING THE PASTRY SHELLS: Prick the bottom of the pastry shells with a fork. Line with a circle of wax paper and fill with pie weights or dried beans. Bake in the preheated oven for 10 minutes. Remove the weights and paper and return the pastry shells to the oven for 1 minute to ensure that the insides are well cooked. Take them out of the oven and unmold onto a cooling rack.

THE FRUITS: Peel, wash, and hull as necessary. Cut into pieces or rounds, depending on the size, and keep at room temperature.

THE SABAYON: Follow the recipe on page 53, flavoring the sabayon with sweet white wine, kirsch, or pear liqueur, according to your taste. When the sabayon has puffed up, sprinkle on the five spice powder and keep at room temperature while you assemble the tartlets.

Preheat a salamander or the broiler to very hot.

PRESENTATION: Arrange the fruits in the tartlet shells, coat generously with two-thirds of the sabayon, and glaze lightly under the hot broiler or salamander for a few seconds. Immediately place the tartlets on warmed plates and pour the remaining sabayon in a ribbon around them. Arrange three wild strawberries and a small sprig of mint on each tartlet and serve at once.

SPECIAL EQUIPMENT:

6 tartlet molds, 5 in/12 cm
diam., ¾ in/2 cm deep

6 in/16 cm plain cookie
cutter

122

CHOCOLATE AND RASPBERRY TART

Tarte au chocolat et aux framboises

THIS IS ONE OF MY CLIENTS' FAVORITE DESSERTS. IN WINTER, THE
RASPBERRIES CAN BE REPLACED BY FINELY SLICED POACHED PEARS.

INGREDIENTS: ❄
9 oz/250 g Sweet Tart
  Pastry (page 20)
Flour for dusting
9 oz/250 g raspberries
1 cup/250 ml heavy cream

GANACHE
7 oz/200 g dark couverture
  or best-quality bittersweet
  chocolate, finely chopped
5 tsp/25 g liquid glucose or
  light corn syrup
4 tbsp/50 g butter

A few Chocolate Curls
  (page 154) (optional)
A pinch of confectioners'
  sugar

Serves 8
Preparation time: 20
  minutes
Cooking time: 10
  minutes

PREPARING THE PASTRY SHELL: On a lightly floured surface, roll out the
pastry into a circle about ½ in/2 mm thick. Roll the pastry around
the rolling pin, then unroll it over the flan ring so as not to spoil the
shape. Line the ring with the pastry and pinch up the edges with your
fingertips to make an even border standing above the top of the ring.
Slide the tart shell onto a baking sheet and leave in the refrigerator to
rest for at least 20 minutes.

BAKING THE PASTRY SHELL: Preheat the oven to 350°F/180°C.
  Prick the bottom of the pastry shell with a fork. It is not necessary
to line it with paper or fill it with pie weights. Bake for 10 minutes.
  Meanwhile, reserve a dozen of the best raspberries for decoration
and halve the rest. Slide the cooked pastry shell onto a cooling rack,
carefully remove the ring, and leave at room temperature. When the
tart shell is cold, cover the bottom with the halved raspberries.

THE CHOCOLATE GANACHE FILLING: Put the cream in a saucepan and
bring to a boil. Take the pan off the heat and add the chocolate and
glucose, stirring with a whisk to make a smooth cream. Now whisk
in the butter, a small piece at a time.

SPECIAL EQUIPMENT:
A flan ring, 9½ in/24 cm
  diam., ¾ in/2 cm deep

NOTES:
You can use a Shortbread
pastry (page 21) instead of
sweet tart pastry, but it is
much more fragile and
delicate to work with.
  Instead of one large tart,
you might prefer to make
small tartlets.

FINISHING THE TART: As soon as the ganache is ready, pour it into the tart shell and let cool at room temperature. Once cold, refrigerate for an hour or two before serving.

PRESENTATION: Dust the chocolate curls with confectioners' sugar and arrange them on the tart. Decorate the tart with the reserved raspberries and serve on a china or silver plate.

RICOTTA CHEESE TART
Tarte au fromage

I ADORE THIS "GRANNY FOOD" TART. IN SUMMER, I MAKE IT WITH PUFF PASTRY TRIMMINGS, BUT IN WINTER I PREFER THE EXTRA SWEETNESS OF SWEET TART PASTRY.

INGREDIENTS:
12 oz/350 g Sweet Tart Pastry (page 20)
Flour for dusting
⅔ cup/150 g soft ricotta cheese (whatever fat content you prefer)
¼ cup/50 g sugar
⅔ cup/150 ml milk
3 eggs, separated
Juice of 1 lemon
Zest of 1 lemon, thinly slivered and blanched
2 tbsp/20 g flour, plus extra for dusting
3½ tbsp/30 g cornstarch
2½ tbsp/20 g confectioners' sugar

SERVES 8
Preparation time: 25 minutes
Cooking time: 35 minutes

THE PASTRY SHELL: On a lightly floured surface, roll out the pastry into a circle about ½ in/2 mm thick. Use it to line the flan ring, and place on a baking sheet. Refrigerate for 20 minutes.
Meanwhile, preheat the oven to 350°F/180°C.

THE CHEESE FILLING: In a bowl, whisk together the ricotta cheese, sugar, milk, egg yolks, lemon juice and zest, flour, and cornstarch. Beat the egg whites stiffly and delicately fold them into the mixture with a spatula. Fill the pastry shell with the mixture and bake the tart in the preheated oven for 20 minutes. Reduce the oven temperature to 300°F/150°C and bake for a further 15 minutes.
Take the tart out of the oven and immediately place it on a cooling rack. Carefully lift off the flan ring and let the tart cool at room temperature until barely cold.

PRESENTATION: Lightly dust the top of the tart with confectioners' sugar and place it on a fine china plate. Serve it just cold, but never chilled.

SPECIAL EQUIPMENT:
A flan ring, 8½ in/22 cm diam., ¾ in/2 cm deep, lightly greased

NOTES:
Never refrigerate this tart, or it will lose all its flavor.
I sometimes substitute a few drops of orange flower water for the lemon zest.

RICE TART SCENTED WITH
LAPSANG SOUCHONG AND LITCHIS

Tarte au riz au parfum de lapsang souchong et fruits de litchies

THIS TART IS PARTICULARLY DELICIOUS IN WINTER. I SOMETIMES SPRINKLE ON A VEIL OF SUGAR AND LIGHTLY CARAMELIZE THE TART WITH A BLOWTORCH TO REINFORCE THE SCENT OF THE TEA. OBVIOUSLY IT DOES NOT THEN NEED GLAZING WITH LITCHI SYRUP. THIS CREAMY DESSERT NEEDS NO ACCOMPANYING SAUCE OR COULIS.

INGREDIENTS:

12 oz/350 g Sweet Tart
  Pastry (page 20)
Flour for dusting
Eggwash (1 egg yolk mixed
  with 1 soup spoon milk
  and a pinch of salt)
3 cups/750 ml milk
6 tbsp/75 g short-grain rice
6 tbsp/75 g sugar
3 tbsp/10 g Lapsang
  Souchong tea, wrapped in
  a piece of cheesecloth
6 oz/180 g litchis in syrup
  (drained weight; reserve
  the syrup)
½ cup/100 ml heavy cream,
  whipped to a ribbon
  consistency

Serves 8
Preparation time: 30
  minutes
Cooking time: 30 minutes

THE PASTRY SHELL: On a lightly floured surface, roll out the pastry into a circle ⅛ in/3 mm thick. Use it to line the flan ring and place on a baking sheet. Refrigerate for 20 minutes.

Meanwhile, preheat the oven to 400°F/200°C.

BAKING THE PASTRY SHELL: Prick the bottom of the pastry shell in several places with a fork. Line the bottom with wax paper, fill with pie weights or dried beans, and bake in the preheated oven for 20 minutes.

Remove the weights and paper and delicately brush the inside and bottom of the pastry shell with a little eggwash. Return it to the oven and bake for another 5 minutes. Place the tart shell on a cooling rack, remove the ring, and leave at room temperature.

COOKING THE RICE: Heat the milk in a small saucepan. As soon as it comes to a boil, scatter in the rice like rain and cook gently for 15 minutes, stirring occasionally with a spatula. Add the sugar and cheesecloth-wrapped tea and cook gently for another 15 minutes, stirring from time to time. Take the pan off the heat, remove the tea, and let the rice cool slightly in the pan for 10–15 minutes.

FILLING THE TART: Reserve one-third of the best litchis for decoration and halve them. Coarsely dice the remainder and stir them into the rice with a spatula, then delicately fold in the whipped cream. Gently pour the mixture into the pastry shell. Arrange the halved litchis tastefully on top and let the tart cool at room temperature for at least an hour.

When the tart is cold, boil the litchi syrup to reduce it slightly and let it cool for a few minutes. With a pastry brush, use a little to glaze the top of the tart very lightly.

PRESENTATION: Place the tart on a serving plate and serve it cold but not chilled.

SPECIAL EQUIPMENT:
A flan ring, 8½ in/22 cm
  diam., ¾ in/2 cm deep,
  lightly greased

NOTE:
If fresh litchis are available,
use about twenty. Just peel
and pit them; they will not
need poaching in syrup,
although you should glaze
them with syrup from a can
of litchis.

PINE NUT AND PRALINE TART

Tarte aux pignons et pralines

SERVE THIS DELICIOUS TART BY ITSELF OR WITH A HONEY SAUCE (PAGE 55)
IN SUMMER, AND A WARM OR COLD CHOCOLATE SAUCE (PAGE 55)
IN WINTER.

INGREDIENTS:

11 oz/300 g Flan Pastry
(page 22)

Flour for dusting

½ cup (1 stick)/120 g
softened butter

7 oz/200 g tant pour
tant (equal weights of
ground almonds and
confectioners' sugar, sifted
together, eg: 1⅓ cups nuts
and ¾ cup + 1 tbsp
sugar)

3 eggs

6 oz/175 g mixed candied
fruits, at least 2 varieties
(eg: angelica, oranges,
cherries), finely diced

6½ tbsp/60 g golden
raisins, macerated in ¼
cup/60 ml Armagnac for
6 hours

1⅓ cups/120 g pine nuts

16 pralines

Confectioners' sugar for
dusting (optional)

Serves 8

Preparation time: 25
minutes

Cooking time: 30 minutes

PREPARING THE PASTRY SHELL: On a lightly floured surface, roll out the pastry into a circle ½₂ in/2 mm thick. Roll it around the rolling pin, then unroll it over the ring, so as not to spoil the shape. Line the ring with the pastry and pinch up the edges between your forefinger and thumb to make a smooth, even border raised slightly above the rim of the ring. Slide the pastry shell onto a baking sheet and let it rest in the refrigerator for at least 20 minutes.

THE FILLING: In a bowl, work the softened butter with a spatula until smooth, then stir in the tant pour tant and then the eggs, one at a time. When the mixture is well blended, add the candied fruits and the macerated raisins.

Preheat the oven to 400°F/200°C.

BAKING THE TART: Prick the bottom of the pastry shell with a fork, pour in the filling, and spread it evenly with a metal spatula. Cover the surface with the pine nuts, then space the pralines evenly around the edge. Press the pine nuts lightly with your fingertips to push them down on the filling, and bake the tart in the hot oven for 10 minutes. Lower the oven temperature to 325°F/170°C and bake for a further 20 minutes.

Take the tart out of the oven and leave until almost completely cold before removing the flan ring.

PRESENTATION: Place the tart on a plate and dust lightly with confectioners' sugar if desired. It is best served barely warm; on no account refrigerate it.

SPECIAL EQUIPMENT:

A flan ring, 9½ in/24 cm
diam., ¾ in/2 cm deep

APRICOT DARTOIS
Dartois aux abricots

CANNED APRICOTS ARE ALWAYS OF EXCELLENT QUALITY, WHICH IS WHY I
USE THEM FOR THIS DESSERT.

INGREDIENTS: ✳
1 lb/450 g Jean Millet's or
   Quick Puff Pastry (pages
   24 and 25)
Flour for dusting
5 oz/150 g Frangipane
   (page 43)
Eggwash (1 egg yolk mixed
   with 1 soup spoon milk
   and a pinch of salt)
9 oz/250 g (drained
   weight) canned apricot
   halves in syrup
Confectioners' sugar for
   dusting
1¼ cups/300 ml Red Fruit
   Coulis (see Fruit Coulis,
   page 51)

SERVES 6
Preparation time: 20
   minutes
Cooking time: 25 minutes

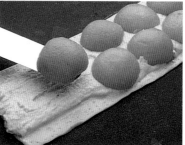

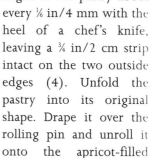

PREPARING THE DARTOIS BASE: On a
lightly floured surface, roll 7 oz/
200 g of the pastry into an 11 ×
5 in/27 × 12 cm rectangle. Roll
this around the rolling pin, then
unroll it onto a baking sheet
lightly dampened with cold water.
Prick the pastry with a fork.

Using a spoon, spread the
frangipane along the length of
the pastry, leaving a clear ¾ in/
2 cm border on either side (1).
Brush these pastry borders with
eggwash. Pat dry the apricots
and arrange them on the
frangipane (2).

Roll out the remaining pastry
into an 11 × 5½ in/27 × 13 cm
rectangle. Fold the pastry in half lengthwise without applying
pressure (3). Make incisions down the length of the pastry about
every ⅙ in/4 mm with the
heel of a chef's knife,
leaving a ¾ in/2 cm strip
intact on the two outside
edges (4). Unfold the
pastry into its original
shape. Drape it over the
rolling pin and unroll it
onto the apricot-filled
rectangle (5). Lightly press the
edges together with your
fingertips and refrigerate the
dartois for 30 minutes.

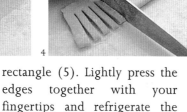

BAKING THE DARTOIS: Preheat the
oven to 400°F/200°C.

Using a chef's knife, trim off
about ⅛ in/3 mm pastry along
the length of the rectangle. Delicately and sparingly brush the top of
the pastry with eggwash. Liberally brush the sides with more
eggwash. With the tip of a small, sharp knife, make light, diagonal
incisions in the borders, then along the edges (6).

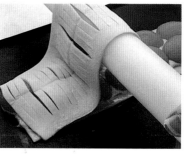

NOTES:
The dartois can be prepared
the day before and kept in
the refrigerator. Bake and
glaze it shortly before
serving. It is best served just
warm.

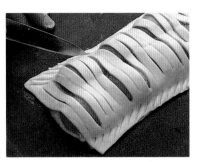

6

Bake in the preheated oven for 25 minutes. Increase the temperature to 425°F/220°C, dust the dartois with confectioners' sugar, and return it to the oven to bake for 1–2 minutes, or place it under a hot salamander or broiler for a few seconds, until beautifully glazed.

PRESENTATION: Serve the dartois on a long plate and cut it with a very sharp knife. Serve the red fruit coulis separately.

129

LATTICED MIRABELLE TARTLETS

Tartelettes fines aux mirabelles en cage

ALTHOUGH THESE SIMPLE, LIGHT TARTLETS ARE BEST MADE WITH THE TINY
FRESH MIRABELLES IN AUTUMN, THEY ARE ALSO EXCELLENT MADE WITH
BOTTLED MIRABELLES IN WINTER OR OTHER LARGER PLUMS.

INGREDIENTS: ❋
1 lb/450 g trimmings of
  Jean Millet's or Quick
  Puff Pastry (pages 24
  and 25)
Flour for dusting
4 oz/100 g Pastry Cream
  (page 39)
84 pitted mirabelles, poached
  in syrup or bottled, or 18
  large fresh sweet plums,
  pitted, each cut into 6,
  and poached in syrup for
  30 seconds
Eggwash (1 egg yolk mixed
  with 1 soup spoon milk
  and a pinch of salt)

Serves 6
Preparation time: 35
  minutes
Cooking time: 18 minutes

PREPARING THE PASTRY BASES: On a lightly floured surface, roll out two-thirds of the pastry to a thickness of ½ in/2 mm. Using the cookie cutter, cut out six rounds and turn them over onto a baking sheet lightly dampened with cold water. Refrigerate for 20 minutes.

THE LATTICE STRIPS: On the lightly floured surface, roll out the remaining pastry into a rectangle about 6½ × 3¼ in/16 × 8 cm and ⅛ in/3 mm thick. Place on a baking sheet and refrigerate for 30 minutes.

ASSEMBLING THE TARTLETS: Preheat the oven to 375°F/190°C.

Prick the pastry bases with a fork and divide the pastry cream among them, spreading it evenly with a spoon. Arrange fourteen well-drained mirabelles or three segmented plums on the pastry cream. Brush the pastry rectangle with eggwash, cut it lengthwise into ⅛ in/3 mm strips, then halve these widthwise. Arrange five strips slantwise on each tartlet, then another five to form a lattice. Trim the lattice if necessary. Refrigerate for 10 minutes.

BAKING THE TARTLETS: Bake the tartlets in the preheated oven for 18 minutes, until golden brown. Use a metal spatula to transfer them delicately to a cooling rack and keep at room temperature.

PRESENTATION: Place the tartlets on plates and serve them plain, while still slightly warm.

SPECIAL EQUIPMENT:
5 in/12 cm plain cookie
  cutter

NOTE:
The tartlets can be prepared
right up to the final stage a
day in advance and kept in
the refrigerator. Bake just
before serving, or during the
meal.

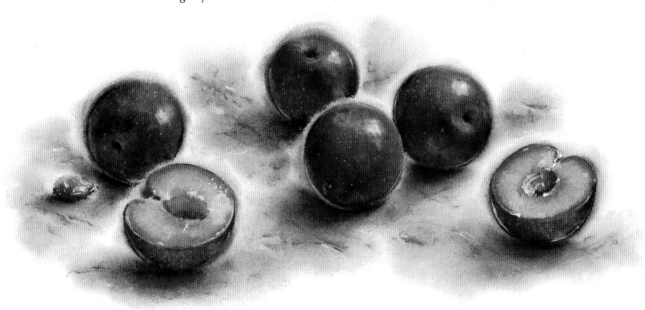

PRINCESS TART WITH BLUEBERRIES

Tarte princesse aux myrtilles

SERVE THIS DELICIOUS TART AT ROOM TEMPERATURE TO ENHANCE THE
SUBTLE FLAVORS OF BLUEBERRIES, ORANGE, AND CHIBOUST CREAM WITH A
THICK, RICH DOUBLE COATING OF CARAMEL.

INGREDIENTS:

9 oz/250 g Flan Pastry
(page 22)
Flour for dusting
Eggwash (1 egg yolk mixed
with 1 soup spoon milk
and a pinch of salt)
1⅞ cups/450 ml heavy
cream
4 eggs
½ cup + 2 tbsp/125 g
sugar, plus ½ cup/100 g
for caramelizing the tart
Finely grated zest of
½ orange
7 oz/200 g blueberries
½ quantity freshly-made
Chiboust Cream (page
39)

Serves 8
Preparation time: 35
minutes
Cooking time: 25 minutes

THE PASTRY SHELL: Preheat the oven to 425°F/220°C.

On a lightly floured surface, roll out the pastry into a circle
1/12 in/2 mm thick. Place the flan ring on a baking sheet and line it
with the pastry. Pinch up the edges to make an attractive, evenly
crimped border. Refrigerate for about 20 minutes.

BAKING THE PASTRY SHELL: Prick the bottom of the pastry shell with a
fork, line with a circle of wax paper, and fill with pie weights or dried
beans. Bake in the hot oven for 15 minutes.

Remove the weights and paper. Brush all over the inside of the tart
shell with eggwash and return it to the oven to bake for a further 5
minutes. Leave it in the ring at room temperature.

Reduce the oven temperature to 400°F/200°C.

THE FILLING: In a bowl, lightly mix the heavy cream, eggs, ½ cup + 2
tbsp/125 g sugar, and the finely grated orange zest.

BAKING THE TART: Reserve the twenty-six best blueberries, spread the
remainder over the bottom of the tart shell, and pour on the cream
filling. Immediately bake in the heated oven for 25 minutes. Take the
tart out of the oven and neaten the border with a sharp knife, then
carefully lift off the flan ring. Place the tart on a wire rack and let cool
at room temperature.

THE CHIBOUST CREAM AND GLAZE: Roll the band of rodoïde or acetate
around the tart and secure it with two pieces of sticky tape. Spread
the freshly-made Chiboust cream over the tart up to the top of the
band, and smooth the surface with a metal spatula. Chill in the freezer

for 30 minutes or in the
refrigerator for at least 1 hour. Fill
the pastry bag with the remaining
Chiboust cream.

After freezing or refrigerating
the tart, carefully remove the
sticky tape and the rodoïde band
by sliding a knife blade between it
and the Chiboust cream. Heat the
salamander or broiler to as hot as
possible.

Sprinkle ¼ cup/50 g sugar over
the Chiboust cream on top of the

SPECIAL EQUIPMENT:

A flan ring, 9½ in/24 cm
diam., ¾ in/2 cm deep,
lightly greased
Pastry bag with a plain
½ in/1 cm tip
32 × 1½ in/80 × 4 cm
band of rodoïde or acetate
Salamander or broiler
Blowtorch (optional)

NOTES:

The uncaramelized tart
freezes well for up to a week.
Transfer to the refrigerator at
least 3 hours before
caramelizing the top to bring
it slowly to the correct
temperature. Why not make
two tarts and freeze one to
enjoy a few days after the
first?

tart and caramelize it lightly by passing the salamader ¼ in/1 mm above the surface of the cream, or by placing the tart under the very hot broiler.

Repeat the operation to make a second coating of caramel, using all but 5 tsp/20 g of the sugar. Let the tart cool at room temperature for a few minutes, then pipe the remaining Chiboust cream into twenty-six rosettes all around the edge. Sprinkle these with the remaining sugar and caramelize them with a blowtorch or leave them plain. Top each rosette with an attractive blueberry.

PRESENTATION: Place the tart on a round serving plate and slice it with a very sharp knife as soon as it has been caramelized, or certainly within an hour.

FIG AND FRESH ALMOND TARTLETS

Tartelettes aux figues et amandes fraîches

THESE SUMMER TARTLETS ARE SIMPLE TO MAKE; THEY LOOK RAVISHING AND
HAVE A DELICATE FLAVOR. THEY ARE PERFECT IN JUNE AND JULY WHEN FIGS
ARE IN FULL SEASON AND FRESH ALMONDS APPEAR IN THE MARKETS.

INGREDIENTS:

9 oz/250 g Tart Pastry
(page 20)
Flour for dusting
1¼ lbs/600 g Pastry Cream
(page 39)
½ cup/100 ml heavy cream,
whipped to a ribbon
consistency
7 very ripe figs, about
2½ oz/65 g each
48 fresh almonds, shelled
and skinned, for decoration
½ cup/50 g sliced almonds,
toasted
ALMOND COULIS
70 fresh almonds, shelled
and skinned
1¼ cups/300 ml heavy
cream
Juice of 1 lemon
2 tbsp milk (optional)

Serves 6
Preparation time: 55
minutes
Cooking time: 10 minutes

PREPARING THE PASTRY SHELLS: On a lightly floured surface, roll out the
pastry to a thickness of ½ in/2 mm. Cut out six rounds with a plain
5 in/13 cm cookie cutter and use them to line the tartlet molds.
Refrigerate for 20 minutes.

Meanwhile, preheat the oven to 350°F/180°C.

BAKING THE PASTRY SHELLS: Prick the bottoms of the pastry shells with
a fork. Line them with a circle of wax paper and fill with pie weights.
Bake for 10 minutes, then remove the weights and paper and unmold
the tartlet shells onto a cooling rack.

THE ALMOND COULIS: Coarsely chop the 70 almonds with a heavy
chef's knife and place in a food processor with the cream. Process for
1 minute to make a slightly grainy coulis. Transfer to a bowl, stir in
the lemon juice, and refrigerate.
If the coulis is too thick, thin it
with the milk.

FILLING THE TARTLETS: Using a
whisk, mix the pastry cream with
the lightly whipped cream.
Divide the mixture among the
pastry shells, making a little
mound in the center. Cut six of
the figs into eight segments
and arrange these on the tartlets,
leaving the stem end protruding
slightly over the edge of the
pastry shells.

Cut the remaining fig into 6
rounds and place one in the
center of each tartlet. Split 24 almonds lengthwise and place 8 halves
between the fig segments on each plate. Halve the remaining almonds
horizontally and arrange them on the fig round like daisy petals.

PRESENTATION: Place the tartlets on individual plates; they look
wonderful on claret-colored and slightly opaque plates. Pour the
almond coulis around the tartlets, decorate with toasted sliced
almonds, and serve immediately.

SPECIAL EQUIPMENT:

Plain 5 in/13 cm cookie
cutter
6 tartlet molds, 4 in/10 cm
diam., ¾ in/2 cm deep

NOTE:

If you cannot find fresh,
milky almonds in their green
shells, use skinned
(blanched) dried almonds
soaked in cold milk for
several hours. These cannot,
however, compare with the
velvety smoothness of fresh
almonds.

CHOCOLATE BOATS

Barquettes chocolat

THESE LITTLE BOATS ARE SIMPLE TO PREPARE AND MAKE AN EXCELLENT
LUNCHEON DESSERT. SERVE THEM ALONE OR WITH A COFFEE-FLAVORED
CREME ANGLAISE (PAGE 40).

INGREDIENTS: ❋
5 oz/160 g Shortbread
    Pastry (page 21) or Sweet
    Tart Pastry (page 20)
Flour for dusting
4 oz/120 g Frangipane
    (page 43)
7 oz/200 g Chocolate
    Chantilly Cream
    (page 42)
3 tbsp/15 g unsweetened
    cocoa powder

Serves 6
Preparation time: 25
    minutes
Cooking time: 15 minutes

LINING THE MOLDS: Arrange the barquette molds in a row. On a lightly
floured surface, roll out the pastry into a rectangle 16 in/40 cm long,
5 in/12 cm wide, ½ in/2 mm thick. Roll the pastry around the
rolling pin, then unroll it over the line of molds. Use your lightly
floured thumb to push the pastry delicately into each mold. Roll the
rolling pin across the top of the molds to cut the pastry. Using a piece
of floured pastry trimming, press down the pastry to ensure that it
takes on the shape of the mold. Refrigerate for 20 minutes.

Meanwhile, preheat the oven to 350°F/180°C.

BAKING THE PASTRY BOATS: Prick the bottom of the pastry shells with a
fork, then use a metal spatula to fill them with frangipane and smooth
the surface. Bake in the preheated oven for 15 minutes. Remove the
pastry boats from the oven, unmold immediately, and arrange on a
cooling rack. Let cool completely.

SPECIAL EQUIPMENT:
6 barquette molds, 3½ in/
    9 cm long, 2 in/5 cm
    wide, ⅝ in/1.5 cm deep

NOTES:
The pastry boats can be
frozen up to a week. Remove
from the freezer 2 hours
before serving and place in
the refrigerator. Dust with
cocoa at the last moment.

Sweet tart pastry is easier
to work than shortbread
pastry, but has a less delicate
and fine flavor.

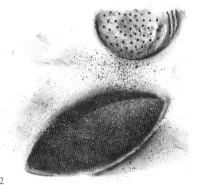

1   2

FILLING THE PASTRY BOATS: Use a metal spatula to heap the chocolate
Chantilly into 1 in/2.5 cm high mounds on the pastry shells and
spread it along their length to resemble little boats (1). Keep in the
refrigerator.

PRESENTATION: Generously dust the Chantilly with cocoa (2). Arrange
the boats on individual plates and serve very cold.

Chapter Nine

Ice Creams and Sorbets

Ices originated in China before the 16th century. Their popularity spread all over the world and continues to grow. Nowadays, a wide range of reasonably-priced ice cream makers is available for domestic use, enabling you to make an ice cream or sorbet in less than half an hour, so it is perfectly feasible to whip up a homemade ice even after a day's work. It is simplicity itself to make sorbets from fruit or vegetables, sweetened, plain, or flavored with aromatics. Concocting a sorbet is rather like creating a cocktail. Being low in calories, sugar, and cholesterol, sorbets make the perfect "diet" dessert.

Custard-based ice creams are best churned just before serving. Since the recipes in this chapter are intended for domestic consumption only, my ice creams contain no stabilizers or preservatives, which makes them all the more delicious. However, the custard mixture can be pasteurized if you wish by poaching it at 175°F/79.4°C for 15 seconds.

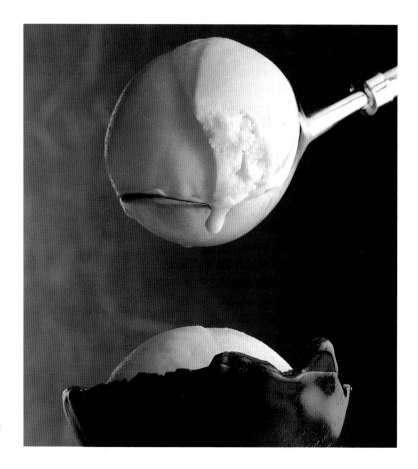

Ice cream in chocolate shells (see recipe page 143)

VANILLA ICE CREAM
Glace vanille

INGREDIENTS:
CREME ANGLAISE:
6 egg yolks
½ cup + 2 tbsp/125 g
  sugar
2 cups/500 ml milk
1 vanilla bean, split

½ cup/100 ml heavy cream

Makes just under 1½
  pints/700 ml
Preparation time: 15
  minutes

THE CREME ANGLAISE: Make a Crème Anglaise with the listed ingredients, following the method on page 40. Strain through a conical strainer and let cool, stirring occasionally.

CHURNING THE ICE CREAM: Churn in an ice cream maker until slightly thickened, then add the heavy cream and churn for another 10–15 minutes.

PISTACHIO ICE CREAM
Glace pistache

I ADORE THE COMBINATION OF PISTACHIO AND VANILLA ICE CREAM AND OFTEN SERVE THEM IN TANDEM. THIS ICE CREAM ALSO FEATURES IN MY TRIO OF ICE CREAMS IN CHOCOLATE SHELLS (PAGE 143).

INGREDIENTS:
½ quantity Crème Anglaise
  (page 40), made without
  vanilla
2 oz/60 g pistachio paste,
  or ¾ cup/80 g pistachios,
  skinned and finely crushed
  in a small mortar
⅓ cup/75 ml heavy cream

Serves 6
Preparation time: 20
  minutes, plus about 15
  minutes churning

THE CREME ANGLAISE: Follow the method on page 40, omitting the vanilla. As soon as the crème anglaise is ready, pour it onto the pistachio paste or crushed pistachios, whisking continuously. Let cool completely, stirring from time to time.

CHURNING THE ICE CREAM: Pass the crème anglaise through a conical strainer and churn in an ice cream maker. As soon as it begins to thicken slightly, add the heavy cream and continue to churn for about 10–15 minutes, depending on your machine.

PRESENTATION: Serve the ice cream in shallow dishes. If you like, garnish with a few skinned and caramelized pistachios (see Pistachio Crème Brûlée, page 67).

MEADOWSWEET ICE CREAM
Glace reine des prés

MEADOWSWEET FLOWERS HAVE A SUBTLE, AROMATIC PERFUME AND WERE ONCE USED
FOR FLAVORING BEER, MEAD, AND WINE. I HAVE USED THEM TO MAKE ICE CREAM
SINCE I WAS CHEF TO MADEMOISELLE CECILE DE ROTHSCHILD IN THE 1960S.

INGREDIENTS:
½ quantity Crème Anglaise
(page 40), made without
vanilla
⅓ oz/10 g dried
meadowsweet flowers
⅓ cup/75 ml heavy cream

Serves 6
Preparation time: 15
minutes, plus about 15
minutes churning

THE CREME ANGLAISE: Follow the method on page 40, omitting the
vanilla. As soon as the crème anglaise is ready, add the meadowsweet
flowers and let infuse for 20 minutes, then pass the crème anglaise
through a conical strainer. Let cool completely, stirring from time to
time.

CHURNING THE ICE CREAM: Churn the crème anglaise in an ice cream
maker. When it begins to thicken slightly, add the heavy cream and
continue to churn for about 10–15 minutes more, depending on
your machine.

PRESENTATION: Serve this ice cream plain in shallow dishes.

NOTE:
Meadowsweet is sold in
almost every pharmacy in
France and is available in
other countries from
herbalists. It has anti-
rheumatic and diuretic
properties and is often drunk
as an infusion, using ⅔–1
oz/20–30 g per 1 quart/1
liter of boiling water.

CARAWAY ICE CREAM
Glace carvi

I ENJOY THIS CARAWAY-FLAVORED ICE CREAM ON ITS OWN OR AS AN
ACCOMPANIMENT TO CHOCOLATE DESSERTS, SUCH AS BITTER CHOCOLATE
AND CARAMELIZED WALNUT DELIGHT (PAGE 162).

INGREDIENTS:
½ quantity Crème Anglaise
(page 40), made without
vanilla
⅓ cup/50 g caraway seeds
⅓ cup/75 ml heavy cream

Serves 6 (makes about
3½ cups/850 ml)
Preparation time: 20
minutes, plus about 15
minutes churning

THE CREME ANGLAISE: Follow the method on page 40, omitting the
vanilla. As soon as it is ready, add the caraway seeds and let infuse for
5 minutes. Pass the crème anglaise through a conical strainer and let
cool, stirring from time to time.

CHURNING THE ICE CREAM: Pour the cooled crème anglaise into an ice
cream maker and churn until slightly thickened. Add the cream and
churn for another 10–20 minutes, until firm.

Almond Ice Cream with a Border of Figs
Glace au lait d'amandes et cordon de figues

THE COLOR AND FLAVOR OF A RASPBERRY COULIS SERVED SEPARATELY IN A SAUCEBOAT WILL COMPLEMENT THIS DELICIOUS ICE CREAM, ALTHOUGH IF THE FIGS ARE REALLY RIPE AND OOZING JUICE, IT WILL NOT BE NECESSARY.

INGREDIENTS:

½ quantity Crème Anglaise
  (page 40)
1⅓ cups/100 g ground
  almonds
½ cup/100 ml heavy cream
3 fresh figs, peeled
2 tbsp best quality chocolate
  liqueur (optional)
12 almonds, peeled, soaked
  in milk, and split

Serves 6
Preparation time: 20
  minutes, plus about 15
  minutes churning

THE CRÈME ANGLAISE: Follow the method on page 40. As soon as the crème anglaise is ready, take the pan off the heat and add the ground almonds. Place in a bowl and leave until completely cold, whisking from time to time.

CHURNING THE ICE CREAM: Pass the crème anglaise through a conical strainer and churn in an ice cream maker. As soon as the mixture thickens slightly, add the heavy cream and churn for another 10–15 minutes, depending on your machine.

PRESENTATION: Cut each fig into eight segments and, if desired, moisten them with chocolate liqueur. Fill six shallow bowls with almond ice cream. Arrange the fig segments in a border around the edge, place four almond halves on the ice cream, and serve.

Fromage Blanc Sorbet with White Pepper
Sorbet au fromage blanc poivré

THIS UNUSUAL SORBET IS EXCELLENT SERVED WITH BERRY FRUITS, SUCH AS WILD STRAWBERRIES AND RASPBERRIES. COMPLEMENT THE FLAVOR WITH SOME HAZELNUT TUILES (PAGE 172).

INGREDIENTS:

1½ cups/350 ml Sorbet
  Syrup (page 144)
1¾ cups/400 g fromage
  blanc or ricotta cheese
  (whatever fat content you
  prefer)
3½ tbsp lemon juice,
  strained
¾ tsp/2 g white
  peppercorns, finely crushed

Serves 6
Preparation time: 10
  minutes, plus about 15
  minutes churning

PREPARATION: Lightly mix the cold sorbet syrup into the fromage blanc, then add the lemon juice and crushed peppercorns. Transfer the mixture to an ice cream maker and churn for about 15 minutes, depending on your machine. Serve immediately, or keep in the freezer until ready to serve.

PRESENTATION: Scoop the sorbet into a glass bowl or individual dishes, using an ice cream scoop dipped into ice water to make each ball.

NOTE:
Churn the sorbet soon after adding the pepper to the mixture, or the flavor will be too strong.

IGLOO WITH VANILLA ICE CREAM AND MIRABELLES
Igloo glace vanille aux mirabelles

CHILDREN ADORE THIS INTRIGUING AND ORIGINAL DESSERT, WITH ITS WONDERFUL FLAVOR COMBINATION OF MERINGUE, ICE CREAM, AND PLUMS. IT CAN BE SIMPLIFIED BY MAKING ONE LARGE IGLOO, USING A SALAD OR MIXING BOWL AS A MOLD. THE PREPARATION WILL BE LESS FIDDLY; MAKE A MUCH LARGER CHIMNEY TO FLAMBÉ THE IGLOO, AND CUT INTO PORTIONS AT THE TABLE.

INGREDIENTS:

2½ pints/1.25 liters Vanilla Ice Cream (page 137)

1 quantity freshly made Meringue Topping made with Egg Whites (page 35)

11 oz/300 g (drained weight) canned or freshly poached mirabelles in syrup, chilled

⅞ cup/200 ml syrup from the mirabelles

1 vanilla bean, cut into very fine slivers (optional)

½ cup/125 ml mirabelle eau-de-vie

8 small bands of rice paper, 4 × ¾ in/10 × 2 cm, rolled up to form chimneys

Serves 8

Preparation time: 1 hour 15 minutes, plus freezing

LINING THE MOLDS: Chill a baking sheet and eight serving plates. Line the 8 molds with the vanilla ice cream, spreading it with a soup spoon. Make a hemispherical cavity about 1¼ in/3 cm diameter, ¾ in/2 cm deep in the center of each, then freeze for at least 1 hour.

After this, cut a ½ in/1 cm hole in the bottom of the ice cream in each mold and lift out the ice cream in the cutter; the resulting hole will be the chimney. Immediately return the molds to the freezer.

ASSEMBLING THE IGLOOS: Prepare the meringue topping and fill the pastry bag and a paper piping cone with the mixture.

Reserve about twenty of the best mirabelles for decoration. Fill the cavities in the igloos with the remaining well-chilled and well-drained mirabelles. Run a blowtorch lightly over the outside of the molds and unmold the igloos onto the chilled baking sheet. Place the rice paper chimneys in the holes in the igloos.

Pipe the meringue topping over the igloos and smooth the surface with a metal spatula, taking care not to block the chimneys. Replace in the freezer to chill for 30 minutes to ensure that the ice cream does not melt. The igloos are now ready to serve. Just pipe on the outline of ice blocks, using the meringue in the paper cone.

PRESENTATION: Transfer the igloos onto well-chilled serving plates, with the aid of a triangular metal spatula. Use the remaining meringue in the pastry bag to form an entrance porch to each igloo, and decorate these in the same way as the igloos. Brown lightly with the blowtorch.

Arrange 5 mirabelle halves on one side of each plate around the igloo, with the vanilla slivers and mirabelle syrup. At the table or sideboard, lightly warm the mirabelle eau-de-vie, pour into the chimneys, and ignite. Serve immediately.

SPECIAL EQUIPMENT:

8 hemispherical molds, 3½ in/9 cm diam., 1¾ in/4.5 cm deep, chilled in the freezer

Plain ½ in/1 cm cookie cutter

Pastry bag with a plain ¼ in/5 mm tip

Blowtorch

NOTE:

It is essential to work fast when coating the igloos with the meringue, so that the ice cream does not melt. The kitchen should not be too warm.

TRIO OF ICE CREAMS IN CHOCOLATE SHELLS

Tierce de glaces dans leur coque de couverture

AN ICED DESSERT FOR A GRAND OCCASION. THREE FLAVORS OF ICE CREAM IN
DELICIOUS BITTER CHOCOLATE SHELLS, TIPPED WITH A TOUCH OF GOLD AND SERVED
WITH STRAWBERRY JUICE. A FITTING GRAND FINALE TO AN ELEGANT MEAL.

INGREDIENTS: ❋

14 oz/400 g bitter
   couverture, tempered (page
   154), or best-quality
   bittersweet chocolate,
   melted and kept liquid

2 sheets of gold leaf
   (optional)

½ quantity Pistachio Ice
   Cream (page 137)

½ quantity Caraway Ice
   Cream (page 138)

½ quantity Almond Ice
   Cream (page 139)

12 pistachios, skinned

A pinch of caraway seeds

4 almonds, skinned, soaked
   in milk for 1 hour, then
   split

⅞ cup/200 ml Strawberry
   Juice (page 51)

2 limes, all peel and pith
   removed, cut in sections

Serves 4

Preparation time: 35
   minutes

THE CHOCOLATE SHELLS: One at a time, dip the bottom two-thirds of the
molds into the liquid chocolate. Let the excess run off for a few
seconds before inverting the molds onto a wire rack. Leave the
chocolate to harden in a cool place (but not in the refrigerator).

As soon as the chocolate has hardened, repeat the operation to
make a second coating (see above). Refrigerate the shells for 1 hour.
Once the chocolate has set, detach the plastic wrap from inside the
molds, then carefully lift the shells off the molds. Very delicately peel
off the plastic wrap from inside the shells.

Arrange the shells on a wire rack and, if desired, dab a touch of
gold leaf here and there on the borders of the shells.

PRESENTATION: Place three chocolate shells on each plate and fill each
one generously with a portion of different ice cream. Sprinkle a few
caraway seeds over the caraway ice cream, place three pistachios on
the pistachio ice cream, and two almond halves on the almond ice
cream.

Pour the strawberry juice onto the plates and scatter on the lime
sections. Serve immediately.

SPECIAL EQUIPMENT:

12 round stainless steel or
   china molds, approx.
   2 in/5 cm diam. at the
   base, 3¼ in/8 cm diam.
   at the top, 2 in/5 cm
   high; the whole exterior
   surface wrapped in plastic
   wrap to give a smooth
   surface

NOTES:

Each chocolate shell weighs
about ⅔ oz/20 g, so you
will have up to 5 oz/150 g
melted couverture left over.
However, you must start
with the full quantity for
dipping the molds.

   Bittersweet chocolate will
not give the same glossy
sheen as couverture.

SORBET SYRUP
Sirop à sorbet

THIS SYRUP IS USED FOR MAKING ALL TYPES OF SORBET.

INGREDIENTS:
3¾ cups/750 g sugar
2⅔ cups/650 ml water
¼ cup/90 g liquid glucose
  or light corn syrup

Makes about 1½ quarts/1.4
  liters
Preparation time: 5 minutes

In a saucepan, bring all the ingredients to a boil, stirring occasionally with a spatula. Boil for about 3 minutes, skimming any impurities from the surface if necessary. If you have a saccharometer, the reading should be 30° Beaumé or 1.2624 density. Strain the syrup through a conical strainer and use when completely cold.

SPECIAL EQUIPMENT:
Beaumé scale saccharometer
  (optional)

NOTE:
The syrup will keep for 2
weeks in the refrigerator in
an airtight container or
covered with plastic wrap.

BANANA SORBET
Sorbet à la banane

YOU NEED VERY RIPE BANANAS FOR THIS SORBET, BUT IF THEY HAVE ANY
BLACK PATCHES, CUT THESE AWAY WITH A SHARP KNIFE.

INGREDIENTS:
1 lb 2 oz/500 g ripe
  bananas (peeled weight)
Juice of 2 lemons
1 cup/250 ml milk
⅞ cup/200 ml Sorbet Syrup
  (page 144)
Flavorings (optional): ½
  vanilla bean, split, or 3½
  tbsp rum, or ⅛ tsp ground
  cinnamon

Serves 8 (makes about
  2¼ lbs/1 kg)
Preparation time: 25
  minutes, plus about 20
  minutes churning

THE SORBET MIXTURE: Cut the bananas into rounds and mix immediately with the lemon juice to prevent the fruit from oxidizing and turning black. In a saucepan, bring the milk to a boil and immediately add the bananas and sorbet syrup. Simmer at 203°F/95°C for about 5 minutes. At this stage, you can add your chosen flavoring, then remove from the heat.

Remove the vanilla bean and purée the mixture in a blender for 2 minutes, until it is homogeneous and smooth, then pass it through a conical strainer. Let cool completely at room temperature, stirring with a spatula from time to time.

CHURNING THE MIXTURE: The sorbet mixture should be churned as soon as the bananas have cooled, as they will cause it to oxidize and turn brown. Churn the cold mixture in an ice cream maker for about 20 minutes, depending on your machine. The sorbet should have a firm consistency.

PRESENTATION: Serve this sorbet plain in shallow dishes, or garnished with half a banana lightly brushed with Chocolate Sauce (page 55).

SPECIAL EQUIPMENT:
Cooking thermometer

NOTE:
I give the peeled weight of
the bananas as the skins vary
in thickness depending on the
variety of the fruit.

PINEAPPLE SORBET IN A PINEAPPLE SHELL

L'Ananas en sorbet dans sa coque

INGREDIENTS: ❋

1 very ripe pineapple, about
   3 lbs/1.4 kg
1 cup/250 ml Sorbet Syrup
   (page 144)
Juice of 1 lemon
6–8 crystallized violets

THE RIBBON (OPTIONAL)
1 tbsp melted butter
2½ oz/70 g Tulip Paste
   (page 28)
A pinch of unsweetened cocoa
   powder

Serves 6
Preparation time: 45
   minutes, plus 25 minutes
   for the ribbon

PREPARING THE PINEAPPLE: Divide the pineapple lengthwise into 60% and 40%, making sure that the larger piece, which will be used as the shell, stands stably on the work surface. Keep the leaves attached.

Using a knife with a fine blade, cut around the flesh ½ in/1 cm inside the skin to release the flesh, then use a spoon to detach the rounded bottom part, enabling you to remove the pineapple flesh in one piece. Prepare the other piece of pineapple in the same way.

Reserve the larger shell in the refrigerator and discard the smaller shell. Cut the pieces of pineapple flesh into ¼ in/5 mm semi-circular slices. Cut the best of these into 12 triangular pieces. Heat the sorbet syrup, poach the pineapple triangles for 20 minutes, then let cool in the poaching syrup at room temperature. When they are cold, drain them, reserving the syrup for the sorbet.

THE SORBET: Put all the raw pineapple pieces and pulp into a food processor with half the sorbet syrup. Process for 2 minutes to make a thick coulis, then pass through a fine strainer into a bowl and add the rest of the syrup and the lemon juice. Churn in an ice cream maker for about 20 minutes, until firm. Transfer the sorbet to a container and chill in the freezer while you make the ribbon.

THE RIBBON: Preheat the oven to 350°F/180°C.

Lay a strip of parcel tape on a baking sheet, then lay the other two parallel to it, spacing the strips 1½ in/4 cm apart. Brush the gaps between the tape very lightly with melted butter. Chill the baking sheet in the refrigerator for a few minutes, then spread some plain tulip paste as thinly as possible over the two buttered gaps.

Color the remaining paste with the cocoa, place in a paper piping cone, and pipe slightly diagonal lines onto the bands of plain paste. Remove the parcel tape and bake the ribbons in the preheated oven for about 4 minutes, until pale golden brown. Take the ribbons out of the oven and, using scissors, immediately cut one of the bands into three equal lengths and fold them into a bow. Cut the second band slightly on the slant into two equal lengths, then slightly crumple them to resemble the two free ends of a ribbon. Keep at room temperature.

PRESENTATION: Spoon half the sorbet into the pineapple shell, then fill it with balls of sorbet, using two different-sized scoops. Top with two small balls in the center. Arrange the candied pineapple triangles among the balls (you can caramelize them with a blowtorch if you wish). Decorate the balls of sorbet with crystallized violets. Place the pineapple on a large serving plate and arrange the pastry ribbon and bows over the pineapple leaves. Serve immediately.

SPECIAL EQUIPMENT:
3 strips of parcel tape,
   12 × 2 in/30 × 5 cm
   (for the ribbon)
Paper piping cone (for the
   ribbon)
Blowtorch (optional)

NOTES:
The ribbon is an extra refinement that can be omitted, although it looks so attractive that I think it is worth the effort.

All the preparation for this dessert can be done the day before; just churn the sorbet before, or better still, during the meal to give a deliciously soft texture.

Fill the pineapple shell at the last moment; it only takes 5 minutes. For a marvelous buffet dish, stand the pineapple shell in a shallow dish on a bed of crushed ice.

APPLE SORBET
Sorbet aux pommes

INGREDIENTS:
11 oz/300 g apples,
    preferably Granny Smiths
1¼ cups/300 ml water
6½ tbsp/80 g sugar
2 tbsp/40 g liquid glucose
    or light corn syrup
Juice of ½ lemon
½ vanilla bean, split

Serves 6
Preparation time: 10
    minutes, plus about 15
    minutes churning

COOKING THE APPLES: Wash in cold water and cut each apple into 6 or 8 segments. Place in a saucepan with all the other ingredients. Cover and cook over low heat until the apples are almost puréed. Remove the vanilla bean, then liquidize everything else in a blender for 2 minutes to make a very liquid purée. Pass this through a fine conical strainer and let cool at room temperature.

CHURNING THE SORBET: As soon as the apple purée is completely cold, churn it in an ice cream maker for 15–20 minutes, depending on your machine. The sorbet should still be quite soft and velvety, so do not churn it for too long.

PRESENTATION: Serve the sorbet as it is, or scoop out the flesh from small raw apples and fill the cavities with apple sorbet.

NOTES:
I do not remove the apple peel or cores, since they contain so much flavor. To enhance this further, you could add 3½ tbsp Calvados at the end of churning.

Adjust the quantity of sugar to suit the sweetness or tartness of the apples.

ICED MELON SURPRISE
Melon glacé en surprise

INGREDIENTS:
4 very ripe melons,
    1 lb 2 oz–1¼ lbs/500–
    600 g each
½ cup/100 ml Sorbet Syrup
    (page 144)
Juice of ½ lemon
1 quantity Spun Sugar
    (page 182)
24 wild strawberries
Crushed ice (optional)

Serves 4
Preparation time: 25
    minutes, plus about 15
    minutes churning

THE MELONS: Using a knife with a very thin, long blade, divide each melon with six zigzag cuts, starting about two-thirds from the bottom and cutting diagonally into the center (see photo opposite). Discard the melon seeds. Use a ½ in/1 cm melon baller to scoop out six small balls of flesh from inside each lid, and refrigerate.

Scoop out the rest of the melon flesh with a soup spoon and place in a food processor with the sorbet syrup and lemon juice. Purée for about 2 minutes, to make a kind of thick coulis, then pass it through a strainer and keep in the refrigerator until ready to churn into a sorbet.

THE SPUN SUGAR: Follow the recipe on page 182, but do not spin the sugar into angel's hair more than 30 minutes before serving the dessert, or the humidity may cause the strands to soften and lose their ethereal quality.

THE SORBET: Pour the melon coulis into an ice cream maker and churn for 10–15 minutes until semi-firm.

PRESENTATION: Put the melon shells into shallow dishes or a bowl two-thirds filled with crushed ice. Using an ice cream scoop, generously fill the shells with balls of sorbet. Arrange a melon ball and a strawberry between each zigzag. Lay a veil of spun sugar on top of each melon and serve immediately.

NOTES:
My favorite melons are Cavaillon or Charentais, which have by far the best flavor. However, other good quality varieties are available throughout the year.

It is difficult to spin sugar successfully in small quantities, so you will need to use 1¼ cups/250 g sugar for this recipe.

Iced Melon Surprise

Chocolate Sorbet
Sorbet au chocolat

I OFTEN ACCOMPANY MY DESSERTS WITH A CHOCOLATE SORBET, ESPECIALLY
IN WINTER. OF COURSE IT IS ALSO DELICIOUS SERVED ON ITS OWN
ACCOMPANIED BY SOME PETITS FOURS SERVED ON A SEPARATE PLATE.

INGREDIENTS:

1¾ cups/400 ml water

½ cup/100 ml milk

¾ cup/150 g sugar

2 tbsp/40 g liquid glucose
  or light corn syrup

⅓ cup/30 g unsweetened
  cocoa powder

4 oz/100 g bitter couverture
  or best-quality bittersweet
  chocolate, chopped

Serves 8

Preparation time: 15
  minutes, plus about 15
  minutes churning

PREPARATION: Combine the water, milk, sugar, glucose, and cocoa in
a saucepan and bring to a boil, stirring continuously with a whisk.
Simmer over a gentle heat for 2 minutes. Take the pan off the heat,
add the chopped chocolate, and stir with the whisk for 2 minutes,
then pass through a conical strainer into a bowl. Let cool at room
temperature, then refrigerate.

20 minutes before serving, pour the mixture in ice cream maker
and churn for about 15 minutes, until the sorbet has set. Serve at
once, or keep in the freezer.

PRESENTATION: Scoop the sorbet into balls, dipping the scoop in ice
water before making each ball. Serve in a large glass compote dish or
individual glasses

Grapefruit Granita with Crisp Wafer Cookies
Granité de pamplemousse dans sa coque et ses dentelles croustillantes

THIS REFRESHING DESSERT WITH A DIFFERENCE SPARKLES LIKE DIAMONDS.

INGREDIENTS:

3 very ripe grapefruit,
  preferably pink

¼ cup/50 ml Sorbet Syrup
  (page 144)

¾ cup/150 g sugar

4 heaped tbsp Pastry Cream
  (page 39)

Crushed ice for serving

Serves 6

Preparation time: 20
  minutes, plus freezing

EMPTYING THE GRAPEFRUIT SHELLS: Using the tip of a small sharp knife,
make an incision all around the grapefruit without spoiling the
sections. Slide a soup spoon into the incision between the skin and
sections and ease away the flesh without damaging the skin.
Refrigerate the shells. Separate the sections and keep the six best for
the garnish.

THE GRAPEFRUIT GRANITA: Purée the rest of the sections with the sorbet
syrup in a blender for 1 minute, then pass through a conical strainer.
Pour the resulting juice into a shallow stainless steel dish and place in
the freezer. Stir the juice with a fork every 30 minutes until it has
frozen into large crystals; depending on the temperature of your
freezer, this may take 1½ hours (at −13°F/−25°C) or up to 3 hours
(at 14°F/ 10°C).

THE CARAMELIZED GRAPEFRUIT SECTIONS: In a small heavy-based saucepan,
gently cook the sugar without water to a very pale caramel, stirring
continuously with a spatula. Remove from the heat and, using a fork,

SPECIAL EQUIPMENT:

Wafer-thin 2⅜ in/6 cm
  diam. template

Nonstick baking sheet, or a
  sheet of parchment paper

NOTE:

This dessert can equally well
be made with oranges

148

dip the grapefruit sections into the sugar, one at a time. Place on a very lightly oiled baking sheet and keep at room temperature.

Grapefruit Granita with
Crisp Wafer Cookies

THE CRISP WAFERS: Preheat the oven to 350°F/180°C.

Place the template on a nonstick baking sheet or parchment paper, put in a little pastry cream, and spread it with a metal spatula. Move the template along and repeat the operation until you have used all the pastry cream to make at least twelve wafers (more than a dozen will allow for breakages). Bake for 3 minutes, until pale golden. Lift them off the baking sheet with a metal spatula while still hot, and crumple them slightly with your fingertips. Place the crisp wafers on a wire rack.

PRESENTATION: Place a little crushed ice in the bottom of six stemmed glass bowls. Fill the grapefruit shells with the granita and arrange them on the ice. Half-bury a caramelized grapefruit section in the granita. Place a couple of wafers at the base of each glass, or serve them separately. Serve immediately.

Chapter Ten

CHOCOLATE

From prehistoric times, the cacao tree, from which cocoa beans come, has grown wild in Central America. The Mayas were the first people to cultivate the trees, and later the Aztecs used cocoa beans not only to make chocolate-based drinks, but also as currency: one slave cost three beans. Christopher Columbus was the first European to discover the bean, which subsequently became popular in the French court in 1615 through the Spanish Infanta.

Cacao trees are grown in thirty-five tropical countries, but 80% of the world's production comes from six countries, four of them in West Africa – the Ivory Coast, Ghana, Cameroon, and Nigeria, which accounts for 52% of this yield. In less than a century, the yield of cacao trees has increased from 115,000 metric tonnes to more than two million.

Tempering chocolate with a metal spatula (see page 154)

The three varieties of cacao tree are Criollo, Forastero (which represents 70% of the world's production), and Trinitario. Criollo, which produces only 10% of the crop, is the best and most sought-after cocoa. All the trees are very fragile. They need a warm humid climate, but are sensitive to wind, sunshine, disease, and pests, so they are often grown alongside other fruit trees, particularly banana palms, whose broad leaves offer perfect shady protection to this valuable crop.

The process from tree to table is complicated, involving many precise steps, each requiring expertise and constant attention. From a simple bean with very few additions comes a superbly complex, rich, tantalizing taste.

The cocoa pod reaches maturity after five to six months. Each cacao tree produces two annual harvests. In Africa, the main crop is between September and December, with a second small gathering in May and June. The harvest is cracked open within a week of picking and any rotten pods are discarded.

The seeds, which are covered in a sweet white pulp, are fermented under banana leaves for five to seven days, and are stirred regularly to circulate the air. This fermentation is very important to develop the flavor. During the process, the seeds turn from light purple to rich brown.

The next stage is the critical drying process, which enhances the flavor and reduces the humidity to prevent mold. Nowadays, a few factories use industrial blowers to blow warm air onto the seeds, but most are still traditionally sun-dried. After three to seven days drying, the seeds take on their new name of "cocoa beans" and are then shipped from their country of origin to the factory, to be transformed into chocolate.

The beans are cleaned and dusted and waste is removed. To separate the nibs from the shell and germ, the beans are warmed and winnowed. Only the nibs are then roasted or ground, depending on the desired end product. The roasted beans are coarsely ground, then further refined into a mass known as cocoa paste or liquor. This is used as an ingredient in chocolate-making, or is pressed again to separate the liquid (cocoa butter) from the dry particles (cake). The cocoa butter is deodorized and has the color removed, while the cake is ground and sifted into cocoa powder. The cocoa paste is mixed with sugar (and powdered milk for milk chocolate), then ground again to a refined, silky texture.

Now follow two long stages called "conching," which remove any remaining humidity and sourness and fully develop the flavor. Conching can take up to five days. The first process, "dry conching," aerates the cocoa paste, sugar, milk, and flavoring to make the particles even smoother. The second is "liquid conching," when cocoa butter is added. The resulting liquid chocolate is then sent to the manufacturers, or molded into blocks for confectioners.

COUVERTURE: Couverture is the finest chocolate used for commercially- and hand-made chocolates and pâtisserie. French legislation determines the following ingredients for couverture:

Dark chocolate is 31% cocoa butter and 16% pure cocoa. Milk chocolate is at least 31% total fats, and contains a maximum of 55% sugar. White chocolate is at least 20% cocoa butter and maximum of 50% sugar. The finest, richest, most densely flavored couverture can have a 76% cocoa solids content; anything above this percentage will taste too bitter.

Couverture can be melted and remolded after tempering (see page 154). It is used for dipping, decoration, and piping. This prized product of pâtissiers can be as important as their skill. The craft of the master is balanced by the quality of the couverture. The taste of the chocolate is reflected in the price you pay. The fruit aroma of the beans cannot deceive the palate with a poor quality product.

Chocolate-based desserts are among my favorites. Generally, they require more care and time than other desserts, but they feature on everyone's hit parade. I like them crunchy, creamy, shiny, featherlight, melting in the mouth – need I say more?

Clockwise from top left: Decorating Chocolate run-outs: Chocolate Teardrop: Modeling Chocolate rose, leaf, and stem: Honeycomb Chocolate Disks: Chocolate Curls: Chocolate Fans: Dark and White Modeling Chocolate roses and leaves

TEMPERED COUVERTURE

This process applies to all couverture, and gives it a wonderful sheen; however, when a recipe calls only for melted couverture, it is not necessary to temper it. Cooking or baker's chocolate never needs to be tempered, since it cannot achieve the same high gloss as couverture.

Chop the couverture with a heavy knife and melt in a hot cupboard or electric chocolate warmer at the following temperatures:

122°–131°F/50°–55°C for fondant, bittersweet, and bitter couverture; 122°F/50°C for milk chocolate; 113°F/45°C for white chocolate. It is essential to use a chocolate thermometer for this process.

Pour about 80% of the melted couverture onto a marble work surface and work it with a triangular scraper or large metal spatula, continuously bringing it up over itself until it cools to 78.8°–80.6°F/26°–27°C. Use the triangle or spatula to scrape up the chocolate from the work surface and mix it with the untempered couverture. Mix the mass with a spatula until it is all the same temperature (82.4°–84.2°F/28°–29°C for white chocolate, and 86°–89.6°F/30°–32°C for dark or bitter chocolate). If it is a few degrees too hot, pour about one-third back onto the work surface and repeat the operation until it reaches the correct temperature.

The couverture is now ready to use for dipping, coating candies, molding, etc. Keep it at the correct temperature in a chocolate warmer. Ideally, all chocolate work should be done at a room temperature of 64.4°–71.6°F/18°–22°C, and a humidity level of not more than 50–60%.

CHOCOLATE CURLS AND FANS
Copeaux et éventails chocolat

INGREDIENTS:
4 oz / 100 g dark couverture,
   melted to 95°F/35°C
¾ oz / 20 g white couverture,
   melted to 95°F/35°C

Makes a 12 × 8 in/
   30 × 20 cm sheet
Preparation time: 10
minutes

CHOCOLATE CURLS: Invert the heated baking sheet onto the work surface. Using the white chocolate in the piping cone, draw fine, even lines, spacing them close together, or further apart, as you prefer. Pour the melted dark couverture evenly over the lines and smooth evenly with a metal spatula. Refrigerate for 15 minutes.

Place the baking sheet on the work surface and push the scraper between the chocolate and the baking sheet with short, rapid movements to roll the chocolate into curls (see photo opposite).

154

CHOCOLATE FANS: Invert the heated baking sheet onto the work surface. Pour on the melted dark couverture and spread it evenly with a metal spatula. Using the white chocolate in the piping cone, draw fine even lines all over the surface of the dark chocolate. Refrigerate for 15 minutes.

Place the baking sheet on the work surface. Holding one side of the chocolate with your index finger, push the scraper between the chocolate and the baking sheet with a short, rapid movement to pleat the chocolate into fans (see photo above).

SPECIAL EQUIPMENT:
12 × 8 in / 30 × 20 cm baking sheet, preheated to 131°F / 55°C
Metal scraper
Paper piping cone

NOTES:
If the chocolate has become too hard after 15 minutes in the refrigerator, let it soften at room temperature for a few minutes before shaping the curls or fans. They will keep well in a cool place for 5 days.

HONEYCOMB CHOCOLATE DISKS
Alvéoles chocolat

THESE CHOCOLATE DISKS RESEMBLE THE CELLS OF A HONEYCOMB AND GIVE A LIGHT, ALMOST AIRY DECORATIVE EFFECT. TEMPERING THE CHOCOLATE MAKES THEM WONDERFULLY SHINY. USE SMALL DISKS TO DECORATE INDIVIDUAL DESSERTS, OR A LARGE DISK FOR A GÂTEAU.

INGREDIENTS:
2 oz / 50 g dark couverture, tempered (see page 154)
2 oz / 50g white couverture, tempered (see page 154)

Makes twelve 2¾ in / 7 cm diam. disks
Preparation time: 10 minutes

Using a pastry brush, spread the dark couverture all over the bumpy side of the bubble wrap (1), then refrigerate for 15 minutes. After this time, use a metal spatula to spread the white couverture over the dark couverture (2) and refrigerate for at least another 15 minutes.

Carefully peel the plastic-wrap-covered bubble wrap off the chocolate honeycomb. Very lightly warm the cookie cutter over a gas flame and cut out twelve chocolate disks. These can be used immediately.

SPECIAL EQUIPMENT:
12 × 10 in / 30 × 25 cm sheet of plastic bubble wrap, covered with plastic wrap
2¾ in / 7 cm round cookie cutter

NOTES:
The disks can be made with only one type of chocolate, but you will not achieve the pretty speckled or marbled effect obtained with dark and white chocolate.

The honeycomb disks will keep well for 5 days.

MODELING CHOCOLATE
Chocolat plastique

YOU CAN MAKE BEAUTIFUL CHOCOLATE FLOWERS BY TINTING WHITE MODELING
CHOCOLATE WITH FOOD COLORINGS, SUCH AS PINK, YELLOW, AND ORANGE.

INGREDIENTS:

DARK CHOCOLATE

9 oz/250 g dark couverture,
melted to 113°F/45°C

5 tbsp/100 g liquid glucose
or light corn syrup and ¼
cup/60 ml Sorbet Syrup
(page 144), boiled
together and cooled to
95°F/35°C

WHITE CHOCOLATE:

9 oz/250 g white
couverture, melted to
113°F/45°C

1 oz/25 g cocoa butter,
melted and mixed into the
couverture

7 tbsp/150 g liquid glucose
or light corn syrup and 2
tbsp Sorbet Syrup, boiled
together and cooled to
95°F/35°C

Makes about 14 oz/420 g
(9–12 roses)

Preparation time: 10
minutes

MAKING THE MODELING CHOCOLATE: (This method applies for both dark
and white chocolate.) Add the glucose and syrup mixture to the
melted chocolate and mix well with a spatula. Pour the mixture onto
a marble or formica work surface and continue to mix with the
spatula until the chocolate is completely cold and crystallized. Wrap
it in plastic wrap until ready to use.

TO MAKE CHOCOLATE OR MARZIPAN ROSES: Dust the work surface very
lightly with confectioners' sugar.
Roll out 1¼–1½ oz/35–40 g
chocolate or marzipan to a
thickness of ½ in/2 mm, then cut
out nine 1½ in/4 cm disks with a
plain cookie cutter (1). Roll the
trimmings into a small ball.

Roll this ball on the work
surface with your hand into an

oval or "bud." Press one end of
the bud against the work surface
so that it stands upright (2).

Use the modeling tool to thin
down one-half of the edge of
each of the nine disks (3). These
will be the petals.

Wrap the first petal around the
bud, placing the thinned edge at
the top, without completely enveloping the bud (4). Use your thumb
to curve up the thicker edges of the other petals.

Now, always keeping the thinner edge at the top, build up the other
petals over the bud wrapped in its first petal, overlapping them (5).
Do not squeeze too hard; just press lightly with your fingertips to
attach the base of the petals to the bottom of the bud to resemble an
open rose in full bloom.

NOTES:

You will need about 1¼
oz/35 g folding chocolate to
make a rose. If you wish,
tint white folding chocolate
with food colorings to obtain
pinks, yellows, oranges, etc.

Marzipan roses can be
modeled in exactly the same
way as chocolate flowers.
Both will keep well in a dry
place at room temperature
for several days.

5   6

Press the base of the flower with your fingertips to make it open out even more. With a knife, cut ¼ in/5 mm off the base of the rose to make it stable (6).

WHITE CHOCOLATE LAYER CAKE
Délice ivoirine

A SCOOP OF CHOCOLATE SORBET (PAGE 148) GOES WELL WITH THIS DESSERT, WHICH IS ALSO DELICIOUS BY ITSELF. IT LOOKS PLAIN AND UNADORNED, BUT IS RICH AND CREAMY.

INGREDIENTS: ❊
½ quantity chocolate Genoise Sponge batter (page 33)
½ cup/120 ml Sorbet Syrup (page 144), mixed with 3½ tbsp Cognac (optional)
1 quantity White Chocolate Mousse (see White Chocolate Dome, page 165)
7 oz/200 g Chocolate Glaze (page 186)

Serves 22
Preparation time: 35 minutes

THE CHOCOLATE SPONGE: Preheat the oven to 400°F/200°C.

Spread the sponge batter over half the baking sheet (ie: 16 × 12 in/40 × 30 cm). Bake in the preheated oven for 8 minutes. Slide the parchment paper onto a cooling rack and leave the sponge until cold. Cover the cold sponge with a dish towel, then a cooling rack, and invert it.

Peel off the parchment paper. Cut the sponge into two 14 × 4½ in/35 × 11 cm bands (the size of the cardboard frames), trimming off the outside edges. Moisten with sorbet syrup, place in the bottom of the frames, and put them on a baking sheet. Using a metal spatula, fill the frames with white chocolate mousse and level the surface as smoothly as possible. Chill in the freezer for at least 30 minutes.

PRESENTATION: Shortly before serving, take the desserts out of the freezer and immediately use a metal spatula to glaze the tops with warmish (but not too hot) chocolate glaze. Only run the metal spatula once over the surface so that the icing sets immediately. Dip a knife blade into hot water and slide it between the inside of the frames and the mousse, then remove the frames. Cut each band into eleven rectangles and place on individual plates. Serve the dessert very cold, almost frozen.

SPECIAL EQUIPMENT:
2 frames made from rigid cardboard covered with foil, 12½ in/35 cm long, 4½ in/14 cm wide, 1 in/2.5 cm deep
24 × 16 in/60 × 40 cm baking sheet lined with parchment paper

NOTE:
Because of its composition, it is impossible to make a smaller quantity of this dessert successfully, but you can keep one frozen for a week. Glaze it only just before serving.

CHOCOLATE TEARDROPS WITH WHITE CHOCOLATE MOUSSE AND GRIOTTINES

Larmes de chocolat, mousse ivoirine et griottines

I CLASS THIS DELECTABLY ELEGANT, RESTRAINED DESSERT AS ONE OF MY "CHOCOLATIER'S FOLLIES."

INGREDIENTS: ❄

9 oz/250 g bitter
   couverture, tempered (see
   page 154)
1 quantity White Chocolate
   Mousse (see White
   Chocolate Dome, page
   165)
72 griottines (small cherries
   in eau-de-vie syrup)
1 cup/250 ml eau-de-vie
   syrup from the griottines,
   reduced by one-third over
   low heat
1½ oz/40 g Tulip Paste
   (page 28), flavored wih a
   pinch of cocoa powder
½ quantity Chocolate Sorbet
   (page 148)
6 sprigs of mint

Serves 6
Preparation time: 1 hour

THE TEARDROP SHAPES: Using a rocking motion, gently dip one side only of each strip of rodoïde or acetate into the surface of 7 oz/200 g of the tempered couverture (1), or lay the strips on the work table and coat the surface with the thinnest possible layer of couverture.

As soon as the couverture begins to set, stand the first strip upright with the chocolate on the inside, pinch the two ends together in a loop, and secure them with a paperclip to make a teardrop shape (2). Place the teardrops on a baking sheet lined with wax paper and refrigerate for 30 minutes.

FILLING THE TEARDROPS: Using the pastry bag fitted with the plain tip, fill the teardrops one-third full with the white chocolate mousse. Arrange 8 griottines in each teardrop, then fill up with mousse and smooth the surface with a metal spatula. Refrigerate until ready to serve.

THE CHOCOLATE TULIP PASTE: Preheat the oven to 350°F/180°C.

Using the template, spread the paste into six rounds on a nonstick baking sheet. Cook in the preheated oven for 3–4 minutes. Lift off the rounds one at a time with a metal spatula and place them in six of the molds, using the seventh mold to press them into basket shapes to hold the chocolate sorbet.

THE CHOCOLATE FILIGREE: Fill a paper piping cone with some of the remaining melted couverture and pipe very fine filigree patterns no bigger than 1½ in/4 cm diameter onto the sheet of rodoïde or acetate. Place in the refrigerator.

PRESENTATION: Remove the paperclips and plastic strips from the teardrops and put one on each plate. Using the piping cone, pipe a line of chocolate along the length of each drop and fill it with the cold reduced eau-de-vie syrup. Arrange three griottines on each plate and one on each teardrop, and place a sprig of mint beside it. Fill the pastry baskets with a small scoop of chocolate sorbet and place one on each plate. Delicately peel off the chocolate filigree patterns and stand them aslant on the chocolate sorbet. Serve the dessert extremely cold, almost frozen.

SPECIAL EQUIPMENT:
6 strips of rodoïde or acetate,
   10 × 1¾ in/26 × 4.5 cm
1 sheet of rodoïde or acetate,
   12 × 8 in/30 × 20 cm
Pastry bag with a plain
   ½ in/1 cm tip
2⅜ in/6 cm diam. template
7 molds, approx. 3 in/7.5
   cm diam. at the top,
   1½ in/4 cm diam. at the
   base, 1 in/2.5 cm deep
6 paperclips
Paper piping cone

NOTE:
All the elements of this dessert can be prepared a day in advance. Arrange all the different goodies on the plates just before serving.

CHOCOLATE CAPPUCCINO MOUSSES
Mousse au chocolat, glace café

THIS EASY DESSERT CAN BE MADE A DAY OR TWO IN ADVANCE. IF YOU LIKE, YOU CAN ADD A DASH
OF TIA MARIA TO THE COFFEE CREAM, BUT I PREFER IT PLAIN. THE CONTRAST BETWEEN THE
UNSWEETENED COFFEE CREAM AND THE HALF-SET RICH, SUGARY CHOCOLATE MOUSSE IS UNIQUE.

INGREDIENTS: ❋
9 oz/250 g dark couverture
   or best-quality bittersweet
   chocolate
6 egg whites
½ cup + 2 tbsp/125 g
   sugar
4 egg yolks
⅔ cup/150 ml heavy cream
1 tbsp instant coffee powder
1 tbsp unsweetened cocoa
   powder

Serves 4
Preparation time: 20
   minutes

PREPARATION: Chop the chocolate with a chef's knife, place in a bowl, and stand it in a bain-marie set over medium heat. Remove from the heat as soon as the chocolate has melted. Beat the egg whites until half-risen, then, still whisking, add the sugar, a little at a time and beat to a very firm snow. Stir the yolks, then ¼ cup/50 ml of the cream into the melted chocolate and immediately fold in the beaten egg whites delicately with a spatula. As soon as the mixture becomes homogeneous, divide it among the shallow bowls or cups and place in the refrigerator.

PRESENTATION: Just before serving, dissolve the instant coffee in a scant 2 tbsp of water. With a fork or whisk, whip the remaining cream into a light, runny foam, then add the coffee. Top the chocolate mousses with the foam, sprinkle with a little cocoa, and serve immediately.

SPECIAL EQUIPMENT:
4 shallow serving bowls or
   wide-mouthed, shallow
   cups, 4½ in/12 cm
   diam., 2 in/5 cm deep

CHOCOLATE MILLE-FEUILLE DIAMONDS
Diamants de mille-feuille chocolat

THE CRUNCHY TEXTURE OF THE COUVERTURE MAKES A WONDERFUL
CONTRAST WITH THE LUSCIOUS, CREAMY FILLING.

INGREDIENTS: ❋
1 oz/30 g white couverture,
   just melted and tepid
8 oz/220 g dark couverture,
   tempered (see page 154)
4 oz/125 g Coffeee
   Chantilly (page 42)
4 oz/125 g Chocolate
   Chantilly (page 42)
⅞ cup/200 ml Caramel
   Sauce (page 55)

Serves 6
Preparation time: 40
   minutes

THE COUVERTURE DIAMONDS: Lay one sheet of rodoïde on a baking sheet. Fill the paper cone with the tepid white couverture and pipe on a network of vertical, horizontal, and diagonal lines. As soon as they have hardened, spread the tempered dark couverture over them. Lay the second sheet of rodoïde on top and very lightly roll a rolling pin over the surface to eliminate all the air bubbles and even up the surface. Leave in a cool place (but on no account in the refrigerator) until the couverture is set.

Lift off the top sheet of rodoïde. Very slightly warm a thin knife blade over a gas flame and cut three 2¾ in/7 cm wide bands along the length of the couverture. Cut each band slightly on the diagonal into six 1⅜ in/3.5 cm rectangles, lightly warming the knife blade.

Fill one pastry bag with coffee Chantilly and one with chocolate Chantilly. Onto twelve of the rectangles, pipe alternating ½ in/1 cm balls of coffee and chocolate cream.

SPECIAL EQUIPMENT:
2 sheets of rodoïde or acetate,
   9 in/23 cm long,
   8½ in/21 cm wide
Paper piping cone
2 pastry bags with plain
   ½ in/1 cm tips

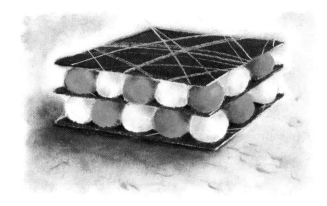

Top six of the cream-filled rectangles with six more cream-filled rectangles, then finish with an unfilled rectangle, placing it with the pattern upward. Leave the mille-feuille diamonds in the refrigerator for at least 30 minutes before serving.

NOTE:
This dessert can be prepared several hours in advance: Stack the plates on rings and keep them in the refrigerator. Spoon the caramel sauce onto the plates at the last moment.

PRESENTATION: Place the diamonds on individual serving plates and spoon some caramel sauce beside them. Serve cold.

CHOCOLATE TRUFFLE TRIANGLES
Palets-triangles

THESE ARE THE RICHEST, MOST INDULGENT CHOCOLATES IMAGINABLE.

INGREDIENTS:
GANACHE
¼ cup/55 ml heavy cream
6 oz/170 g best-quality bittersweet chocolate or dark couverture, melted
6 tbsp/80 g butter, softened and whipped
1 tbsp aged Armagnac (at least 10 years old)

9 oz/250 g bitter couverture, tempered (page 154), for dipping

Makes 12 triangles, about 1¼ oz/35 g each
Preparation time: 40 minutes

THE GANACHE: In a small saucepan, boil the cream for 1 minute, then cool at room temperature to 95°–104°F/35°–40°C. At this stage, pour the cream onto the melted chocolate and whisk to make a completely homogeneous mixture. Keep in a cool place.

When the ganache has cooled to 68°F/20°C, whisk in small pieces of butter, one at a time. Finally add the Armagnac and whisk until the ganache is smooth and very shiny.

SHAPING THE GANACHE: Pour it into the tray or inside the rulers and smooth the surface with a metal spatula. Chill in the refrigerator for 3 hours.

DIPPING THE TRIANGLES: Invert the tray onto a board and peel off the plastic wrap or slightly warm a knife blade over a gas flame, slide it between the inside of the rulers and the ganache, and remove the rulers. Slice the ganache rectangle in half along its length to make two bands. Cut each band into three 2¼ in/5.5 cm squares, making six squares in all. Slightly warm the knife blade again and cut each square diagonally to make twelve 2¼ × 2¼ × 3¼ in/5.5 × 5.5 × 8 cm triangles. Using the dipping fork, dip the triangles one at a time into the tempered couverture. Let the excess drip off before placing the triangles on the lined baking sheet. Cover them immediately with the rodoïde triangles (this will make them beautifully shiny) and press lightly with a broad metal spatula. Keep in a cool place away from any humidity, which would ruin the shine on the chocolate coating.

PRESENTATION: Remove the rodoïde triangles only just before serving the chocolates so that they remain very glossy. Serve them piled in a pyramid on a round plate.

SPECIAL EQUIPMENT:
A two-pronged fork for dipping
A tray covered with plastic wrap, 6½ in/16.5 cm long, 4½ in/11 cm wide, ½ in/1.2 cm deep, or 4 metal confectioner's rulers placed on a baking sheet covered with plastic wrap
Chocolate thermometer
Twelve 2½ × 2½ × 3½ in/ 6.5 × 6.5 × 9 cm triangles of rodoïde or acetate
Baking sheet lined with parchment or wax paper

NOTE:
The chocolate-dipped triangles will keep well in a cool place for 5 days.

BITTER CHOCOLATE AND CARAMELIZED WALNUT DELIGHT WITH CARAWAY ICE CREAM

Délice au chocolat amer et cerneaux de noix, glace carvi

YOU CAN TRULY BE PROUD OF THIS MARVELOUS DESSERT. THE SUBLIME COMBINATION OF CHOCOLATE MOUSSE, WALNUTS, AND ICE CREAM AMPLY JUSTIFIES THE TIME SPENT ON ITS PREPARATION.

INGREDIENTS: ❀

CHOCOLATE MOUSSE:

4 tsp water

½ cup/100 g sugar

1 egg, plus 2 extra yolks

1 cup + 2 tbsp/275 ml heavy cream, whipped to a ribbon consistency

6 oz/175 g bitter couverture or best-quality bittersweet chocolate, warmed to 98.6°F/37°C

CARAMELIZED NUT CRUNCHES:

¾ cup/75 g walnut halves, plus 6 tbsp/75 g sugar

20 walnut halves, plus 1¼ cups/250 g sugar

2 oz/60 g Tulip Paste (page 28)

12 × 8 in/30 × 20 cm sheet baked Joconde Sponge (page 31)

5 oz/150 g Chocolate Glaze (page 186)

½ quantity Caraway Ice Cream (page 138)

2 cups/500 ml Honey Sauce (page 55)

Zests of 2 limes, cut into thin slivers and blanched twice

Oil for greasing

Serves 10

Preparation time: 1½ hours, plus 2 hours freezing

THE CARAMELIZED NUT CRUNCHES: Put the 6 tbsp/75 g sugar without any water into a small, heavy-based saucepan, and melt over low heat, stirring with a spatula to obtain a pale, nutty caramel. Add the ¾ cup/75 g walnuts and mix well. Pour onto a lightly-oiled baking tray and leave at room temperature. When the nuts have cooled, crush them coarsely with a rolling pin to make small nut crunches.

THE TULIP PASTE BASKETS: Preheat the oven to 350°F/180°C.

Using the template, spread ten small circles of tulip paste on a non-stick baking sheet, flattening them with a metal spatula. Bake for 3–4 minutes, then immediately lift off the circles one at a time with a metal spatula and place them in ten of the molds, pressing down lightly with the eleventh mold to shape little shallow baskets for the ice cream.

THE JOCONDE SPONGE: Using the cookie cutter, cut out ten circles from the baked sponge. Place these in the dessert rings, arrange on a baking sheet, and leave at room temperature.

THE CHOCOLATE MOUSSE: Put the water in a saucepan, add the sugar, and bring to a boil over low heat. Wash down the inside of the pan with a pastry brush dipped in cold water, and cook the sugar until the temperature reaches 240°F/115°C. Now work the egg and yolks in a bowl, either by hand or with an electric mixer. As soon as the sugar reaches 250°F/121°C, remove from the heat, let the syrup rest for 1 minute, then pour it gently onto the eggs, whisking continuously until completely cold. Add the melted chocolate, then stir in the nut crunches with a spatula. Finally, fold in the whipped cream. Fill the dessert rings with this chocolate mousse, smooth the surface with a metal spatula, and freeze for at least 2 hours.

THE CARAMELIZED WALNUTS AND CARAMEL DECORATION: In a small, heavy-based saucepan, heat the 1¼ cups/250 g sugar without water over low heat, stirring continuously, until pale caramel. Immediately remove from the heat. Dip the 20 walnut halves in the caramel, one at a time, and use a fork to transfer them to a lightly oiled baking sheet. If the caramel becomes too thick while you are dipping the walnuts, reheat it over very low heat. Keep the caramelized walnuts in a dry place.

Dip the tines of a fork in the caramel (reheated if necessary) and swirl the sugar into whatever shape you like – spirals, criss-crosses, etc. – as

SPECIAL EQUIPMENT:

10 dessert rings, 2½ in/ 6.5 cm diam., 1¼ in/ 3 cm deep

11 molds approx. 3 in/ 7.5 cm diam. at the top, 1½ in/4 cm diam. at the base, 1 in/2.5 cm deep

2⅜ in/6 cm diam. wafer-thin template

2½ in/6.5 cm round cookie cutter

Candy thermometer

Nonstick baking sheet, or a sheet of parchment paper

Blowtorch (optional)

NOTES:

All the separate elements of this dessert can be prepared several hours before the meal.

The mousses freeze well for a week, so make them a few days in advance.

it runs off onto a nonstick baking sheet or a sheet of parchment paper. Repeat to make about ten caramel decorations. Keep in a dry place.

GLAZING THE MOUSSES: Pour a little chocolate glaze onto one unmolded mousse and smooth the surface with a metal spatula. Glaze all the mousses in this way.

PRESENTATION: Gently heat the outside of the rings with a blowtorch, or run a knife blade dipped in hot water between the rings and the mousses. Remove the rings by rotating them gently upward.

Place a mousse on each plate, then a basket filled with a 1½ in/4 cm scoop of caraway ice cream. Arrange a caramel decoration aslant on the ice cream and place one walnut half on the mousse and another on the ice cream. Spoon a little honey sauce and some lime zest between the mousses and baskets of ice cream, and serve at once.

WHITE CHOCOLATE DOMES WITH RASPBERRY PARFAIT AND DARK CHOCOLATE CURLS

Dômes aux deux chocolats et ses framboises

I PARTICULARLY LOVE THIS DESSERT FOR ITS SMOOTH SHAPE AND THE VISUAL AND GASTRONOMIC CONTRAST BETWEEN THE PURITY OF THE WHITE MOUSSE AND THE RICHNESS OF THE DARK PARFAIT. ALTHOUGH IT DOES TAKE TIME, IT IS QUITE SIMPLE TO PREPARE, AND THE PLEASURE IT GIVES YOUR GUESTS WILL BE TINGED WITH ENVY AND ADMIRATION OF YOUR SKILL.

INGREDIENTS:

Italian Meringue (page 37), made with 6½ tbsp/100 g egg whites and 6 tbsp/75 g sugar

1 quantity Raspberry Parfait (see Cardinal Gâteau, page 103)

WHITE CHOCOLATE MOUSSE

7 oz/200 g white couverture or best-quality bittersweet chocolate, chopped

4 tbsp/50 g butter, melted

2 cups/450 ml heavy cream, whipped to a ribbon consistency

12 oz/350 g raspberries

12 × 8 in/30 × 20 cm sheet of baked Joconde Sponge (page 31), cut into ten 3¼ in/8 cm circles

80 Chocolate Fans or Curls (page 154)

10 mint sprigs

7 oz/200 g thick Raspberry Coulis (see Fruit Coulis, page 51)

Serves 10

Preparation time: 30 minutes

THE ITALIAN MERINGUE: Follow the recipe on page 37. Do not make the meringue in advance; it should be freshly made and just cold.

THE RASPBERRY PARFAIT: Make this after you have prepared the meringue, following the recipe on page 103. Do not prepare it more than 30 minutes in advance.

THE WHITE CHOCOLATE MOUSSE: Put the white couverture in a small bowl and stand it in a bain-marie. Heat over medium heat to 104°F/40°C, stirring occasionally.

Whisk the melted butter into the warm couverture without overworking it. Still using a whisk, fold in one-third of the cold whipped cream, then the meringue. Finally fold in the rest of the cream very delicately until the mousse is perfectly blended.

ASSEMBLING THE DOMES: Using the pastry bag, pipe about 2 oz/50 g mousse into the bottom of the molds. Using a metal spatula, spread the mousse up the insides of the molds to cover them completely, then place in the freezer to harden for 10–15 minutes.

THE RASPBERRIES: Reserve about thirty of the best for decoration. Arrange six raspberries in the bottom of each mold on top of the hardened mousse. Fill up the molds with the raspberry parfait and smooth the surface with a metal spatula. Top each one with a joconde sponge circle, pressing it delicately and lightly with your fingertips onto the parfait. Cover the molds with plastic wrap and keep in the freezer until ready to serve.

PRESENTATION: Heat the outside of the molds for 2 or 3 seconds with a blowtorch, or by dipping them briefly into boiling water. Invert the molds onto serving plates and unmold the domes. Arrange the chocolate fans or curls around the base. Place three raspberries and a mint sprig on top of each dome. Pour a little raspberry coulis around the domes on one side of the plates and serve very cold, but not frozen.

SPECIAL EQUIPMENT:
Chocolate thermometer
10 hemispherical molds, 3½ in/9 cm diam., 1¾ in/4.5 cm high
Pastry bag with a plain ½ in/1 cm tip
Blowtorch (optional)

NOTE:
This dessert can be frozen for at least a week, so you could serve the domes at more than one meal.

CHAPTER ELEVEN

PETITS FOURS

Petits fours come in many forms, but of course they are always small. Their colors range from glowing to brilliant to understated, depending on the type. They are particularly delicious when freshly made, since they hate humidity, heat, and especially the cold. Sadly, not many people really appreciate them, and still fewer have mastered the art of preparing them.

But what delight, what luxury to nibble one or two petits fours with your coffee! It is a mistake to offer too much choice; my advice is to serve only two or three well-made varieties.

In this chapter, you will find a large selection of petits fours. Some are more appropriate to certain seasons than others. For example, you would serve Black Currant Jellies in summer and Chocolate Tuiles in winter. My own personal favorites to serve with coffee are the *petits fours secs* or chocolate petits fours, such as Hazelnut Tuiles, Little Lemon Cakes, and Chocolate Quenelles.

Petits fours also go very well with ice creams and sorbets and certainly justify the time spent in preparing them.

Dipping a pineapple segment into syrup

166

CANDIED PINEAPPLE SEGMENTS
Fruits déguisés à l'ananas

A PETIT FOUR TO SHOW OFF YOUR SKILLS, WHICH IS WELL WORTH THE
EFFORT INVOLVED IN THE PREPARATION.

INGREDIENTS:
1 pineapple, about 3¼ lbs/
    1.5 kg
4 oz/120 g marzipan, made
    with 33% almonds
Confectioners' sugar for
    dusting

SYRUP:
2 cups/400 g sugar
1 cup/250 ml water
COOKED SUGAR:
1¼ cups/250 g sugar
2½ tbsp/50 g liquid glucose
    or light corn syrup
½ cup/100 ml water

Makes 20
Preparation time: 1 hour 10
    minutes

SPECIAL EQUIPMENT:
Small copper sugar pan, or a
    heavy-based saucepan
Two-pronged fork for dipping
Plain ⅝ in/1.5 cm round
    cookie cutter
Candy thermometer
1 lightly-oiled baking sheet

PREPARING THE PINEAPPLE: Using a very sharp knife, cut off the two ends of the pineapple and remove all the skin from the fruit. Cut eight attractive slices, about ¼ in/5 mm thick, from the peeled pineapple. Remove the fibrous core with the cookie cutter.

POACHING THE PINEAPPLE RINGS: Dissolve the sugar in the water to make a syrup and bring to a boil. Drop in the pineapple rings and poach gently at 194°F/90°C for 1 hour. Remove from the heat and let the pineapple cool slightly in the syrup. When the rings are barely warm, arrange them delicately on a draining rack and leave until completely cold.

Dust the work surface with confectioners' sugar. Roll out the marzipan to the same diameter as the pineapple and ⅛ in/3 mm thick. Pile four pineapple rings on the marzipan. Trim off any excess marzipan from around the edge and the center with a small, sharp knife, following the contours of the pineapple. Turn over the four rings and top with the remaining rings so that the marzipan is sandwiched between the two. Cut each "sandwich" into five regular segments and place on a wire rack.

COOKING THE SUGAR: Combine the water, sugar, and glucose in the sugar pan and bring to a boil over low heat. Skim the surface and wash down the inside of the pan with a pastry brush dipped in cold water. Put in the thermometer and cook to 303.8°F/151°C. Remove from the heat and let the sugar bubble down for 2 minutes.

Insert the dipping fork into the center of the pineapple segments and dip them in the cooked sugar, one by one (see photo, opposite). As soon as they are coated with sugar, take them out and let them drain for 2 or 3 seconds. Place on a lightly-oiled baking sheet and leave until cold.

PRESENTATION: Ideally, the pineapple segments should be served on a silver platter, to set off the beautiful sheen of the sugar coating.

BLACK CURRANT JELLIES
Pâte de fruits

THESE PETITS FOURS ARE AMONG THE SIMPLEST TO MAKE, YET ONE OF THE TASTIEST. IT IS A RARE PERSON WHO EATS FEWER THAN FOUR OR FIVE IN ONE GO! YOU COULD USE STRAWBERRIES OR APRICOTS INSTEAD OF BLACK CURRANTS; THEY ARE PARTICULARLY DELICIOUS WHEN THE FRUITS ARE IN HIGH SEASON.

INGREDIENTS:
7 oz/200 g fresh or frozen
   black currant pulp
   (drained weight)
¾ cup + 2½ tbsp/180 g
   sugar
½ oz/15 g pectin mixed
   with 5 tsp sugar
¼ cup/50 g sugar

Makes 35
Preparation time: 15
   minutes

THE JELLY MIXTURE: In a heavy-based saucepan, heat the black currant pulp to 122°F/50°C. Add the ¾ cup + 2½ tbsp/180 g sugar and bring to a boil. Skim the surface, add the pectin and sugar mixture, and cook to 217.4°F/103°C. Take the pan off the heat and let the fruit bubble down for 10 seconds.

Pour the mixture into the tray or rulers and let cool at room temperature for at least 2 hours.

PRESENTATION: Remove the jelly from the tray or rulers and cut into thirty-five ¾ in/2 cm cubes. Roll them delicately in the ¼ cup/50 g sugar and arrange on a plate, alone or with other petits fours.

SPECIAL EQUIPMENT:
Candy thermometer
A tray, 6 in/14 cm long,
   4 in/10 cm wide,
   ⅝ in/1.5 cm deep, lined
   with plastic wrap, or 4
   metal confectioner's rulers,
   placed on a baking sheet
   covered with plastic wrap

NOTES:
Fruit jellies will keep for a
week in a cool but not
humid place.
   If you want to make a
larger quantity, cook the
mixture to 221°F/105°C
instead of 217.4°F/103°C.

CANDIED GRAPEFRUIT PEEL
Aiguillettes de pamplemousse confites

ONLY THE GRAPEFRUIT PEEL IS USED FOR THIS RECIPE, SO SERVE THE CHILLED SECTIONS WITH A COUPLE OF SPOONS OF THE POACHING SYRUP FOR A REFRESHING DESSERT.

INGREDIENTS:
1 grapefruit, about 12 oz/
   360 g, washed
2 cups/400 g sugar
1¼ cups/300 ml water

THE GRAPEFRUIT: Using a very sharp knife with a flexible blade, cut off a ¼ in/5 mm sliver from the top and bottom of the fruit. Starting from the top of the grapefruit and following its contour, cut off about five strips of peel, 2⅜ in/6 cm long and 2 in/5 cm wide, removing all the pith and membrane from the fruit. Cut each strip into five long, thin batons.

NOTES:
These delicious petits fours
keep well at room
temperature for 3 days, but
will lose some of their soft
texture after a day or two.

168

¼ cup/50 g sugar

Makes 25
Preparation time: 25
   minutes
Cooking time: 1½ hours

POACHING THE BATONS: Place in a saucepan, cover with cold water, and bring to a boil. Refresh, drain, and repeat the process four times.

Put the sugar and water in a saucepan and gently bring to a boil. Immediately drop in the five-times-blanched grapefruit batons. Poach gently without boiling at about 194°F/90°C for about 1½ hours.

Leave the batons to cool slightly in the poaching syrup. Place on a wire rack while still just warm and drain until completely cold, then roll them in the ¼ cup/50 g sugar.

PRESENTATION: Place the batons in paper petits fours cases and serve with coffee, by themselves or with other petits fours.

SPECIAL EQUIPMENT:
Candy thermometer

MINI-TARTLETS WITH BERRY FRUITS
Mini-tartelettes aux fruits rouges

I CAN NEVER HAVE ENOUGH OF THESE PETITS FOURS. DECORATE THEM WITH BLACK CURRANTS, GRAPES, WILD STRAWBERRIES, OR WHAT YOU WILL.

INGREDIENTS: ❋
Flour for dusting
4 oz/120 g Sweet Tart
   Pastry (page 20)
1 soup spoon strawberry or
   raspberry jam
6 oz/170 g Frangipane
   (page 43)
½ cup/100 ml heavy
   cream, whipped with 1½
   tbsp/10 g confectioners'
   sugar
20 attractive raspberries,
   small strawberrries, small
   clusters of red currants, or
   blueberries
20 small mint leaves

Makes 20
Preparation time: 20
   minutes
Cooking time: 8 minutes

MAKING THE TARTLETS: Preheat the oven to 350°F/180°C.

On a lightly floured work surface, roll out the pastry to a thickness of ½ in/2 mm. Cut out twenty rounds and line the molds with them. Using a paper cone, pipe a little jam into the bottom of the pastry shells. Fill with frangipane and bake in the preheated oven for 8 minutes. Unmold the tartlets onto a cooling rack.

PRESENTATION: Just before serving, pipe a rosette of whipped cream onto each tartlet. Decorate with the fruit of your choice and a mint leaf. Arrange the tartlets on a china plate or, better still, on a silver platter with other petits fours.

SPECIAL EQUIPMENT:
20 tartlet molds, 1¾ in/
   4.5 cm at the top, 1 in/
   2.5 cm diam. at the base,
   ½ in/1 cm deep
Paper piping cone
Pastry bag with a fluted
   ½ in/1 cm tip
2 in/5 cm fluted round
   cookie cutter

NOTE:
The pastry cases must be freshly baked, so it is essential to serve the tartlets the day they are made.

PROVENÇAL CARAMEL CUPS

Coques au caramel provençales

MY FRIEND DANIEL GIRAUD FROM VALENCE GAVE ME THE RECIPE FOR THESE
PROVENCAL PETITS FOURS, WITH THEIR CRISP CHOCOLATE SHELLS AND DIVINELY SOFT
CARAMEL CENTERS. THEY ARE A GREAT FAVORITE AT THE WATERSIDE INN.

INGREDIENTS:

7 oz/200 g milk chocolate
  couverture, tempered (page
  154)
⅓ cup/70 g sugar
4 tsp/20 g butter
2 tbsp heavy cream

THE CHOCOLATE CUPS: Dip the outside of the paper cases one by one into the tempered couverture and place on a baking sheet lined with plastic wrap. Let harden in a cool place, but not the refrigerator. Repeat the operation to give a second coating of chocolate. When this has hardened, delicately peel off the paper cases one by one. The chocolate cups will weigh about ⅙ oz/5 g each. Keep them in a cool place away from any humidity.

SPECIAL EQUIPMENT:

Small heavy-based saucepan
20 rigid paper bonbon cases,
  1½ in/4 cm at the
  opening, 1 in/2.5 cm at
  the base, ⅝ in/1.5 cm
  deep

2 oz/60 g fondant
1 tbsp/20 g highly
 perfumed clear honey
¼ cup/25 g toasted sliced
 almonds

Makes 20
Preparation time: 40
 minutes

THE CARAMEL FILLING: Put the sugar in the pan and dissolve it over low heat without water, stirring continuously with a spatula. As soon as it turns to a pale golden caramel, remove from the heat. Stir in the butter, then the cream, and finally the fondant and honey. Stir until the mixture is smooth and homogeneous, then add the almonds and fold them in delicately so as not to break them too much. Let the mixture cool completely in a cool place. Fill the chocolate cups with the cold filling and keep in the refrigerator until ready to serve.

PRESENTATION: Arrange the caramel cups on a small plate or tray and serve with coffee. They will be much appreciated.

Left to right: Provençal Caramel Cups, Piped Almond Petits Fours, Chocolate Tuiles, Little Lemon Cakes, Candied Pineapple Segments, Chocolate Quenelles, Mini-Tartlets with Berry Fruits, Hazelnut Tuiles, Macaroons, Black Currant Jellies with Candied Grapefruit Peel

CHOCOLATE QUENELLES
Quenelles au chocolat

DO NOT HESITATE TO PROVIDE THREE OR FOUR OF THESE WONDERFUL
CHOCOLATE TREATS PER PERSON.

INGREDIENTS:

1 quantity Ganache (see
Chocolate Truffle
Triangles, page 161),
made with Scotch whisky
instead of Armagnac
5 oz/150 g bitter couverture,
melted
1 cup + 2½ tbsp/100 g
unsweetened cocoa powder,
sifted

Makes about 32
Preparation time: 20
minutes

THE GANACHE: Prepare it following the recipe on page 161. As soon as
it is ready, form it into small quenelles, using two teaspoons, and
place them on a sheet of wax or parchment paper. Refrigerate for at
least 2 hours.

FINISHING THE QUENELLES: Using a fork, dip them quickly one at a time
into the melted couverture, then roll them in the cocoa and place on
a wire rack. Keep in a cool place until ready to serve.

PRESENTATION: It is best to serve the quenelles in little paper cases so
that your guests are not showered with cocoa as they pick them up.
Serve them alone or with other petits fours.

NOTE:

The quenelles will keep in a
cool place for 5 days.

HAZELNUT TUILES
Tuiles noisette

THESE TUILES ARE DELICIOUS SERVED WITH ICE CREAM OR ON THEIR
OWN WITH COFFEE.

INGREDIENTS:
4½ tbsp/70 g egg whites
7 tbsp/90 g sugar
5 tsp/15 g flour
1¼ cups/100 g very finely
ground hazelnuts
4 tsp hazelnut oil

Makes about 50
Preparation time: 15
minutes
Cooking time: 10 minutes

THE PASTE: In a small bowl, beat the egg whites 5 or 6 times with a
fork until slightly frothy. Add the sugar, mix it in with a spatula, then
mix in the flour and ground hazelnuts and finally the hazelnut oil.
Cover with plastic wrap and leave at room temperature for 1 hour.
    Meanwhile, preheat the oven to 425°F/220°C.

SHAPING AND BAKING THE TUILES: Work the mixture with a spatula for a

SPECIAL EQUIPMENT:
1 wafer-thin template,
    2¾ in/7 cm diam.
2 lightly greased, well-
    chilled baking sheets
1 gutter-shaped tuile mold,
    or a rolling pin

NOTE:
The tuiles will keep well for
a week in an airtight
container in a dry
atmosphere, so you can treat
yourself to some homemade
petits fours with your
morning coffee.

few seconds. Lay the template on one chilled baking sheet, put in a little tuile mixture, and level it out to the sides with a metal spatula. Move the template a little way along and use all the mixture to make about twenty-five tuiles in this way.

Place the tuiles in the hot oven and lower the temperature to 400°F/200°C. Bake for about 5 minutes, until very pale golden. Take the tuiles out of the oven and immediately, using a metal spatula, lift them one at a time onto the tuile mold or rolling pin. Let cool. Shape and bake a second batch in the same way.

PRESENTATION: Arrange the tuiles on a plate and dust with a light veil of confectioners' sugar or serve them plain.

CHOCOLATE TUILES
Tuiles au chocolat

THESE TUILES SHOULD BE STORED IN A COOL, DRY PLACE . . . BUT THEY MAY NOT REMAIN THERE FOR LONG. ONCE YOU HAVE TASTED ONE, THE SHEER PLEASURE WILL TEMPT YOU TO EAT AT LEAST ANOTHER FOUR, SO I SUGGEST YOU PROVIDE THIRTY TUILES FOR SIX PEOPLE!

INGREDIENTS:
9 oz/250 g dark or white couverture or best-quality bittersweet chocolate, chopped
⅔ cup/75 g slivered almonds, toasted and cooled

Makes 30
Preparation time: 15 minutes

PREPARING THE TUILES: Temper the couverture (following the method on page 154) and stir in the toasted almonds. Place the template on one of the strips of rodoïde and fill with about 1 tablespoon of the chocolate and almond mixture. Move the template a little distance away and spread in the mixture again, repeating the process to make a maximum of five tuiles per strip.

As soon as you have prepared the first strip, slide it onto the tuile mold or rolling pin to curve the rodoïde and thus the tuiles, and let cool. Lift the tuiles off the rodoïde only after the chocolate has set and just before serving, so that they keep their brilliant shine.

SPECIAL EQUIPMENT:
Cardboard template, 2⅜ in/6 cm diam.
6 strips of rodoïde or flexible acetate, about 4 in/10 cm wide
Gutter-shaped tuile mold or rolling pin

NOTE:
Before spreading dark couverture in the template, you could smear the rodoïde strips with a little melted white couverture, using the tip of your index finger to give an attractive marbled effect of white on brilliant brown. This will make the tuiles even prettier.

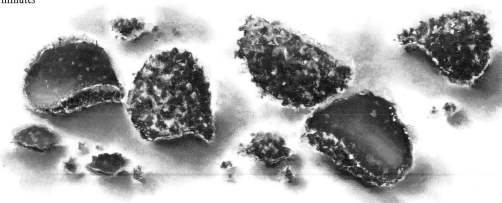

SOFT MACAROONS
Macarons tendres ou "Progrès"

INGREDIENTS:

7 oz/200 g tant pour tant (equal weights of ground almonds and confectioners' sugar, sifted together, eg: 1⅓ cups nuts and 1 cup sugar)

5 tsp/15 g flour

4½ tbsp/37.5 g cornstarch

3 tbsp tepid milk

¾ cup/175 ml egg whites

¾ cup/150 g sugar

⅔ cup/60 g sliced almonds

2 tbsp/15 g confectioners' sugar

Makes about 35

Preparation time: 25 minutes

Cooking time: 12 minutes

PREPARATION: Preheat the oven (preferably a convection fan oven) to 325°F/160°–170°C.

Combine the tant pour tant, flour, cornstarch, and milk in a bowl and carefully blend with a spatula.

Beat the egg whites until half-risen, then beat in the sugar, a little at a time, until the whites are very firm and almost like meringue. Delicately and gradually fold the egg whites into the tant pour tant mixture with a slotted spoon. As soon as it becomes homogeneous, stop working the mixture, and put it into a pastry bag with a plain tip. It must be used immediately.

PIPING AND COOKING THE MACAROONS: Line the baking sheets with your chosen paper and pipe on seventy 1½ in/4 cm balls of the macaroon mixture, spacing them 1½ in/4 cm apart. Sprinkle the macaroons with a few sliced almonds, then dust with a light veil of confectioners' sugar. Bake in the preheated oven for 12 minutes.

Remove the macaroons from the oven and slide the paper onto cooling racks. When the macaroons are cold, assemble them in pairs, pressing them very lightly together.

PRESENTATION: Arrange the macaroons on a plate lined with a doily and serve them alone or with other petits fours.

SPECIAL EQUIPMENT:

Pastry bag with a plain 2¾ in/7 cm tip

Four 12 × 8 in/30 × 20 cm, or two 24 × 16 in/ 60 × 40 cm baking sheets, lined with wax or parchment paper

NOTES:

Make large macaroons by piping them into 2⅜ in/ 6 cm balls. Sandwich these with a praliné-flavored Buttercream (page 41).

Macaroons freeze well for 3 or 4 days, but they are at their delectable best served on the day they are made, when they are divinely melting, and almost creamy

PISTACHIO MACAROONS
Macarons à la pistache

INGREDIENTS:

3 cups/350 g confectioners' sugar

4 cups/300 g ground almonds

1½ cups/350 g egg whites

2 cups/250 g confectioners' sugar

3 oz/85 g pistachio paste

2 drops of green food coloring

Makes 90

Preparation time: 35 minutes

Cooking time: 20 minutes

THE MACAROON MIXTURE: Preheat the oven to 240°F/120°C. Process the 3 cups/350 g confectioners' sugar and ground almonds for 1 minute at medium speed in a food processor, then sift. Follow the method for Chocolate Macaroons (opposite) until the egg whites are stiffly beaten with all the 2 cups/250 g confectioners' sugar. Mix the food coloring into the pistachio paste, soften with a little beaten egg white, then mix into the rest of the egg whites without overworking. Shower the dry ingredients from a height onto the pistachio-flavored egg whites, folding them in with a skimmer. Mix gently until the mixture is very slightly runny and completely homogeneous.

PIPING AND COOKING THE MACAROONS: Pipe ninety 1 in/2.5 cm balls of mixture onto the wax paper. Cook for 20 minutes, following the method for Chocolate Macaroons.

PRESENTATION: Pile the pistachio macaroons in a pyramid on a plate.

SPECIAL EQUIPMENT:

Four 24 × 16 in/60 × 40 cm baking sheets

2 sheets of wax paper

Pastry bag with a plain ½ in/1 cm tip

CHOCOLATE MACAROONS
Macarons chocolat

THE NAME "MACAROON" DERIVES FROM THE VENETIAN *macarone*,
MEANING A FINE PASTE.

INGREDIENTS:

DRY INGREDIENTS

4 cups + 2½ tbsp/500 g
confectioners' sugar, plus
an extra ⅔ cup/75 g

½ cup + 1 tbsp/50 g
unsweetened cocoa powder

3⅔ cups/275 g ground
almonds

1 cup/250 g fresh egg
whites

½ oz/15 g powdered egg
white

Makes 110
Preparation time: 25
minutes
Cooking time: 10 minutes

THE DRY INGREDIENTS: Put the 4 cups + 2½ tbsp/500 g confectioners' sugar, the cocoa, and ground almonds in a food processor and process at medium speed for 1 minute, then sift coarsely onto a sheet of wax paper. Keep at room temperature.

THE EGG WHITES: Beat the fresh egg whites in an electric mixer until half-risen, then add the ⅔ cup/75 g confectioners' sugar and beat until stiff. Immediately add the powdered egg white and continue to beat for another 3 minutes.

Meanwhile, preheat the oven to 500°F/250°C.

Sprinkle the dry ingredients onto the egg whites and fold in delicately with a slotted spoon to make a perfectly smooth, very slightly runny paste.

PIPING THE MACAROONS: Pipe the mixture onto the 2 sheets of paper to make one hundred and ten 1 in/2.5 cm balls.

COOKING THE MACAROONS: Carefully slide the paper onto two baking sheets and double up each sheet on another one (hence the need for four baking sheets). Place in the very hot oven, immediately reduce the temperature to 300°F/150°C, and cook for 10 minutes.

As soon as the macaroons come out of the oven, run a trickle of cold water between the wax paper and the baking sheet so that the macaroons can be detached more easily (this is not necessary with parchment paper). Leave them like this for 10 minutes, then carefully lift off the macaroons and assemble them in pairs, pressing them together very lightly.

PRESENTATION: Pile the macaroons in a pyramid on a plate and serve them alone or with other petits fours.

SPECIAL EQUIPMENT:
2 sheets of wax or
parchment paper
Four 24 × 16 in/60 × 40 cm
baking sheets
Pastry bag with a plain
½ in/1 cm tip

NOTES:
Ideally, the macaroons should be cooked in a convection fan oven.

Do not be put off by the large quantities in this recipe. It is difficult to prepare macaroons successfully in smaller quantities. They freeze well for a couple of weeks; peel them off the paper, stick them together, and immediately arrange them on a tray, wrap in plastic wrap, and freeze. To serve, leave the wrap over the macaroons until they are completely thawed so that they remain shiny and do not lose their luster. They will also keep well for several days in an airtight container. Store at room temperature in a very dry place.

CANNELÉS
Les Cannelés

CANNELÉS, A CLASSICAL SPECIALTY FROM BORDEAUX, ARE QUITE UNLIKE ANY OTHER PETITS FOURS;
THEY ARE CRUNCHY ON THE OUTSIDE AND SOFT IN THE CENTER, WITH A MOST DELICIOUS FLAVOR.
THEY ARE NOT EXACTLY LIGHT — BUT EVEN THE MOST BEAUTIFUL GIRL IN THE WORLD DOESN'T
HAVE EVERYTHING! BOTH MY BROTHER AND I LOVE THEM; THE RECIPE WAS GENEROUSLY DONATED
BY MY FRIEND MANUEL LOPEZ FROM THE PATISSERIE LOPEZ IN LIBOURNE.

INGREDIENTS:

1 cup/250 ml unsweetened condensed milk, or 1½ cups/350 ml full cream sweetened condensed milk

2¾ cups/540 g sugar (or 2¼ cups/440 g if using sweetened condensed milk)

1⅓ cups/240 g flour

3 whole eggs, plus 2 extra yolks

5 tbsp rum

2½ cups/600 ml water

4 tbsp/60 g butter

½ cup/60 g whole milk powder

Makes 36
Preparation time: 15 minutes, plus at least 24 hours chilling
Cooking time: about 55 minutes

THE CANNELÉ MIXTURE: Combine the condensed milk, sugar (if using sweetened condensed milk, use only 2¼ cups/440 g sugar), flour, whole eggs and yolks, and the rum in a large bowl and mix with a spatula.

Put the water, butter, and powdered milk into a saucepan and bring to a boil, whisking continuously. Pour the boiling liquid onto the egg and condensed milk mixture, still whisking all the time. Mix thoroughly until very smooth, then pass through a conical strainer and let cool completely. Transfer the mixture to an airtight container and refrigerate for at least 24 hours.

Preheat the oven to 400°F/200°C.

GREASING THE MOLDS: In a saucepan, melt the beeswax over very low heat, then mix in the oil. Warm the molds in the oven for a few seconds. Lightly brush the insides of the molds with the beeswax and oil mixture, then place them upside-down on a cooling rack for about 5 minutes, until the wax has set. Arrange the molds on a chilled baking sheet.

BAKING THE CANNELÉS: Give the cannelé mixture a good whisk, then fill the molds to within ½ in/2 mm of the top. Bake in the oven for 30 minutes, then turn the baking sheet through 180° and bake for another 20–25 minutes, until the cannelés are deeply colored. Immediately unmold them onto a cooling rack.

PRESENTATION: Serve the cannelés just warm, arranging them on a plate lined with a doily. They can be served with other petits fours, but are delicious on their own.

SPECIAL EQUIPMENT:
36 cannelé or croquette molds, 1¾ in/4.5 cm diam., 1¾ in/4.5 cm deep
Equal small quantities of peanut oil and beeswax, for greasing the molds

NOTE:
The uncooked mixture will keep in the refrigerator for 4 or 5 days, which allows you to bake the cannelés as and when you want them.

PIPED ALMOND PETITS FOURS

Petits fours pochés aux amandes

INGREDIENTS:

5 oz/150 g marzipan, made
   with 50% almonds
1 tbsp/15 g egg white
13 whole blanched almonds
2 tbsp Sorbet Syrup (page
   144), (optional)

Makes 26
Preparation time: 15
   minutes
Cooking time: 4 minutes,
   plus 8 hours resting

PREPARING THE PETITS FOURS: Put the marzipan and egg white on the work surface and work together with the palm of your hand. Place in the pastry bag and pipe onto the baking sheet into the shape of thirteen commas and thirteen teardrops, 1 in/2.5 cm long. Place an almond on each teardrop. Leave on the baking sheet for about 8 hours at a temperature of 86°–95°F/30°–35°C, so that a crust forms on the surface.

COOKING THE PETITS FOURS: Preheat the oven to 450°F/230°C for 20 minutes before cooking the petits fours, then bake for 4 minutes. As soon as they come out of the oven, run a little cold water between the paper and the baking sheet, and brush the petits fours with sorbet syrup if you wish. It will give them a sheen, but also sweeten them a little. After 5 minutes, remove the petits fours one by one and place on a wire rack.

PRESENTATION: Arrange the petits fours on a plate or platter, alone or mixed with other varieties.

SPECIAL EQUIPMENT:
Pastry bag with a fluted
   ½ in/1 cm tip
Baking sheet lined with
   parchment or wax paper

NOTE:
These easy-to-make petits
fours will keep well at room
temperature for 3 days.

LITTLE LEMON CAKES

Petits cakes citron

INGREDIENTS:

1 egg

A small pinch of salt

7 tbsp/85 g sugar

Zest of ½ lemon, very finely grated

3 tbsp heavy cream

2 tbsp/25 g butter, melted and cooled

½ cup/70 g flour, mixed with ⅟₃₀ oz/1 g compressed fresh yeast

LEMON ICING:

½ cup + 1 tbsp/70 g confectioners' sugar, sifted and mixed with the juice of ½ lemon

Makes 20

Preparation time: 15 minutes

Cooking time: 5 minutes

MAKING THE CAKES: Preheat the oven to 400°F/200°C.

Put the egg, salt, sugar, and lemon zest in a bowl and work lightly with a whisk. Add the cream, then the flour and yeast mixture and mix until smooth, then add the butter.

Cover the bowl with plastic wrap and let the mixture rest at room temperature for 30 minutes. Fill the pastry bag with the mixture and pipe it into the molds. Bake in the preheated oven for 5 minutes. Unmold the cakes onto a cooling rack as soon as they are cooked. Using a pastry brush, coat them lightly with lemon icing and return them to the oven for 15 seconds. Put them back on the rack until completely cold.

PRESENTATION: Serve the cakes alone or with other petits fours.

SPECIAL EQUIPMENT:

20 small molds, 1¾ in/ 4.5 cm at the top, 1 in/2.5 cm at the base, ½ in/1 cm deep

Pastry bag with a plain ½ in/1 cm tip

NOTE:

These refreshing little cakes will keep in an airtight container for 3 days.

LITTLE RAISIN CUPS

Friands de sultanas en caissettes

INGREDIENTS:

9 oz/250 g tant pour tant (equal weights of ground almonds and confectioners' sugar, sifted together, eg: 1⅔ cups nuts and 1 cup sugar)

1 egg, plus 2 extra yolks

½ cup (1 stick)/100 g butter, melted and cooled

¼ cup/35 g moist golden raisins

¼ cup/35 g flour, sifted

3 egg whites

A pinch of sugar

Confectioners' sugar for dusting

Makes 50

Preparation time: 20 minutes

Cooking time: 7 minutes

MAKING THE LITTLE CUPS: Preheat the oven to 400°F/200°C.

In the electric mixer, beat the tant *pour* tant, egg, and yolks with the paddle beater until the mixture becomes pale and has a runny ribbon consistency. Fold in the melted butter with a spatula. Roll the raisins in the flour and mix them and the flour into the mixture.

In the electric mixer, beat the egg whites with a pinch of sugar until very stiff. Fold them gently into the mixture with a spatula. As soon as the mixture is homogeneous, put it into a pastry bag without a tip and fill the paper cases two-thirds full. Stack two baking sheets and arrange the filled cases on them. Bake in the preheated oven for 7 minutes, then immediately transfer the raisin cups to a cooling rack.

PRESENTATION: Dust the cups lightly with confectioners' sugar and serve with other petits fours.

SPECIAL EQUIPMENT:

Electric mixer with a paddle beater

50 round paper bonbon cases, 1 in/2.5 cm diam., ¾ in/2 cm deep

NOTE:

If you prefer, omit the raisins and put a cherry or raspberry in eau-de-vie on top of the mixture just before baking.

The baked raisin cups can be frozen for up to a week in an airtight container.

Chapter Twelve

DECORATION AND SUGARWORK

The craft of decoration and sugarwork deserves an entire tome to do it justice. Artwork in pâtisserie is more diverse, complex, and imaginative than in any other area of cooking, yet it is relatively simple and enormously pleasurable to master the skills involved. Once you have done so, you will be delighted with the decorative effects you can achieve.

Decorative techniques include COOKED SUGAR, which can be poured, pulled, blown, and made into rock, ball, and spun sugar, and; PASTILLAGE for molding, assembling models, collage, and as soft paste for piping. CHOCOLATE AND MARZIPAN can be sculpted, modeled, and molded into flowers and other shapes. PIPED DECORATIONS include decorative writing and ornamentations made with piped Buttercream or Decorative Choux Paste. PAINTING WITH A BRUSH is done primarily on Pastillage or Marzipan, using food coloring or chocolate.

Aniseed Parfait (see recipe page 72) with spun sugar caramel

ROYAL ICING
Glace royale

NUMEROUS DESSERTS CAN BE DECORATED WITH A PIPING OF THIS ICING,
EITHER WHITE OR TINTED WITH FOOD COLORINGS.

INGREDIENTS:
3 tbsp/50 g egg whites
2 cups/250 g confectioners'
  sugar, sifted
Juice of ¼ lemon, strained

Preparation time: 5 minutes

Put the egg whites in the bowl of an electric mixer and beat at low speed, adding the sifted sugar a little at a time, then the lemon juice. Beat until the mixture is firm and slightly risen; the icing is ready when it forms a very straight, fine point whichever way up you hold the beaters. If it is too thick to form a point, add a touch more egg white. If it is too thin, so that the point flops over when you hold it upward, add a little more confectioners' sugar.

NOTE:
Royal icing is best used immediately, but it will keep in the refrigerator for several days. Store in an airtight container or a bowl covered with plastic wrap to prevent a crust from forming.

SPUN SUGAR CARAMEL
Sucre décor fourchette

DRIZZLE THIS SUGAR OVER LIGHTLY-OILED HEMISPHERICAL MOLDS TO MAKE
SUGAR CAGES TO PLACE OVER AN ICE CREAM OR SURPRISE DESSERT. THIS
ATTRACTIVE DECORATION IS SIMPLICITY ITSELF TO MAKE (SEE PHOTO OPPOSITE).

INGREDIENTS:
⅓ cup/80 ml water
1 cup/200 g sugar
3 tbsp/60 g liquid glucose
  or light corn syrup
Food colorings, according to
  taste

Makes about 12 oz/350 g

MAKING THE CARAMEL: In the pan, gently heat the water, sugar, and glucose. As soon as the syrup comes to a boil, wash down the inside of the pan with a pastry brush dipped in cold water. Add a few drops of food coloring, put in the thermometer, and cook until the sugar reaches 311°F/155°C. Take the pan off the heat and let the sugar cool for 3 minutes.

MAKING THE DECORATION: Place the parchment paper on a baking sheet. Dip the tines of a fork into the sugar and let it drizzle off the fork into lines or criss-crosses, to make the pattern you require. Repeat the operation to make as many decorations as you need. When they are cold, use them to decorate your dessert.

SPECIAL EQUIPMENT:
Copper sugar pan, or a small
  heavy-based stainless steel
  saucepan
Candy thermometer
A sheet of parchment paper

SPUN SUGAR
Sucre filé

THIS DELICATE, BRILLIANT SUGARWORK IS EXTREMELY SIMPLE TO ACHIEVE AND ADDS AN AIR OF GREAT
FESTIVITY TO A DESSERT. SINCE IT IS VERY PLIABLE, IT CAN BE FORMED INTO ALL SORTS OF ATTRACTIVE SHAPES
(SEE ICED MELON SURPRISE, PAGE 146), AND CAN ALSO BE USED TO MAKE THE PISTILS FOR SUGAR FLOWERS.

INGREDIENTS:

6 tbsp water

1¼ cups/250 g sugar

3 tbsp/65 g liquid glucose
or light corn syrup

1 tbsp peanut oil or pure
vaseline, for greasing

Preparation time: 15
minutes

COOKING THE SUGAR: Pour the water into the pan and add the sugar. Stir with a spatula, then place over low heat until the sugar has completely dissolved. As soon as it begins to bubble, skim the surface. Do this several times, taking care to rinse the skimmer in a bowl of very clean water each time.

Wash down the inside of the pan with a scrupulously clean pastry brush dipped in cold water to prevent the formation of sugar crystals. (These could fall back into the pan during cooking and make the sugar grainy, which might cause it to form lumps as you spin it.)

Now add the glucose, partially cover the pan with a lid, and cook the sugar over high heat. Put in the candy thermometer and stop cooking when the temperature reaches 305°F/152°C. Let the sugar bubble down and cool for 2 minutes. It is vitally important that it is at the correct temperature and consistency – if it is too hot or too thin, it will fall in little drops and not form threads; if too cold, it will be too thick to spin.

SPECIAL EQUIPMENT:

Copper sugar pan, or a
heavy-based stainless steel
saucepan

Candy thermometer

2 forks, or a small whisk
with the wires all cut to
the same length

NOTE:

Spun sugar is very sensitive
to moisture, so it is
important not to work in a
humid atmosphere.

PREPARING THE WORK SURFACE: Protect the surface with several sheets of wax paper. Lay a lightly oiled broom handle between two chairs or stools, or simply use an oiled rolling pin, holding one end carefully in your hand.

SPINNING THE SUGAR: Dip the tines of the forks or the ends of the whisk into the sugar and flick them rapidly back and forth above the broom handle or rolling pin. The sugar will run down and spread and spin into threads on either side. When all the sugar has run off, repeat the operation and continue until the handle or rolling pin is fairly well covered with sugar threads (see photo, left). Do not overfill it.

Collect up all the sugar threads and place them on a lightly-oiled baking sheet if you intend to use them quickly, or store in an airtight container if you want to keep them for a few days. Place some silica gel, quicklime, or carbide in the bottom of the container and cover it with foil before putting in the spun sugar.

PASTILLAGE

EXPERIENCE IS NOT IMPORTANT WHEN MAKING PASTILLAGE, BUT PRACTICE MAKES PERFECT WHEN IT COMES TO MOLDING AND CUTTING OUT SHAPES. PASTILLAGE LOOKS LOVELY PAINTED WITH FOOD COLORINGS, BUT CAN ALSO BE LEFT WHITE.

INGREDIENTS:

4 cups + 2½ tbsp/500 g confectioners' sugar, sifted

6 tbsp/50 g cornstarch or potato flour (potato starch), sifted, plus extra for the work surface

1 egg white

1 soup spoon water

2 gelatine leaves, soaked in cold water for 20 minutes and well drained

Juice of ½ lemon, strained

Food colorings (optional)

Makes about 1½ lbs/650 g

Preparation time: 10 minutes

Drying time: 24—48 hours, depending on the thickness

MAKING THE PASTILLAGE: Put the confectioners' sugar and cornstarch or potato flour on a very smooth work surface and make a well.

Heat the egg white and water slightly in a bain-marie, stirring with your fingertips to stop it coagulating. Remove from the bain-marie, add the prepared gelatine, and stir until completely dissolved.

Still stirring with your fingertips, pour this mixture into the center of the well, add the lemon juice, and mix, gradually drawing the sugar and cornstarch into the center to make a firm but malleable paste. If it is too soft, add a little more sugar; if too firm, add another drop of lukewarm water. Add any food colorings at this stage. Immediately wrap the pastillage in plastic wrap to prevent it from drying out or cracking.

MOLDING THE PASTILLAGE: This must be done on a very smooth work surface (such as marble or formica), dusted with cornstarch or potato flour. Roll out the pastillage to the appropriate size and thickness, and cut out your desired shapes, using stencils if you wish.

DRYING THE PASTILLAGE: Immediately transfer the cut shapes to a very smooth baking sheet lined with wax paper and let dry at room temperature for 24—48 hours. Turn the pieces over when nearly dry to ensure that the underside is also dry; well-dried pastillage is much stronger. Once the pastillage is completely dry, you can polish the surface with very fine glass paper to achieve a porcelain-smooth finish.

PRESENTATION: You could shape several pieces to make one large model (eg: a house), sticking them together with royal icing (page 181) piped from a paper cone. A painted medallion makes a wonderful presentation for a child's birthday cake (see photo opposite).

SPECIAL EQUIPMENT:

A very smooth pâtisserie rolling pin, preferably plastic

1 or more very sharp knives

NOTE:

Do not keep pastillage for too long after shaping because it dries out quickly and will crack. It is best used immediately after kneading, but it can be kept in the refrigerator, tightly wrapped in plastic wrap, for 24 hours.

Pastillage seal and painted medallions

BUBBLE SUGAR
Sucre bullé

THIS MODERN SUGARWORK DECORATION WILL AMAZE THE UNINITIATED. IT IS RATHER TEMPERAMENTAL: SOMETIMES IT MAKES LARGE BUBBLES, SOMETIMES SMALL ONES. TO DATE WE HAVE NO IDEA WHY IT CHANGES, BUT BOTH RESULTS ARE EQUALLY EFFECTIVE.

INGREDIENTS:
2½ cups/500 g sugar
½ cup/150 g liquid glucose or light corn syrup
⅞ cup/200 ml water
A few drops of food coloring, according to taste

Makes about 1¾ lbs/850 g

COOKING THE SUGAR: Follow the method for Spun Sugar Caramel (page 181). When the sugar temperature reaches 316°F/158°C, pour it immediately in small quantities and as thinly as possible onto the sheet of parchment paper and, holding the sheet by the corners, tilt it to make the sugar run, but do not tap it. Take great care that the sugar does not run off the paper because it could burn your fingers.

When the sugar has cooled, peel it off the paper. It does not matter if it breaks into different-sized pieces; it will look even more attractive.

PRESENTATION: Arrange the thin sheets of bubble sugar on the serving plates to enhance the visual effect of your dessert.

SPECIAL EQUIPMENT:
Candy thermometer
A sheet of parchment paper

POURED SUGAR
Sucre coulé

POURED SUGAR MODELS ARE THE STARS OF DECORATIVE SUGARWORK AND ARE SIMPLICITY ITSELF TO MAKE. AN ATTRACTIVE MODEL ON A STAND WILL TAKE ONLY HALF AN HOUR.

INGREDIENTS:
1 lb 2 oz/500 g sugar cubes
⅞ cup/200 ml water
6 tbsp/125 g liquid glucose or light corn syrup
Food colorings, as required
A little peanut oil

PREPARING THE TEMPLATE FOR THE MODEL: Lay the sheet of parchment or foil on the work surface and on it roll out the modeling paste. The larger the model you intend to make, the thicker the paste should be. Using a stencil, cut out the shapes needed for your model with the tip of a very sharp knife (see the fish, right), or use confectioner's rulers to make an outline. The base for the model can be any shape, but it must be large enough to give adequate support and stability. Lightly brush the inside edges of the paste or rulers with oil.

COOKING THE SUGAR: Cook the sugar as for Spun Sugar Caramel (page 181). Put in the thermometer and cook until the temperature reaches 284°F/140°C. Add the food colorings you require and heat to 312°F/156°C. Take the pan off the heat and let the sugar bubble down for 2 minutes. It is now ready to use without delay.

Pour the sugar in a steady stream into the template or rulers. Prick any air bubbles with the tip of a fine knife. Let the sugar cool for about 20 minutes, then lift off the modeling paste or rulers. If you wish, pipe on decorations with royal icing (page 181). Peel off the paper or foil and assemble your model.

SPECIAL EQUIPMENT:
Copper sugar pan, or a
   heavy-based stainless steel
   saucepan
Candy thermometer
Modeling paste (eg:
   plasticine), or metal
   confectioner's rulers
A sheet of parchment paper
   or foil
Stencils of your chosen shape

PULLED SUGAR
Sucre tiré

ANY KIND OF SUGARWORK DEMANDS CARE AND PATIENCE. COOKED SUGAR IS VERY HOT, SO BE CAREFUL NOT TO BURN YOURSELF. PRACTICE MAKES PERFECT, BUT THE ESSENTIAL QUALITIES NEEDED FOR SUGARWORK ARE LOVE AND THE DESIRE TO PRODUCE A BEAUTIFUL OBJECT, SENTIMENTS THAT I HAVE FELT SINCE THE AGE OF SIXTEEN.

INGREDIENTS:
1¼ lbs/600 g fondant
1¼ cups/400 g liquid
   glucose or light corn syrup
Food colorings, as required
   (optional)

Makes 2¼ lbs/1 kg

In the pan, gently heat the fondant and glucose to boiling point. Skim the surface and wash down the inside of the pan with a pastry brush dipped in cold water. Increase the heat, put in the thermometer, and cook to 293°F/145°C. Add your chosen food coloring or leave the mixture plain for a white color. Take the pan off the heat.

Let the sugar bubble down for 2 minutes, then pour it onto the parchment or marble. As soon as the sugar begins to harden at the edges, use a metal spatula or triangular metal scraper to fold them into the middle; do this four or five times. After a few minutes, the sugar will become malleable. Hold one end of the sugar and, using your fingertips, pull the mass outward without squeezing, then fold it back onto itself and repeat about 25 times, until it becomes very glossy and smooth. After a few folds, as the sugar becomes less hot, it will hold better. Roll it up into a ball; it is now ready to use.

Place the pulled sugar under a sugar lamp or near the open oven door. Using your thumb, pull off small pieces to shape into flower petals or leaves, to make beautiful sugar roses, for example (see photo, left).

SPECIAL EQUIPMENT:
Copper sugar pan, or a
   heavy-based stainless steel
   saucepan
Candy thermometer
A sheet of parchment paper,
   or a marble slab lightly
   greased with pure vaseline

NOTES:
This fondant-based recipe is easier to work than the classic pure sugar and glucose recipe.

Pulled sugar flowers will keep well in a dry airtight container lined with silica gel, carbide, or quicklime, covered with foil.

Page 184, left: Spun Sugar Caramel cages:
Right: Bubble Sugar behind Poured Sugar fish

Left: Pulled Sugar roses and leaves: Right: Marzipan roses, stems, and leaves

DECORATING CHOCOLATE
Cacao décor

THIS SHINY CHOCOLATE IS USED FOR WRITING AND CREATING DECORATIVE
PATTERNS AND EFFECTS.

INGREDIENTS:
½ cup/100 g sugar
3 tbsp/60 g liquid glucose
   or light corn syrup
½ cup/100 ml water
5 oz/150 g cocoa paste,
   finely chopped

Makes about 12 oz/350 g
Preparation time: 5 minutes

Boil the sugar with the glucose and water to make a syrup, then cool to 122°F/50°C. Strain it through a conical strainer onto the cocoa paste. Whisk until homogeneous and very smooth, but take care not to overwork the mixture, or it will lose its elasticity and brilliance. The decorating chocolate is now ready to use for piping or writing.

SPECIAL EQUIPMENT:
Copper sugar pan, or a
   heavy-based stainless steel
   saucepan
Candy thermometer

NOTE:
Decorating chocolate can be
kept in an airtight container
in the refrigerator for 2
weeks. Spoon out as much as
you need and heat in a bowl
in a bain-marie or for a few
seconds in the microwave

Left: Decorating Chocolate
runouts

CHOCOLATE GLAZE
Glaçage chocolat

THIS GLAZE WILL GIVE YOUR CHOCOLATE DESSERTS AND GATEAUX A
BEAUTIFUL SHINY FINISH.

INGREDIENTS:
1 cup/250 ml Sorbet Syrup
   (page 144)
4 oz/120 g bitter or dark
   couverture or best-quality
   bittersweet chocolate,
   chopped
½ cup/40 g unsweetened
   cocoa powder, sifted

Makes about 14 oz/400 g
Preparation time: 10
   minutes

In a bowl set in a bain-marie over medium heat, heat the chocolate to 104°F/40°C. Heat the syrup with the cocoa, whisking continuously. When it reaches 122°F/50°C, pour it into the melted chocolate, still whisking just until the glaze becomes smooth and shiny. It is now ready to use.

NOTE:
The glaze will keep in an
airtight container in the
refrigerator for up to a week.
Reheat it in a bain-marie or
microwave oven for a few
seconds before using, taking
care not to heat it to more
than 104°F/40°C or to
overwork it.

Right: Chocolate Fans atop
Chocolate Glaze

DECORATIVE CHOUX PASTE

Pâte à choux à décor

INGREDIENTS:

2½ tbsp/35 g butter, diced

3½ tbsp water

3½ tbsp milk

A pinch of salt

7 tbsp/60 g flour

2 eggs

Makes about 5 oz/150 g

Preparation time: 20
minutes

Cooking time: 6–10
minutes, depending on the
size of the decorations

COOKING THE PASTE: Preheat the oven to 320°F/160°C.

Combine the butter, water, milk, and salt in a saucepan and bring to a boil over high heat. Take off the heat and mix in the flour with a whisk to make a very smooth paste. Return the pan to the heat and stir with a spatula to dry out the paste for 30 seconds.

Beat in the eggs one by one, then rub the paste through a very fine strainer into a bowl, using a plastic scraper.

PIPING THE PASTE: Pipe the choux paste into your chosen pattern directly onto the parchment paper. Bake in the preheated oven for 6–10 minutes, until lightly browned. For raised shapes, such as shells, pipe and bake the shapes flat, then mold them around an appropriately shaped mold as soon as they come out of the oven.

SPECIAL EQUIPMENT:
Pastry bag with a plain
¹⁄₁₂–⅛ in/2–3mm tip, or
a paper piping cone
Parchment paper

NOTE:
This choux paste will keep
for a week in a dry, airtight
container.

Clockwise from top left:
Decorative Choux Paste
shooting star: Tulip Paste
ribbon: Decorative Choux
Paste run-outs: Puff Pastry
palm trees

NOUGATINE

ALTHOUGH I NORMALLY MAKE NOUGATINE WITH SLIVERED ALMONDS, SLICED ALMONDS CAN ALSO BE USED, AND WILL LOOK BETTER IF YOU ARE MAKING A LARGE PRESENTATION PIECE.

INGREDIENTS:

5¼ cups / 500 g sliced almonds or 4⅓ cups / 500 g slivered almonds

3⅓ cups / 660 g sugar

4 tbsp / 60 g butter (optional)

2 tbsp peanut oil

Makes 2¾ lbs / 1.2 kg

Preparation time: 25 minutes

COOKING THE NOUGATINE: Preheat the oven to 350°F/180°C.

Spread the almonds on a baking sheet and toast in the oven until lightly browned. Cook the sugar in the pan over low heat, stirring gently and continously with a spatula, until it melts to a light golden caramel. Add the almonds and stir over low heat for 1 minute, then stir in the butter until completely absorbed (this is not essential, but will give the nougatine an added sheen). Pour the nougatine onto an oiled baking sheet.

SHAPING THE NOUGATINE: Place the baking sheet toward the front of the warm oven, leaving the oven door half-open. The warmth will keep the nougatine malleable. Work with one small piece at a time, of a size appropriate to the shape you want. Roll

out each piece on a warm, lightly oiled baking sheet or lightly oiled marble surface. It is essential to work quickly, since the nougatine rapidly becomes brittle. If you have a microwave oven, heat the nougatine for only a few seconds to soften it. Alternatively, place a sugar lamp just far enough away from the nougatine to keep the mass warm while you mold the individual pieces.

Roll the nougatine into the appropriate thickness for your desired shape, but never thicker than ⅛ in/3 mm. Quickly cut out your chosen shapes using the cutters or the blade or heel of a chef's knife.

To mold the nougatine, drape it very rapidly over the mold so that it follows the shape and contours. Leave until completely cold before removing from the mold.

SPECIAL EQUIPMENT:

Copper sugar pan, or a heavy-based saucepan

Cookie cutters, dessert rings, or a chef's knife (have these ready on hand before you start making the nougatine)

Heavy rolling pin

1 or 2 lightly-oiled baking sheets

Sugar lamp or microwave oven (optional)

NOTES:

Like all sugar-based confectionery, nougatine should be stored well away from any humidity. In damp conditions, it will keep for at most 2 days. 1 teaspoon Nougasec (see page 190 for stockist) added to the sugar will keep the nougatine dry for at least a week.

Nougatine Basket with Yellow Peaches (see recipe page 76)

SPECIALIST EQUIPMENT AND FOOD SUPPLIERS

Bridge Kitchenware Corp.
214 East 52nd Street
New York, NY 10022
Tel: 212–688–4220
American and imported cooking equipment, including a large selection of molds. Catalog available at nominal fee against first purchase.

Dean & DeLuca
121 Prince Street
New York, NY 10012
Tel: 212–431–1691
American and imported bakeware and cooking equipment.

Kitchen Bazaar
4455 Connecticut Avenue NW
Washington DC 20008
Tel: 202–363–4625
American and imported bakeware and appliances. Catalog available.

Kitchen Glamor
26770 Grand River Ave.
Redford Township, MI 48240
Tel: 313–537–1300
American and imported baking equipment.

Maid of Scandinavia
3244 Raleigh Avenue
Minneapolis, MN 55416
Tel: 800–328–6722
Mainly American baking supplies. Catalog available at nominal charge.

Sur La Table
84 Pine Street
Pike Place Farmer's Market
Seattle, WA 98101
Tel: 800–240–0853
American and imported bakeware and kitchen items. For catalog, call 800–243–0852.

Williams–Sonoma
P.O. Box 3792
San Francisco, CA 94119
Tel: 415–652–9007
American and European bakeware, appliances, gadgets. Catalog available.

Zabar's
2245 Broadway
New York, NY 10024
Tel: 212–787–2000
American and imported gourmet foods, bakeware, cookware, and appliances. Catalog available.

INDEX

191